THE PRICE

MY RISE AND FALL AS NATALIA, NEW YORK'S #1 ESCORT

This book is based on the true life exploits of Natalie McLennan. All dates, place names, titles and events in this account are factual to the best of Ms. McLennan's recollection. However, to protect the rights of those whose paths have crossed the author's and in accordance with the wishes of certain participants, some of the names have been changed in order to protect their privacy. What follows is her true story.

ISBN-10: 1-59777-594-0
ISBN-13: 978-1-59777-594-6
Library of Congress Cataloging-In-Publication Data Available

Book Design by: Sonia Fiore

Printed in the United States of America

Phoenix Books, Inc.
9465 Wilshire Boulevard, Suite 840
Beverly Hills, CA 90212

10 9 8 7 6 5 4 3 2 1

THE PRICE

MY RISE AND FALL AS NATALIA, NEW YORK'S #1 ESCORT

By NATALIE "NATALIA" McLENNAN

TABLE OF CONTENTS

PROLOGUE
THE AUDITION

"Nat, get in a cab, I need you to meet someone," said the voice on the other end of the phone. "I've just met the most beautiful girl I've ever seen in my life."

Typical Jason tact, I thought to myself.

Yes, I know, he was my pimp, and I was an escort, and yes, I know that for most people we were living in some sort of beyond good-and-evil, bizarro world where normal morality and feelings don't apply, but just suspend your disbelief for a minute. Imagine your boyfriend saying that to you about another girl? Messed up, right? I guess I had kind of gotten used to it. It was like one of those quirks you think is cute at the beginning of a relationship, like a guy calling you "pumpkin," but eventually you grow to hate it.

So I feigned enthusiasm, "Really? That's so cool."

When I arrived at the hotel, Jason brought me into the lobby and told me to check out a girl working behind the desk.

"Don't stare!" he said.

He had just given this girl, Ashley he said her name was, one of his metal business cards and was standing in the lobby, watching her like a wolf. The cards were silver, razor-thin and read: New York Confidential: Rocket Fuel for Winners.

I checked her out. I had to hand it to him: Jason had the eye. She was hot. We milled around for a little while longer trying to look inconspicuous before Jason finally said, "Okay, let's go. I just wanted you to see her. I'm hungry."

We arrived home at the loft, hung out for a bit, had sex, I ordered sushi, did our weekly alcohol order (about a dozen bottles of Veuve Clicquot, a dozen bottles of Grey Goose, and half a dozen bottles of Johnny Walker Blue) and then who should call?

The little lamb from the hotel.

I was relieved that she called so quickly. If this girl was going to work out, Jason wouldn't need to sell her on the idea; she'd have to come to us. An hour later, she arrived at the loft. I was perched on my throne in my private sanctuary in front of a vanity mirror surrounded by twenty bright lights, all my fabulous clothes and shoes scattered around me, revitalized from doing a huge line of coke and feeling like the queen of my castle. I quickly checked myself out in the mirror. My rich, brown curls were perfect and shiny. My big brown eyes and pink lips were accentuated with mascara and some Lip Venom gloss. My skin looked great, especially considering how much I partied, and I'd had a manicure and pedicure done that morning to make myself appear fresh, even if my body was telling me otherwise. I have smallish breasts and a large surgery scar on my stomach, but I've always been reasonably happy with my figure. Some clients thought I was too skinny, but I was living in New York—everyone's a little underweight or else they're considered fat.

I was actually excited Ashley had shown up. She was even cuter than I remembered. Her face was adorable. She was tanned, with shiny, flowing brown hair. I could tell she was young, and I could sense that I was more street-smart than she was, but she had that hungry glimmer in her eye that told me she was game for anything. The fact was, I was happy to see anyone who seemed nice. It was lonely at the top, and I needed some friends.

Jason brought her into our bedroom to meet me in my closet. He always brought new people there to meet me. In smaller spaces, you can tune into a person's energy so much better.

Ashley's eyes lit up when she saw the theater dressing room-style lights around my mirror.

"This is so cool! I've always wanted a mirror like this."

"Me too," I said, smiling.

I patted the stool next to mine. She sat down and Jason leaned against the wall, trying not to be overbearing. He knew when to let girls be girls.

"I'm Natalia."

"Ashley."

Jason turned to me: "I told Ashley that you're the number one-rated escort in the U.S. How cool would it be if Ashley became number two?" He laughed his Jason laugh.

I looked at Ashley to gage her reaction. Her eyes were sparkling. Jason had taken the words right out of her mouth. I had never seen this before. Every other girl who had come to work for the agency had either worked as an escort before or, like most of our girls, was new but had to be sold on the idea and have her hand held at every step.

Ashley appeared to be happier to have found us than we were to have her.

For the first time, I felt a little threatened. This business was all about attitude—guys feed off your enthusiasm, your raw energy and, for lack of a better term, positive vibe. This girl had the looks and the glow. I had always kept my jealousy and other ugly girlish instincts in check, but she was almost too good to be true. I had to tell myself to chill out.

"Wait, wait. Before we go there, Ashley, I'm going to have to see you naked," Jason interjected.

My eyes darted back to her.

She squinted a little, trying to figure how to react.

"That's normal, right?" she asked.

She looked to me.

"I got naked for him. I've never worked anywhere else, so I can't really say, but it's normal here," I said.

I left out the part that when I got naked, it was during a twenty-four-hour MDMA-fueled threesome with Jason's girlfriend at the time. Not that I'd mind doing that again—with Ashley—but the agency was moving into a new era. We were getting serious about the operation. Just the other night, Jason and I checked into a room at the Gansevoort that we'd been using all day for clients and hired an escort for ourselves to see how the competition was doing. Everything she did was just wrong. She was candid and honest about all the wrong things—no one wants to hear about your drug problem or the fact you don't talk with your family. We made mental notes and gave our girls a refresher on what not to do.

"If you want, I'll stay in the room, too," I offered.

If a new girl was really shy, I'd stay in the room with my back turned. It made them more comfortable.

"It's okay. I don't mind taking my clothes off," she chirped.

She disappeared with Jason into the bedroom. I threw on a mix CD, and in two minutes they were back.

"So?" I joked, "It's a no, right?"

It had been totally unnecessary for Ashley to do the naked thing. It was obvious she had a near-perfect body, but it was a reminder to her who called the shots.

Everyone laughed and I got a bottle of champagne. I popped it, poured some for all of us and raised my glass. After I swigged, I got back to business.

"Every girl starts at $800 an hour. If and when that changes is dependent on the reviews you earn. Reviews are posted by clients on a site called TheEroticReview.com, and they have a huge impact on your success. Our clients are rich, handsome, smart and fun. I've been really lucky, and I've gotten a string of great reviews."

"The best reviews ever written," Jason added.

"What makes them the best?" Ashley asked.

I explained the rating system. "My rate has gone up from $800 to $1200 an hour because I earned so many great reviews. You'll have to start at $800, but if everything works out, it won't take long for you to earn more than that."

I was the pioneer, the girl who had made all this possible. The agency had grown so quickly in the last month, partly as a result of my reputation, that the demand far exceeded our supply of great girls.

We talked about how she should dress for appointments, and I showed her some examples of what I wore on bookings. She freaked over my shoes.

I asked her what she wanted her name to be. She really didn't know. She was drawing a blank. Jason started throwing out names: Melissa, Brooke ("we already have a Brooke," I reminded him), Morgan....

I looked at her. She had Dior sunglasses on her head and had a sort of well-bred, suburban look to her. Her curves were extreme, her body screamed sexy, and her voice was a little throaty and cute.

I had the perfect name.

"Victoria."

We smiled at each other, already seeing the fabulous future that awaited us.

CHAPTER ONE
CANADIAN CHAMP

The Canadian Junior National Tap Dancing Championships were exactly what you'd imagine them to do be: pale, overweight showbiz moms and their robotic brats battling for a shot out of Canadian mediocrity. My mother wasn't an obnoxious showbiz mom, but she had been taking me to dance lessons since I could barely walk. It was 1996 and I was now sixteen. So this was her moment as much as it was mine. She was a bundle of nerves as I took the stage to perform a swing dance number my instructor had choreographed especially for the competition.

Swing is best with a partner. But I spun and jumped and tapped like it was 1942 and I was at the Savoy Ballroom. As I walked off-stage, I knew the girl from Manitoba with her poodle skirt and bows had no chance.

When they announced I was national champ, my mom starting balling like I had just beat out Kerri Strug for Olympic gold. She held me as tight as she ever had and whispered in my ear, "Honey, I am so proud of you."

I wish I could have bottled up that moment and kept it under my pillow.

* * *

My mom had it rough. One snowy night right before Christmas, my dad, who owned a tow truck business, told her he was going to help get a friend's car out of a drift. He never came home.

At least that's how my mom tells the story. I wasn't even a year old, so I don't really remember, at least not consciously. My earliest clear memory comes two years later. I was three. My dad had moved to upstate New York with his new girlfriend and had come around to take us to see his mother on Christmas Day. My mom loaded my nine-year-old brother and me into my dad's big American car. We were bundled up in our snowsuits, and it was freezing, the windows were all fogged up, and I couldn't see outside. I was scared and confused.

I turned to my brother and asked, "Who is that man?"

"That's our dad," he answered.

My father didn't say anything.

He dropped us off at his mother's and drove off.

That was the last time I saw him, and it wasn't until a few years ago that I discovered he had moved to Texas. My entire childhood I had no idea where in the world he lived, or if he was even still alive.

After he left, my mom would still make us go over to our grandmother's every Christmas. To make matters even worse, we had to take the bus in the peak of the Canadian winter. My mother would revert back to being this wounded bird around my grandmother. Each year, shortly before we left, she would muster up the courage and ask, "Do you know where Bill is?" and my grandmother, a petite, proper Scottish immigrant, would give the same curt answer, "No, I have no idea."

My mom would look down and mumble, "Oh, okay. Thanks."

My grandmother would look off into the distance and then change the subject.

My mom ran a mini-daycare out of our apartment. There were always half a dozen kids running around, which is great when you're little. You never run out of kids to play with. But when you're a teenager living in a small two-bedroom apartment and waking up every morning to babies screaming, it's easy to forget that your mom is trying really hard and really easy to start hating your life.

She tried to make sure we had the right clothes, the right school, the right friends, but it was hard. We were social outcasts—poor English-speakers in a heavily French part of Montreal. My mom became hypersensitive about everything, especially our appearance. No matter how broke we were, she always made sure my clothes were spotless and perfectly pressed, and my unruly curly hair was tamed and bowed.

My dad's leaving was especially hard on my brother. As I got older, I began to feel that he blamed me for our dad leaving. My dad bolted shortly after I was born, after all. I could see how a six-year-old could make the correlation, and he probably wasn't too off base.

My mom tried to shield us from all of the pain. She never said anything bad about my dad. So she never really said much of anything about him at all. He became like a phantom. All I have are these snapshots in my head, all tainted with anger and confusion.

My final memory of anything connected to my dad comes from when I was five. It was my birthday, and he'd sent me a present. My mom had to force me to open the package, a Cabbage Patch doll—one of three I would get that day. Later, when I would play with them, I'd always make sure his doll was the one who had to wear the clothes I didn't like and never got served tea at the Cabbage Patch parties.

My mom never dated again. Even though I was a little girl and had no business knowing anything about adult relationships, I remember thinking it was because she was scared she would get hurt again—scared we would all get hurt again. She just closed herself off from the world of romance and sex. She gained weight and lost all her confidence as a single woman, and she focused all of her attention on raising my brother and me.

I lived in a perpetual state of "no." If I asked to go to a friend's house for a sleepover, the first response was always no. She always erred on the side of safety, trying to be the father figure. I had to argue or bargain or try any other tactic I could think of in order to stand a chance of getting what I wanted.

For my brother, this parenting style worked. But for me, it backfired. It created a rebellious streak that kicked in at the slightest attempt at control.

My mom's solution was dance lessons. I was three when she first took me to learn how to tap dance.

I was a little *phenom*. I took classes three times a week and private lessons at the teacher's house on weekends. Instructors would show me the steps once, and I would repeat them right back at them. It blew their minds. At age twelve, I started going to competitions. I wasn't really into competing, but I loved to perform. And when I started to win, I could see how happy it made my mom, so I kept doing it—and kept winning.

It was grueling and deathly boring at times, and on numerous occasions, I begged her to let me quit. But she would lay down the law, "I never force you to do anything, but this is the one activity you have to stick with."

She would threaten to take away what little else I had, like school dances, if I didn't keep on.

Tap led to other things, like acting and singing. When I was twelve, Disney came to town and held a huge open audition for the Mickey Mouse Club.

It was a big deal. I got my picture on the front page of the *Montreal Gazette* for dazzling the judges and getting to the final round. As I waited for word from the producers, I remember having this fantasy that one day my dad would see me on TV and think to himself, "Wow, I really screwed up not being her dad."

When I didn't get the role[1], I sat in my room under a big poster of Joey McIntyre of *New Kids on the Block*, crying my eyes out until I suddenly realized that I wasn't crying about not getting the gig. *Who wants to be a lame-ass Mouseketeer anyway?* I was crying because I wasn't going to get the chance to show my dad what an awesome, talented daughter he had walked out on.

Screw him, I finally said to myself, *he's not someone who deserves to be in my life. He is the only who is missing out.*

I resolved that I would do everything in my power from that point on not to have a sad life, just to prove to him that he couldn't hurt me.

*   *   *

As I entered my teenage years, the "no's" from my mom became more and more common, and my rebellious streak went into overdrive.

I had two identities. To my mom and our family friends, I was the responsible, hardworking, dutiful daughter. I would bring home my tap trophies and report cards with straight A's, and somehow my mom never noticed my bloodshot eyes and the skirts that kept getting shorter and shorter. I had an older girlfriend who

---

[1] Britney Spears and Justin Timberlake were cast in the same North American talent search.

had a boyfriend who was a dealer. She'd supply me with pot, 'shrooms, acid, anything she could get her hands on, which I would then sell to my classmates at the elite magnet school my mom was so proud I'd been accepted into. My illicit lunch money gave me a sense of independence and made me something of a legend around campus. I was the bad girl whom all the guys loved, and the girls were sort of scared of. No one could figure out how I got such good grades yet could be so wild. It all came so easy. And when you keep getting away with it, after time, you start to believe you're invincible.

At my mom's insistence, I kept tap dancing, and kept winning.

The tap competitions weren't quite JonBenét-land, but whenever there's a stage full of young girls in leotards eager to please older men, there's going to be a creepy factor—especially if the girls have started to blossom. I had woken up one morning and found that I had gone from being a cute and pure pre-teen to a brown-haired young Britney. If you think teenage boys are obsessed with sex, you've never met a girl who's hit her sexuality early. It hits us hard. I wanted it bad, all of the time. By the time I was sixteen, my hormones were raging out of control. I could never tell my mom, but part of why I kept doing those competitions was that I liked all the other little girls' fathers imagining my naked body under my tights. It turned me on.

My coup de grâce came when I won the Canadian Nationals. I was proud of the accomplishment, but I would have been happier if I had been the best at something I actually cared about.

A year later, I graduated from high school and finally had enough of tap dancing. I was a national champ. I had even gotten the chance to dance with Gregory Hines at the Montreal Jazz Festival. Where else could it take me? I retired my tap shoes and got accepted to Montreal's Dome Theatre School, second only to the National Theatre School of Canada.

I fell in love with acting. At the Dome, I didn't smoke, drink or do any drugs for three years. I didn't need to. I was so consumed by what I was studying, I had no interest in anything else.

*   *   *

After I graduated from the Dome, I stayed in Montreal, while my actor boyfriend at the time left for New York to try and conquer America. Despite the obvious odds stacked against me and every other aspiring Kim Cattrall (yes, she's Canadian), I thought I'd have a better shot as a big fish in a small (albeit often frozen) pond. I was the only actor in my class to have an agent a year before graduation—and not just any agent. He represented another Canadian, Elisha Cuthbert, Jack Bauer's hottie daughter on *24*.

Six months later, my boyfriend called me to tell me he'd finally scored his first part. He invited me down to New York to see him in action. After the show, a musical in which he ended up naked on stage, I went outside to wait for him to get dressed. I was sitting on the stoop when a middle-aged woman dressed in a flowy dress, lots of scarves and lots of bangles walked up to me.

"Excuse me, are you an actor?" she asked in an upper-class English accent that screamed *thespian*.

I *was* sitting on the steps of an acting school.

I answered, "Yes," and let her continue.

"Would you like to audition for a play? I'm directing a Shakespeare."

Without thinking, I replied, "Uh, thanks. But I'm just here on vacation. I actually live in Montreal."

"Right," she said. "Well, cheers, good luck."

And then she walked into the theater.

I sat there for about thirty seconds, and then jumped up. *What the hell was I thinking? How many people get offered an audition for a play in New York while sitting on a stoop?* It was right out of some kind of showbiz fairy tale. I ran after her.

"Excuse me, excuse me," I yelped. "Actually, I would be interested in that part!"

I auditioned for her on the spot, wowing her with my repertoire of contemporary and classical monologues, including a Lady Macbeth.

*   *   *

My mom wasn't thrilled when I told her about my latest role. As much as she was my biggest fan, allowing me to move to New York on the drop of a dime was not her idea of responsible parenting. However, I wasn't her little girl anymore, and she knew it.

So I landed in Manhattan with no plan whatsoever. I crashed on the couch of two Canadian girls who lived in Spanish Harlem and got a job answering phones at a snobby Upper East Side hair salon.

I figured out quickly why the lady in the wispy dress and jangling jewels was recruiting off the street. The company was a mess. The actors had huge egos and no talent, and despite her impressive accent she didn't know her Bard from her butt.

But it was a break. A random, non-paying minor role in a crappy off-off-Broadway production of *The Tempest,* but I had made it out of Canada.

After the play wrapped, I got my own place and a regular gig with another small theater. I even went on to perform at Juilliard, playing Mustardseed in *A Midsummer Night's Dream.*

* * *

Fast-forward three years to 2003. The fairy tale was over. My actor boyfriend was long gone and for the last two years I had been seeing a native New Yorker named Paul. He was an MIT graduate and during our honeymoon period, he had embodied the loving, supportive boyfriend persona every girl dreams of. He had helped me overcome the daunting obstacles newcomers face when confronted by the harsh reality of New York, doing things like getting me a cell phone when I didn't have credit history and taking trips home to Canada with me at Christmas time.

More recently, he had begun to drink like Falstaff. I was barely making rent busting my ass as a bartender, and I wasn't getting any decent auditions, let alone good roles. The only parts I did get were in obscure experimental productions in crappy black-box theaters above delis. I was actually in a play called, *Platonov! Platonov! Platonov! or the Case of a Very Angry Duck*—and I didn't even play the duck.

About once a day, I'd get this cramping knot in my stomach that pierced my whole body. I was a ball of panic, anxiety and frustrated creative energy ready to explode.

Paul and I began fighting—a lot. His temper got more and more unpredictable. As we drifted apart, I delved deeper and deeper into the dark underbelly of the city's nightlife demimonde, losing myself in harder and harder drugs. After I got off work at the bar, I'd hit the clubs and then the after-hours scene. I had a cell phone full of fake friends I could call any night of the week and instantly tap into a well of seemingly limitless debauchery.

It was like I had been recruited. I quickly became a crowd favorite of the city's elite hardcore party people—club promoters, bankers, rock stars, real estate developers, and trust fund kids—who all loved to have as many girls around as possible. I was happy, pretty, liked to dance, get high, kiss girls, and best of all, I was drama free. I was always on the list at the clubs, and when they closed, I always got the 4:30 a.m. call or text when they needed more girls to keep the night interesting.

My first after-hours marathon was at the Tribeca loft of Edward Albee, the playwright and legend of American theater. His protégé hosted an extended bender while Albee was out of town. Wearing only sunglasses and undies, I rolled around on the gorgeous hardwood floor for three days, giggling in disbelief that I was tripping my 32B tits off on mushrooms and ecstasy at Edward Albee's house. And so it went. One night I would find myself in a penthouse looking out over all of downtown Manhattan sharing lines with an heir to a banking fortune, a Jamaican drug dealer, a semi-famous actor and a pouty model from Estonia who had just done the cover of French *Vogue*. The next, I'd end up in a fifth-floor walkup in the East Village freebasing with a girl named Billy.

It was like a secret club where the instant intimacy evaporated into thin air the moment the sun came up or the drugs ran out—whichever came first.

So I'd try to trick time. I'd attempt to will a wormhole to that magical place where my buzz would never fade, and the sun would never rise. Inevitably, no matter how hard I tried, the night would morph from the orange glow of the streetlight, to the gray of dawn, to that unholy white blast of day that shoots through the blinds no matter what lengths you go to block it out. With the sun's cue, I'd gather up my stuff, check my nose in the mirror by the elevator and try to steady myself for the urban machine that had kicked into gear below. Cursing my one mistake, I'd ask myself: *Why didn't I bring my sunglasses? If only I had sunglasses, I'd be able to face the fact that my life was going nowhere.*

CHAPTER TWO
MY FIRST TIME

When I got the chance to try out for the lead in a play about the late great Andy Warholista Edie Sedgwick, one of my childhood heroes, I jumped at the opportunity.

My callback for *Andy and Edie* was in a dingy basement performance space on the Lower East Side. I had heard that the playwright, a writer for *Women's Wear Daily*, had a reputation as a troubled genius. So I brought him a present—a shell casing from a 9mm. I knew I had to do something to get his attention if I were going to be considered for the part of the skinny, blonde Edie. Bearing curves and curly dark-brown hair, I'm more or less her physical opposite. I did my monologue, handed the director the bullet, and walked out the door. I can tell in a second when I have guys in the palm of my hand. This guy was smitten.

Plus, it was January 30th—my birthday.

I needed a drink, so I headed to a bar nearby where one of my favorite people in New York was waiting for me with a group of my friends. Who better to celebrate my twenty-fourth year on planet Earth than with a guy who had seen most of it?

The blue-blooded grandson of a railroad tycoon, Peter Beard is a bon vivant who loves beautiful women, animals, art and anthropology. He discovered the supermodel Iman in an African village; he's been gored by a rhino; he's notorious in the nightlife underworld for having the stamina of an elephant and famous in the art world for his gigantic photomontage paintings.

He'd invited me into his inner circle of models, artists and, well, mostly models. We'd been spending a lot of time together, stoned, making collages on the floor of his loft in Tribeca. (I still have one collage of me and two other naked girls sprawled on his floor. After everything went down, it was the only asset of any real value I owned.)

After a couple of shots of Patron, Peter said, "Come on, Nat, I have to go see someone," and he whisked me out the door of my own party.

We arrived at a second-floor walkup apartment above the Manolo Blahnik store on West 54th Street, between 5th and 6th. It had been crudely converted into a sort of 50s noir workspace, complete with flickering fluorescent lighting and red pleather couches. There was a huge blowup of Frank Sinatra's mug shot in the entryway. It was dingy and gritty in a cool, old-school way. There were a few people lounging around conspiratorially in the shadows. Peter told me it used to be hipster magician David Blaine's office, which made total sense.

I wasn't quite clear on what kind of business was being conducted by the current occupants, but it didn't feel legal. We immediately made ourselves comfortable on the floor, where Peter sits whenever possible.

The boss of whatever it was that was going on sat down beside us. Peter introduced me, "Jason, you have to meet Nat. She's just the most amazing girl in New York right now."

Peter knows how to make a girl feel special.

I smiled at Jason and gave him my hand. He sat down right next to me on the floor and kissed my cheek.

"Nice to meet you."

He grabbed a plate of coke from some random guy next to us and cut big lines for the two of us. He handed me the straw, "Ladies first?"

I hesitated. I never felt comfortable partying in front of new people. But then I remembered I was with Peter Beard. He's like the James Bond of the nightlife world. He has a license to do anything. And if you're rolling with him, so do you.

Jason was thrilled to see Peter and seemed completely uninterested in me: "Peter, we have to talk about pictures. Have you seen our Web site? I need you to shoot my girls."

Peter chuckled and mumbled something about how the space might make a great backdrop, but he never committed.

"Come on, Peter," Jason said. "I need you, man."

I pegged Jason as just another New York rich kid party guy. People in New York have a certain vibe about them when they don't have to work at a day job for their money. He only sat with us for a few minutes before he was called away, but not before he made me put his number in my phone. He told me to give him a call if I ever wanted to make people happy and make lots of money doing it. I didn't quite understand what he was talking about. But as he walked off, Peter mumbled something about "escorts" and shook his head in an aloof, disapproving way.

It was all coming together now.

For fun, Peter and I did a series of photo shoots in Jason's office over the course of the next three nights. Me standing in front of the Sinatra mug shot; me standing in the grungy stairwell; me crawling on the floor like a horny hyena. While all around us an endless stream of hot young things came and went. Peter might have had a haughty attitude about their line of work, but he sure didn't seem to mind hanging out and partying with them.

Jason was never around, but the office manager introduced herself to me as Mona. She looked like a princess out of *Lord of the Rings*: five-ten, long brown hair, blue eyes and the most beautiful doll face I had ever seen. But I never saw her smile. On the third night, Peter had left, and I was sitting around doing a last line when Mona came over to me and said, "Are you going to hang out here or are you going to work?"

I know this is going to sound ridiculous, but I still didn't fully grasp what being an "escort" was all about. Did you have sex? Or did you just "escort" a guy on a date and then decide if you wanted to fuck him? I may have been a wild child in high school, but when it came to sex I was really just a theater geek. I had only recently seen porn, and I had never cheated on Paul.

But I was high, broke, and open to new ideas. I asked her what I could expect to make.

She broke it down like this, "The rate is $700 an hour. You take home forty-five percent. I have a client ready to go. The appointment is for one hour. He's an Asian guy. One of our regulars. Totally harmless. He's waiting to come over and pick you up. If you want to do it, I need to tell him now."

Whoa, this was happening fast. I calculated my cut. In one hour I could make as much as I was making over two nights slaving behind the bar serving drunk assholes.

Fuck it, I thought. *I'll try it. If it's a nightmare, I'll never do it again.*

"Okay," I said, trying to sound confident and upbeat. "That sounds cool."

I asked, "Do I need condoms?" trying to get more of a hint of exactly what was expected of me.

She replied, coldly, "I'm sorry. I can't talk about that with you."

I was totally confused.

You're about to send me out on a $700-an-hour job, but you can't tell me what I'm supposed to do?

"Mona, is Jason here?" I was desperate for a familiar face—someone who would at least offer me some words of encouragement as this was, after all, my first ever client. I felt sixteen again, like when I was about to have sex for the first time.

She turned her back on me and picked up the phone to call the client. Luckily, there was another girl lounging around on the couch smoking and doing lines. Desperate for details, I told her it was my first time and asked if she had any advice. She told me to relax. I had nothing to worry about. She'd seen this client before, and he was all about new girls—he'd love me. He was a nice Asian guy, totally harmless.

I already knew that! But what was I supposed to do exactly?

The buzzer rang. It was my date. I was out the door before I could think about it too much more.

He had a slick, modern apartment with an amazing view of the Chrysler Building. He was skinny, not too tall, about forty years old, dressed in an expensive lightweight gray suit. He made me a drink. I asked if he was going to join me he said no, he didn't drink. I sipped a Grey Goose and cranberry, wishing I was a little less jittery and a little more drunk. The coke I'd been doing all night was making me feel anxious, but I was too timid to down the vodka like a shot and ask for another one. He excused himself for a minute, and I took the opportunity to knock one back and pour another. He returned, took my hand, and led me to the bedroom. He asked me again if this was really my first time, and I told him yes. He seemed to believe me.

Once we were in bed together, something took over, and I was able to be myself. He came and was happy. He laughed a little and said I would do really well in the business.

The girls were right. He was totally harmless. Super polite and pretty lackluster in bed. It was the easiest money I had ever made. My conscience felt clear. Paul and I were over anyway. And if we weren't before, we were now. I was free to do and be whatever I wanted.

I was back at the office in less than two hours. Mona didn't ask how it went. She didn't even say hi. She just wrote me out a check for $310. I had to ask her to leave the name-field blank because I didn't have an American bank account.

It was five-thirty in the morning when I finally got home to Paul. He was passed out drunk on the couch.

*   *   *

My brilliant audition for the Edie play (and the ammo, apparently) scored me the role of Ingrid Superstar, the mysterious factory girl who disappeared in 1987 and was never seen again. But it was a Pyrrhic victory. At each rehearsal, the director became more and more obsessed with me. He would shower me with praise in stalker-esque phone messages, citing my "unending dedication to the theater" and my "intrinsic work ethic and creative vibe."After the twentieth time he tried to get in my pants, I finally told him to fuck off and quit the production. He was one of the most irritating people I have ever met.

His name is Peter Braunstein. Two years later on Halloween, he dressed up like a fireman, broke into the apartment of a woman he worked with at a fashion magazine and sexually tortured her for sixteen hours in some kind of bizarre revenge fantasy. The attack was a huge tabloid cover story in the city, and when he fled, the cable news networks ate it up. After a multi-state manhunt he was eventually caught in Memphis, Tennessee, convicted of sexual assault and sentenced to eighteen years to life in a New York State prison.

I can pick 'em, can't I?

In retrospect I guess I should be happy I escaped that poor woman's fate, especially after I told him he was a loser on numerous occasions. At the time, it just seemed like another chapter in my going-nowhere life.

I tried my best to stay optimistic, but I had this increasing sense that a black cloud was following me.

*   *   *

A month later, I scored a lead role in a low-budget psychological thriller. It seemed like maybe, *just maybe,* my luck was changing. I figured it would be good to get out of the city for a while. But the filmmakers weren't paying me, and I had to keep paying rent on my Manhattan apartment. It was shooting in the middle of nowhere, two hours northeast of Montreal. So by the time the film wrapped seven weeks later, I had blown through my entire savings.

Even worse, Paul was in really bad shape. He progressed from yelling at me to smacking me around. We went from all out screaming matches to full-contact wrestling matches. I never felt more vulnerable, more hopeless, or less in control of my own life. I needed a change, and I needed it fast.

A few days later, as I walked up Second Avenue, fed up with having my throat grabbed, no auditions on the horizon and $78 to my name, I thought about Jason and the ice princess and that quick $310 I had earned doing something I liked doing anyway. I took out my phone and dialed his number. He didn't pick up. I left a rambling message.

Over the next two weeks, I left three messages. I was getting desperate. Rent was due in two weeks, and I didn't have it.

Finally, he called me back. He told me he was sending a car service to pick me up and bring me to his apartment so we could talk. I put on a pair of jeans, a wife beater and some heels. It was the middle of the day—I wanted to look hot, but not like I was trying too hard.

An hour later, a sleek black town car pulled up in front of my apartment. The driver told me we had to make a stop along the way. We pulled up outside a luxury building on Central Park South and waited...and waited.... A half hour went by; I sat silently. Finally, a gorgeous blonde in a small red dress and with the most incredible full, round tits I had ever seen casually strolled out of the building and got in beside me. She looked me up and down, gave me a friendly smile and said her name was Samantha.

The driver said hello like he knew her well and pulled out. As we headed downtown, Samantha and I chatted about clothes and lip-gloss. But mostly about clubs and restaurants and partying: the sum of our existences at that point. I could detect a slight Russian accent, but she was almost completely Americanized. As soon as I saw her big black Dior purse, I knew we didn't shop at the same places. She'd probably never even heard of Century 21.

When the car pulled into the Holland Tunnel, I gave her a quizzical look.

"Where are we going?" I asked.

"Hoboken," Samantha said with a wink.

Jersey? I'd never been. Ever.

Shortly after, we arrived at Jason's pied-à-terre.

By the time we got to the fifth floor of the walkup, I was winded and skeptical. If I had known I was going to Hoboken, I would have told the driver to turn around and take me home.

Decorated in light purple pop-art silhouettes of naked women and plush caramel velour couches with pastel beanbag pillows, the railroad apartment was *Austin Powers* by way of North Jersey. Jason, with his huge, beaming white smile, greeted us as if he were welcoming us to the penthouse at Trump Tower.

He kissed Samantha on the mouth and me on my cheek. He told me he was so happy to see me and asked if I'd seen Peter recently. I told him no, I'd just gotten back to New York from filming my movie. I was busy with auditions and looking for a new apartment. I left out the part about the boyfriend who was hitting me.

For the first hour, his phone rang incessantly, and we barely talked. Girls in short dresses would pop in, drop off money, smoke a cigarette, do a line and then disappear.

Finally, Jason got a break and walked over to me and apologized for not calling me back. I asked him to explain what I could expect to make if I came to work for him.

He said I could make between five and ten thousand dollars—a week.

Really? The calculator in my head whirled. With that kind of money, I could set myself up with a whole new life. I could finally live in New York on my own terms without having to rely on another asshole boyfriend.

"Samantha, why don't you fill Natalie in on how we work," he said, as he walked away to take another call.

At first Samantha was restrained. She told me most of the clients were great, the money was amazing, and there was nothing to be afraid of. I might even get to travel, depending how good I was. All of the things I needed and wanted to hear. But Jason was on the phone a long time. As Samantha became more comfortable with me, and we became more like giggly girlfriends—the pure MDMA we were snorting didn't hurt—she opened up and started getting real.

Samantha proceeded to expound on the nitty-gritty of her personal escort style. For one, she got off by not showering between clients. It was her little inside joke. She also revealed that the clients never interested her sexually or otherwise, no matter how rich or good-looking they were.

"The cash makes me *svet*," she said, her Slavic bleeding through.

"What do you mean?" I asked.

"I mean the cash, the dollars, in my hand. It makes me wet."

Oh, right.

She added that she was thinking about breaking into porn, and that you can really make some money if you become a star.

I was speechless. She was truly all about the Benjamins.

But I loved her. The funny thing about Samantha was that she was so beautiful, clearly educated and actually kind of prim, that when these outrageous things would come out of her mouth it made it so much more shocking and hilarious. She started telling me about her favorite clients, what they did together, where they took her to dinner. She had one client that paid twice her rate. He liked to take her to swingers' clubs, one in particular that I'd heard of and that was known for being really skeezy.

"You're not worried about someone seeing you there?"

"He's paying me minimum $10,000 each time. He could film me for that money and show it to my parents, I wouldn't care."

Samantha's Advanced Escorting for the Postmodern Woman seminar was interrupted by a screaming match that had erupted across the apartment.

Jason was yelling into the phone at the top of his lungs.

"Bruce, I gave you my lawyer's number. I won't waste my time talking to a criminal like you. If you want to be an asshole, talk to my lawyer, that's what I pay him for, to deal with losers like you. If you want to be a gentleman, we can both save a lot of money...I'm listening."

The guy on the other end said something, and Jason's jaw clenched.

"Are you threatening me? Are you threatening me? I know you didn't just do that. Are you asking me to call the cops on you?"

He leaned back in his chair, kicking his leg on his desk, which exposed something around his ankle.

"Oh, my God," I thought to myself. "Is that what I think it is?"

I was pretty sure he was wearing some kind of electronic tracking device. The kind you attach to endangered polar bears on ice floes, or criminals you don't want skipping town. He was a pimp. I guess I shouldn't have been surprised he was also an ex-con. As he continued to pound away at the guy on the other end of the line, I started to freak. *What if he treated me like that?*

I thought if I told him that I didn't like to be spoken to that way, he'd respect me and everything would be okay.

When he finally hung up, I let the dust settle and walked over to him.

"If you want to get me to do what you want to do, you can't be like that with me," I said, trying to sound assertive. "I respond to nice."

"I prefer nice," he said. "It's just some people have to be dealt with in a certain way. That got a little insane, I know. But that guy is insane. We've known each other for a while. That's how we talk. Relax babe."

Satisfied with his answer, I went over a poured myself some more wine. As I would come to learn about myself later, when it came to denial, my mom had nothing on me.

*   *   *

I ended up more or less moving in with Jason, while Samantha disappeared back to the city.

One day, Jason nonchalantly mentioned that his probation officer was going to be stopping by sometime in the afternoon. I freaked. The place was a drug den. There were semi-naked girls lounging around everywhere. But he wasn't fazed. He roused a couple of girls and told them to clean up and went back to working the phones.

As the appointment time neared, he demanded that all of the girls stick around. We put on some clothes and tried not to look like drugged-out hos. It was Jason's way of showing his girls that he had it all under control. More importantly, it was his way of giving the finger to the law.

The probation officer walked in, gave a funny smile, but didn't say anything. There was nothing he could say. He asked Jason a bunch of perfunctory questions and left.

That night, I finally got the nerve to ask Jason what the ankle bracelet was all about. Jason explained that he had been busted at the Newark airport for trying to smuggle in four thousand ecstasy tablets on a flight from Amsterdam. *Hmmm*, I thought, *not quite* Oceans 11. He had done a year and a half in a Jersey prison and was now out on probation. The electronic ankle bracelet made sure he stayed in Jersey. The probation officer visits made sure he was staying clean.

After our little talk, we decided to celebrate. Jason didn't do any coke because he was getting tested the next day. But he could do other drugs they didn't test for, like Ketamine, or Special K, a tranquilizer popular with veterinarians that puts you into a deep trance-like state called a "K-Hole." I thought, "When in Rome, do like the Romans" and, in the kingdom of Hoboken, Jason was Caesar, and Caesar was high on animal anesthetic.

So I did a few bumps, sat down beside him on the couch and was immediately sucked into the weird void so specific to that drug. Your emotions don't even come into it, the rest of you is so messed up. You just sink into yourself like you're slowly drowning in quicksand. Drowning in quicksand may not sound like a good trip—but, trust me, if your body can take it, it's one of the deepest and most intense highs, or I should say lows, around.

Jason and I stayed like that, side by side on the couch, for hours. When we came out of it, everyone else was gone. I looked over at him, and all of a sudden I liked him. I was okay with all of his chaos and aggression— that was just business. I could see he was really a big kid. He seemed unafraid to be himself and open up to me, and I felt like I could be myself, totally uncensored and uninhibited.

He snuggled up to me, and we lay together closer. My mind started racing, *Why did this feel so good?* I told myself to be quiet and melted into him a little more. He was hot in his own bad-boy Jewish way. On one shoulder he has a really intense dragon tattoo, and on the other, Hanuman, the Hindu monkey god of strength and loyalty—star of the Hindu fairy tale, the *Ramayana*. On his wrist he wore a classic Cartier watch. It was a mishmash of totally sexy contradictions.

When he kissed me the first time, I felt like we were meant to be together. It sounds incredibly cheesy, but it was something I'd never thought about anyone else. I fell in love with him right there.

Can you tell the grandkids that their grandparents fell in love over a gram of horse tranquilizer? Probably not. But it was our moment, and it was real.

A couple of hours later, Samantha came back and joined the party. As Samantha and I were cuddling together on his bed after our totally intense threesome, he finally turned to me and asked, "Are you ready to go to work?"

"I'm ready," I said.

He didn't need to convince me.

He convinced me by not convincing me.

He's a sales genius.

And I am a curious cat.

"Great," he said. "And by the way, your new name is Natalia."

"My *new* name?" I said. "But people already call me Natalia—Peter calls me Natalia. I thought the whole point of adopting a second name was to stay under the radar. Or at least become like a character or something, some kind of fantasy for the client?"

"Well, is there another name you want to use?"

I thought about it for a few minutes. I didn't want anything that sounded too stripper-y or porn-esque, like Candy, Angel or Bambi.

What was a killer, sexy name that I felt suited me?

"You're right, Natalia is hot," I said.

It just felt right. It had an exotic ring to it, and it was real. I decided then and there what my mission would be: I would bring my own brand of honesty and realness to my work.

I got up to get dressed and looked at my phone. Yikes. Thirty missed calls from Paul, a few from my mother and some girlfriends. I called back a girlfriend and chatted. I let her know that I was alive, safe, hanging out at a friend's house in Jersey—yes, New Jersey, it's that far away land on the other side of the river—and would be back...eventually.

* * *

Jason got to work. As I listened to him on the phone, he was promising prospective clients that I was drop-dead beautiful, with the best ass he'd ever seen and from what he'd been told, super-talented in bed.

My anxiety started setting in. Drop-dead gorgeous? No one's ever accused me of that. I did have a great ass. And yes, I was wild in bed.

Maybe I could pull it off.

I focused in on my clothes. Samantha had thankfully left me something to wear in case I went to see a client. A backless silk shirt and a short black skirt that actually looked great. I didn't exactly have a perfect purse to carry and that messed with my confidence, which will sound ridiculous to any guy reading this. But women will understand. I shut that part of my brain off and went into the bathroom to check myself out. *Shit!* I had a hickey on my neck. I wondered who was responsible: Samantha or Jason? I had a flashback of sitting on top of Jason with his dick inside me and Samantha behind me with her hands on my hips grinding my hips back and forth and her mouth connecting with my neck and sucking really hard until I came.

Samantha.

Whoa. I shook myself back to the present.

What was I going to do about the hickey? I looked in my makeup bag. I didn't have much with me. I hadn't been planning to stay more than a few hours. In typical New York style, my things were scattered at a few different apartments.

Most of my stuff was at Paul's, where I'd been living for more than two years. Since I'd left Paul, I didn't want to impose on any one friend, so I was kind of bouncing around. I found some concealer and covered it up as best I could. I hadn't even started working and already I was making myself "un-sellable." I went into the living room to show Jason, a stressed expression on my face.

"What? The hickey? You can barely see it," he said.

It was big and purple; of course you could see it.

"Guys will think it's hot. It's like proof that you're a sexual person."

Won't me showing up to have sex for money be proof of that enough? I thought.

The phone rang, and Jason started chatting with another prospective client. He smiled at me and said into the phone, "Hey, do you think, if you're fooling around with a girl, and she has a hickey on her neck that it's hot? That's what I thought. Here, can I put you on the phone with a girl, and you tell her what you just told me?"

He handed me the cordless. I put it to my ear.

"Hi, this is Natalia."

"Hi, Natalia," said a deep, rough voice. Very New York.

"I would not be turned off by a hickey. I'd just want to give you a bigger, badder one."

Wow, I thought, *that's cool.*

I laughed and said, "Well, it was a girl who gave it to me."

"Well, in that case, put Jason on the phone... you're coming over right now."

I laughed and handed the phone back to Jason. This was going to be a fun life. I went back to the bathroom to finish with my makeup. I wiped the concealer off my neck and wore my hickey proudly, like a new tattoo. I was ready for my first appointment. Okay, this was technically the second, there was the Asian guy Mona had sent me to three months prior, back in February, but that didn't really count in my head. I'd done that as an experiment, for research purposes. I thought back to that first appointment and, except for Mona and her attitude, the whole experience had been pretty great.

I could hear Jason filling out the booking sheet with the client, getting all his details. I heard him hang up the phone, and I went back to the living room. I was surprised at how excited I was, my heart even skipped a little, but when I looked down at the sheet, there was some other girl's name on it. Jason saw the confusion on my face and said, "Natalia, I already have an amazing appointment for you lined up, didn't I tell you?"

*   *   *

The first date Jason sent me on was with Kevin, a law school graduate, whose dad had bought him two escorts for his graduation present. He was a nice guy, but completely overwhelmed by Isabella and me.

Isabella was a stunning Colombian girl, nineteen years old, five-foot-nine, and maybe a little skinny for some guys. She swore she hadn't had implants, which was ludicrous because her tits were perfect and stuck out like baseballs. I was the first girl she was ever with. Even though it was my first appointment, I found it very easy because he wasn't intimidating.

Isabella and I were naturals together, and we both knew how to put on a show: making out with each other, eating each other out like sex-crazed demons, sucking his cock together, pushing each other off like we each wanted it for ourselves and couldn't get enough. It wasn't the first time I had done it, but everything felt new and really, really hot.

As I walked out into the night, $600 richer, my underwear ripped, the skirt Samantha had lent me totally stretched out, I didn't justify what I had gotten into by trying to convince myself that I was "saving marriages" by becoming some kind of sex therapist. I wanted to make money and change my life. *Fast.*

CHAPTER THREE
"YOU'VE GOT $650 SHOES ON— ACT LIKE IT"

I excelled at my new job, and it didn't take long before I was "top girl," or Jason's "bottom bitch" in street lingo. This made me very popular with the bookers. Their compensation was 10% of the date they booked: a 2-hour/$2,400 date with me would earn them $240 compared with a 2-hour/$1,600 date with any of the other girls. The system had a built-in positive- feedback loop that favored the top girl.

After a brief chat about what the client was looking for, the booker would direct him to the escort's reviews on TheEroticReview.com, a hugely influential Web site, and ninety percent of the time the client would call back, often within the hour. The power of those reviews was undeniable.

During the 90s, Giuliani cracked down on street prostitution, but he pretty much left the high-end escort trade alone. It seemed every day a new Web site popped up offering to fulfill your wildest sexual fantasies for a premium. As Wall Street recovered from 9/11, the industry was booming, and it was all happening online.

Clients, or "hobbyists" as they are called, guard TheEroticReview.com (or TER, as it was known to insiders) with a geeky sense of ownership that is familiar to anyone who spends time on any kind of hobbyist web forum. It's a great source of information for anyone looking to make an appointment: which escorts to avoid, which agencies were safe to call, and who offered what services. It's sort of like a *Consumer Reports* for horny guys, only instead of vacuums and SUVs, this site happens to rate blowjobs and fake tits. Back in the stone age, before TER went online, clients had very few sources from which to draw information. Men relied on the pictures in the ads in the back of weeklies, which were notorious bait-and-switch scams, or tales from their friends, which were, if not outright lies, dramatically inflated half-truths. What guy wants to admit paying $600 for a limp lay?

The key to the site is that a profile (composed of four parts) is created by the first client, not the agency or the girl herself. This profile includes physical stats: height, weight, hair and eye color, breast size and shape, body type, piercings or tattoos, and whether her pussy is shaved, partially shaved or natural. Then the page lists what services the girl offers. This section and the "Juicy Details" are only viewable by "VIP" members. To get VIP status you have to either pay a membership fee or have a certain number of escort reviews approved and posted by TER administrators. The "services available" section details everything from kissing to anal sex. When an escort changes her hair color or decides not to offer blowjobs without a condom anymore, she has to email TER and ask very nicely to have her profile updated.

Like pretty much every other aspect of the industry, it disempowers the workers, putting the women at the mercy of the clients. Many women suffer from fake reviews posted by ex-boyfriends or a pissed off client, although plenty of bad reviews are based on reality. Reading those can be like stepping into a particularly twisted William S. Burroughs novel.

Here's a career killer:

appearance: 4 - OK if you are drunk
performance: 2 - I should have stayed home
attitude: borderline nuts
atmosphere: freaky in the wrong way

My luck was due to run out. After some excellent luck with outcall, this was the balancing factor. Not only was she not the girl in the photo, she was nothing like the girl in the photo. Rather, she was old, unattractive, half-crazy and a total rip off.

Why I didn't say no at the door, I just don't know. I realized right away she wasn't nearly like the photo. She also looked older. But I'd had a few encounters with older women that were great. Their enthusiasm more than made up for a small sag here or there. Maybe this time, too?

No. No way. About the time we lost our clothes, and I handed over the cash, I started to understand this would be awful. First, she wasn't in her late 20s or even her 30s. Also, everything about her was strange. Even the way she tried to up sell me (no dice) was strange. The covered BJ surely was strange with oddball noises and unsynchronized use of her hands. Time to proceed. She gets on her back, opens her legs to show a full, natural bush (when was the last time I saw that?) and sort of half-hides her face with the pillow.

As if it's not bad enough already, she's jabbering about this and that. Talk about shrinkage. I thought I might just get on with it and get that nut. No way with her yammering maybe in

English, maybe some Asian language—who could tell?

So I pull out and ask for a hand job. The only way I get off is by focusing entirely and exclusively on her nipples, which were nice and fat, the way I love.

Bottom line—should have jerked off as I had originally intended.

Stay away.

The 1-10 rating given by the client is split into two categories: appearance and performance. A 5-4 review (appearance: 5, performance: 4) can wreck an escort's career with the click of a mouse. In the first few months of going out, I got an unprecedented seventeen consecutive 10-10 reviews. I was, apparently, a natural. No one believed that all of my reviews were authentic. Accusations that clients were bribed to write shining reviews, and even that the reviews were completely fictional, abounded.

It was true for other girls that if a client told Jason he was planning to give her, say, an 8-8, Jason would lobby him hard to change it. "Please don't write one because it will only hurt her," I would hear him saying over the phone. "These are sweet girls. Don't be mean to them." In this way Jason was able to keep any less-than-perfect reviews off of the site, but I earned my actual posted reviews fair and square.

My first review was an important one. I had seen about half a dozen clients in my first few days, without any photos or posted reviews. This made Jason's job significantly harder. Jason was like the high-roller wrangler at a big-time casino. The big spenders would be patched through to him, and he'd work his magic. Jason would often spend up to forty-five minutes on the phone with each one, letting his natural ability to bond with strangers build an instant trust and camaraderie. He talked to them as if he were their lifelong friend—one who was only too happy to rent out his girlfriend for a few hours.

What Jason was selling, and I was providing, was more than a lay. It was the GFE (The Girlfriend Experience). It wasn't an original pitch. Other agencies were increasingly using it as high-end clients began asking for more of an "authentic" sexual encounter. GFE is the idea that most guys didn't just want to buy a fuck. These men wanted to hang out with a smart, sensual woman who would listen to them, tell them they were interesting and cool, do whatever they wanted in bed...and then leave.

Jason would make all the girls repeat this mantra three times before they walked into the hotel room to meet a client: "This is my boyfriend of six months, the man I love, I haven't seen him for three weeks.... This is my boyfriend of six months, the man I love."

I was a natural for the part. I was the smart, sassy girl whom you could take anywhere—and then do anything to. I was presentable, playful and baggage-free. I didn't look like a Barbie doll with traffic cones for breasts. I was educated, outgoing and, most importantly, a great listener. Some clients just wanted sex. Others craved the non-sexual part just as much. With me, they didn't have to choose. I delivered both.

*   *   *

Still, I needed a review on TER to be able to consistently command the kind of money we were shooting for.

The particular client Jason called, Steven, had been an agency regular since the beginning and was also an influential reviewer on TER. Steven agreed to a two-hour appointment for $1,600 and promised to write a strong review—if he thought I was great. If not, he would receive a credit with the agency, on the condition that he refrain from writing a bad review and instead give his critique to Jason privately.

Talk about pressure.

Jason insisted I stop at Manolo Blahnik's midtown store en-route to the Hudson Hotel for my date with Steven. The traffic was horrendous and the added stress of buying my first pair of $600 shoes seemed unnecessary. But Jason insisted that men would be impressed when I took off my shoes and saw the label. Jason had called the store and asked the manager to have the shoes ready at the register. Jason told the guy to give me the sexiest black stilettos he had, size seven.

When I finally got there, they had the black stilettos waiting for me. In size eight. A good size too big. They were true hooker shoes. The heel had to have been at least four inches high. I laid out $650 in cash and bolted out the door, my feet slipping out of the straps. When I finally made it to the Hudson, I staggered through the super-hip lobby of the hotel feeling ridiculous and went straight to the elevators. I made it to the twenty-fourth floor. I composed myself and put on my best, albeit wobbly, foot forward.

You've got $650 shoes on, act like it.

Steven opened the door with a warm smile. He told me to relax and take off my shoes. I tried to flash him the label as I slowly took them off. He looked at my ass the whole time.

Maybe Jason didn't know everything.

We made small talk. He gave me some vague non-statements about what business he was in. I told him about my acting gigs. He seemed semi-interested. That lasted all of three minutes.

I slinked up to him on the couch and began rubbing his leg. Then I kissed his neck and started my hand up to his balls. I could feel my panties getting wet. I could feel he had a large, strong cock. He grabbed my ass and pulled off my thong underwear. Despite his age (he was in his early 50s), I liked the way he touched me. My pussy started dripping, and I could barely control myself. When he went down on me, it felt good, and I let myself enjoy it. He treated me like a girlfriend rather than an object to fuck.

Steven and I had sex twice. The second time I let him come in my mouth and then we lay together for a few minutes. We chatted a little more, and I confessed the story of my shoes and my general nervousness about my review, but he laughed and told me not to worry about it.

Steven and I developed a rapport, especially after the sex. He understood this crazy escort world I had just entered and what it must be like for me as a new girl, which made me feel more at ease. As we went through the questions for my TER profile, I imagined I was Meryl Streep sitting across from James Lipton on *Inside The Actors Studio*, answering his slightly ridiculous questions.

He asked me my age, height, weight, etc., and I told him about my tongue piercing (I usually didn't wear it to appointments. It went against the "nice girl" image Jason sold). Then he asked me if I offered "Greek."

"Greek?" I responded.

"Anal," he explained.

When I hesitated to answer, Steven was cool. He said he'd put down, "Don't know." The line of questioning was starting to rattle me. I hadn't really thought through the ramifications of having to do things I didn't want to, things that might actually hurt, for money. So far, I'd only had to fuck and suck decent-looking rich guys who treated me like a queen. I'd even come a couple of times. That's one reason why I think I was so good. The hobbyists, the veteran clients, could spot a fake orgasm a mile away. I didn't come because I was supposed to, I came because it completed the sexual connection with the guy. They noticed and appreciated it.

I wobbled out of the hotel in my big shoes, pleased with my performance, trying not to think about the cradle of Western civilization's penchant for buggery.

*   *   *

Ironically, my ass became my best and most sellable asset. It was the first thing that came out of Jason's mouth when he was selling me to a potential client. His apartment was at the top of a five-story walkup, and I had to trek up those stairs every time I got back from a booking, every time I wanted something that couldn't be delivered or just to get a breath of fresh air. I hated having to go to Jersey, and those stairs, but they did do wonders for my glutes.

I was out at Jason's apartment for a full month before I got up the courage to break free from my old life. Most of my stuff was still at the apartment I shared with Paul.

Finally, I called him and told him I was coming over the next day. When I showed up he was drunk and had a wild look in his eyes. I kept my head down and quickly tried to pick up whatever clothes I could find laying around and tried to make a run for it. But he grabbed me as I got to the hallway. I slipped by and ran down the stairs.

He chased down the stairwell after me, screaming, "You don't know what you're doing! Natalie, let me help you. Where are you going? Where are you going to go? You have nobody, you're going to end up dead!"

I just laughed inside. At this point, Paul had no effect on me. My love for him had evaporated the first time his hand grabbed my throat. I knew what I was doing—his words only made me stronger and more stubborn.

I made it to the front door, but he grabbed me again. I yanked my body so hard to break his grasp that I almost fell down the stoop's stairs. A passerby saw the whole thing and called 911. The police arrived a couple of minutes later and offered to file a report and start the process to have an order of protection (similar to a restraining order) filed against him.

They seemed disappointed when I said no.

It was over between us. I knew I wouldn't see him again. I also knew he wouldn't come looking for me to try and hurt me. I had grown to hate him, but I wanted him to get better and leaving him with an order of protection on his record was the last thing he needed.

We had been through a lot: drug overdoses, money problems, stalling careers.... I convinced him to reconnect with his two kids and to start trying to be a dad again.

However, as soon as I was in a cab with my things and on my way uptown to Samantha's apartment, any pangs of guilt disappeared. As we turned onto Central Park South, memories of all the nasty things Paul had said and done to me came roaring back. He didn't deserve to be arrested, but he sure didn't deserve me. I didn't know where my life was going, but I did know this: Paul was over. I was making more money than I had ever seen in my life and soon would be on my own, in my own apartment, alone. I told myself over and over again this was a great thing, that my life was turning around. *Finally.*

Within a matter of days, Samantha was out as Jason's girl. And he and I began what you might call a capitalist adventure in post-feminist relationship dynamics.

*　*　*

Jason and I were lounging around the Hoboken HQ on a Friday night. The phone wasn't ringing. Jason was tethered to his apartment via his ankle bracelet, and I was joined at the hip to Jason when I wasn't grinding mine with a client.

I was finally crashing after working for basically a month straight. Jason was high on Special K and not much in the way of conversation. He was just passing time until his house arrest expired.

It was in moments like those that thoughts would creep into my head and mess with my emotions. I was thinking about my ex, Paul, and the fighting and crying and pain that we'd put each other through. I'm optimistic by nature, but I had to acknowledge the reality: I didn't have an apartment; I hadn't been to an audition in weeks, and I didn't really have many friends. Plus I had my period. Not the best night.

The phone rang and Jason came to. Jason put the client on hold, "Natalia, I know this guy from way back! His name is Finn. Should I play dumb, or tell him who I am?"

I giggled. Even though he was all business, he still liked to have fun.

Finn and Jason had history. Finn comes from money. A genuine New York prep school, Ivy League over-achiever who preferred being one of downtown

Manhattan's most debauched playboys to a life with a wife and kids on Park Avenue.

Jason told Finn that he was so busy tonight that he only had one girl available and, even though I was the most gorgeous chick he had, I was on my period, so therefore not working.

Finn freaked out, "Send her over, send her over!" I could hear him telling Jason.

Jason covered the receiver and looked at me.

"Really?" I said. "That's kinda freaky."

This was a first: I'd been with guys who didn't *mind* sex during a girl's period, but never someone who was into it.

"She'll be there in half an hour."

Jason took down his address, and I jumped in the shower.

"No! Don't shower!"

"Jason, I don't care if he's into it. I'm taking a shower!"

Finn kept me six hours, until the sun came up at five in the morning. In between our marathon sex sessions, he told me that he had figured out who Jason was. He knew Jason from back in the early 90s when he went by his birth name Jason Sylk and was known as the phone-sex king of Miami. Finn was the publisher of a now-defunct, high-end porn magazine and his family owned something like forty other titles. Finn would go to phone-sex conventions to pick up advertisers, and he'd met Jason at one of them. They'd immediately clicked, he said. Pretty much everyone else in the phone-sex industry was a fat slob. Jason was slick, and Finn liked his charisma. Jason liked Finn's pedigree and penchant for rolling big. He later told me that one night at Caesar's Palace in Vegas, he'd walked up to a table and seen Finn betting $20,000 a hand. Jason ended up spending

$60,000 to $70,000 a month on ads in Finn's magazine and their friendship was forged.

But their decade-old bond didn't stop Finn from warning me to watch out for myself with Jason. In the middle of his warning, he picked up the phone and called Jason. He told him that he had found a diamond in the rough and that he'd be crazy not to make me his partner in the business.

Then he hung up the phone, and we fucked again. I went home to Hoboken, still feeling a little down about life, trying to put his warning out of my mind and focus on the positive—like what a good impression I had made on such an amazing guy.

CHAPTER FOUR
"ROCKET FUEL FOR WINNERS"

One day, as we got back to Jason's apartment from shopping at a huge Staples in Jersey, buying new whiteboards and every other office supply you can think of, I finally asked him what I'd been afraid to since that first week. I couldn't believe I had waited so long, but it never came up. Everyone seemed to already know the story, and Jason acted like it was of little or no importance. But on that day we got stuck in traffic, and Jason started to sweat. He tried to hide it, but he was freaked out of his mind. If he wasn't back in his apartment by noon, he would end up in jail. We made it with just a few minutes to spare. So it seemed like the time to finally ask.

"Why are you under house arrest?"

He sighed, as if he were expecting it, and explained that he and Mona, the head booker who had been so cold to me, had been dating. They had been together about a year, right around the time I'd met him at the 54th Street office, when things between them started to go bad. They were in the middle of their breakup when Mona dropped a bomb. She was pregnant. And he didn't want to have the baby

During their final argument, she made an appointment to get an abortion.

Apparently, there was a lot of screaming and crying. He was vague on the key details. Did she want the baby, and he did not? I didn't have the courage to ask.

Whatever it was over exactly, it got ugly. And she called the cops. When they showed up she told them that he had thrown her down the stairs. He was already on parole for the drug conviction. She didn't press charges, but the damage was already done. He was in violation of his parole. He was placed under house arrest for ninety days, during which he was confined to his apartment, except for three hours in the mornings—hence the ankle bracelet.

Jason claimed that Mona had later written a letter to his parole officer saying it wasn't true, and I believed him. I had been around Jason long enough to know he had a wicked tongue but wasn't capable of violence. I had just left Paul, and my radar was on high alert, but Jason was different. I never felt threatened or scared, even when it all fell apart, and our worlds came crashing down around us eight months later.

Shortly after he confided in me, Jason got his electronic dog collar removed and the terms of his probation loosened. He was no longer under house arrest, but he still had to check in with his parole officer every week and get drug tested. This meant he was finally able to get out of the purgatory that is New Jersey.

I was so happy. I hated going out there. The fifty-dollar cab ride each way alone was bleeding into my income. And because it was so hard to recruit girls to work for the agency—no one trusts a pimp in a Hoboken walkup—I was working inhuman hours.

He wanted to move in together, and I told him straight up that I didn't want to. I reminded him that my motivation for becoming an escort was to become independent and have a place of my own—my own apartment, my own cell phone, my own life.

The plan was for me to help him find a cool apartment in the city that he also could use as an office and a small, but nice, one-bedroom for me.

I was trawling Craigslist when I came across a listing for a loft in Tribeca. It sounded just like what Jason was looking for. When we went to check it out, my jaw dropped. The shady real estate agent claimed it was ten thousand square feet. I had no idea if he was full of it or not. I'm from Canada. I'm metric. But it was the biggest apartment I had ever been in, let alone lived in.[2]

I was in awe, staring up at the fifteen-foot ceilings and wandering from room to room. I went up the stairs to one of the balconies and sat down on the floor, my feet dangling off the edge between the bars of the railings.

Jason looked around for about two minutes, then turned to the agent and asked him what he needed from us to make it ours. The agent told us he'd just need $21,000 cash for the first and last months rent plus a security deposit. On the spot. Plus a cash commission. The broker didn't ask us what we did. He didn't want to know, at least not exactly. He seemed to know that whatever it was, it was illicit. That was how it would be with us as the months went on. There were always certain types of people who got off just being around us. Most of them didn't even partake in any shenanigans. They just liked the idea of being close to something so sexy and dangerous.

Jason took me aside and asked me what I thought. I just looked at him. It was magic. I told him he should definitely take it. He shook his head and said, "No, you don't get it. I want you to move in here with me."

I started to protest, then I looked around again. It was so fabulous.

"How much were you looking to spend on an apartment?" he asked.

I told him $1,500. I knew that was a stretch as one-bedrooms in Manhattan start at $1800 minimum, but I was hoping to get lucky.

---

[2] Later, I found out it was more like 5,000 square feet. A dishonest Manhattan real estate agent—what a shock.

"Okay, you contribute $1,500 a month, I'll cover part of it, and the agency will take care of the rest. If we break up, or you don't want to share a bedroom with me, you can move into the second bedroom and that's it. You can stay as long as you want. If you want to move out after a month, that's fine."

How could I resist? When would I ever be able to live in a place like this and call it mine? I nodded and jumped up and hugged him.

Our new home was on the first floor in the back of an old factory building on Worth Street in Tribeca, conveniently located (for the vice squad cops who would later move a surveillance unit into the apartment above us) seven blocks from One Police Plaza. It was all stark white with big columns placed throughout the main loft's area with floor to ceiling windows along the back wall. From the middle of the loft to the back wall, the ceiling angled down at forty-five degrees, and the sun blazed through beautiful skylights that spanned that part of the ceiling. In the loft's main area there was a grand piano, a large marble bar and full kitchen with a Sub-Zero fridge. There were two huge bedrooms, the larger of which became mine and Jason's. I had a walk-in closet the size of most studio apartments with a huge mirror surrounded by lights, just like a theatrical dressing room.

The room on the right side of the loft we decked out in a sort of Marrakesh-meets-the-Kalahari theme in homage to our friend Peter Beard, the man who introduced us. The office was on the second floor, where two-second floor mezzanines looked down on all of the action, giving the place the feeling of a very hip bordello.

To top it all off there were twenty-six Swarovski chandeliers. Yes, twenty-six. Jason said they cost $3,000 each.

To top it all off, being on the ground floor meant no neighbors to complain about too much traffic in the hallways at all hours.

*   *   *

The Cipriani Downtown is one of those chic eateries that's so not about eating. It's always filled with the jet set crowd talking loudly about their jet-set lifestyles so everyone on the sidewalk knows they summer in Monaco, winter in Gstaad, and party on Puffy's yacht. The owner, Giuseppe Cipriani, is a racecar-driving playboy who always seems to be embroiled in some scandal involving the unions and the mob.

In other words, it was Jason's kind of place.

Jason and I were more or less inseparable unless I was out on an appointment. When my first review hit TER, the phone didn't stop ringing, literally. Everyone wanted to meet the new girl, Jason's next superstar. I was booked solid: at least one appointment every afternoon, usually with a married guy, always at a hotel; two appointments every night; and often a late-night appointment, starting at two or three in the morning and lasting a few hours. It was my new life. I was well on my way to achieving my goal: to save enough money to get out and have my own apartment.

We were drinking Cipriani's famous Bellinis with the beautiful people, including one of the city's biggest club promoters—the kind of guy Jason loved to impress by picking up the check for a table full of near-strangers. The promoter casually asked, "Hey, Jason, what is it exactly you're doing these days?"

Without missing a beat, Jason nonchalantly answered, "I'm the number-one pimp in New York."

My face flushed. The rest of the table, an assortment of models and financier types, people I'd heard of but never met, snapped their heads in attention. The air went dead. Did he really mean "pimp," or was that some sort of white boy, hip-hop reference?

Jason clarified, "My agency has the best girls in the city."

A few people still thought he was joking and laughed. The rest literally turned up their noses while still leaning in to hear what came next. The promoter guy, a consummate social climber, jumped in, itching to crush Jason.

"Everyone, this is Jason Sylk. Or is it Lubell?"

Lubell was Jason's mother's maiden name.

"Itzler, actually." Jason answered.

"Well, Jason Itzler, this isn't another SoHo Models is it?"

"SoHo Models?" one of the models asked.

She was obviously new to the city.

The promoter continued, "Yeah, Jason forced otherwise nice models to get naked on web-cams, totally fucking their chances of ever succeeding in the business."

I had heard of SoHo Models back in the day and narrowly missed hanging out there one night with some friends. I was going away on a month-long yoga retreat the next morning and wisely, for once in my life, went home early. By the time I got back to the city, Jason and SoHo Models had disappeared. Jason had shown me a *Details* magazine exposé about the whole affair. The article claimed that he had lured young model-wannabes to sign up with a legit-sounding modeling agency using the promise of photo shoots with famous photographers he'd met in the nightlife world, like Peter Beard. Once they were on the roster but weren't making any money (because Jason had no real connections in the modeling world), he'd open the office's secret back door to a series of stalls. He'd explain to the girls they could earn some extra cash by doing live web-cam chats (a.k.a. sex shows) with horny guys in Utah or the Ukraine—*no one they'd ever meet, and it wasn't recorded so they didn't have to worry about their parents or friends seeing it.*

The girls made a couple of hundred dollars, no one had to know, and everyone was happy, right? Wrong, at least according to *Details*. The girls told the magazine they were hoodwinked into working in what they called a sex-cam sweatshop. After the article came out, the business tanked, and Jason soon found himself dangling over the side of a six-story building on Canal Street held by the ankles by a guy who worked for a guy whose last name ended in a vowel whom Jason owed money. Apparently, that just doesn't happen in the movies or to Vanilla Ice.

Jason told me that the article was bullshit—the girls wanted to do the web-cams—and I believed him. No one was forcing them to sit in front of those computers, he said. Either way, he told me that he'd learned his lesson. He was not trying to disguise New York Confidential as anything other than what it was. In fact, he was doing the exact opposite.

"Here's my card," Jason said with a friendly smile, handing the promoter one of his newly minted business cards. It was razor-thin metal, engraved with our name, number and motto: "Rocket Fuel for Winners."

The promoter examined it, smirking, but clearly impressed.

It was like the moment in *American Psycho* when the bankers sit around comparing fonts and card stock.

"Those cards are great," I said. "If you get too high to call an escort and actually have sex, you can just cut more coke with them."

The entire table looked at me, and a roar of laughter went up.

I felt like the sharp-tongued minx in a table of wolves.

Then Jason opened his big mouth again.

"Everyone, this is Natalia, the city's top escort."

I wanted to disappear. I had just won these snobs over. And now Jason had to call me out. I fumed the rest of the night.

But the truth is part of me got off on it. I liked being part of his renegade operation. We were like Bonnie and Clyde in Dolce & Gabbana.

I've always been drawn to the extreme, especially when it comes to guys. It may be partly because I'm an artist and thrive on the edge, but I think it goes deeper than that. I was never rich or pretty enough to be one of the cool kids, and I've always felt rejected by the "in" crowd. I don't resent people born to privilege, but I've always felt like there was something boring about having it easy. I like guys who don't fit in. I get turned on by the self-made man.

And Jason was the ultimate self-made, if not completely delusional, man.

He had huge plans for New York Confidential. He wanted to create a *Playboy*-style empire of high-end escort agencies, starting with Vegas Confidential and Miami Confidential and then spreading across the country. He didn't seem to stop for a second to think about the fact that the authorities might look a little differently at someone who sold women by the hour than it did at someone who slipped gauzy photos of them in between hi-fi reviews.

But you had to hand it to him. Jason appeared to literally will things into existence. He told everyone from tables full of strangers in the city's hottest restaurants to his own family that he owned the best, most exclusive escort agency in New York City. And in a matter of weeks, he did.

*   *   *

Everything was shaping up perfectly, when out of the blue, Mona called. She and Jason started chatting like nothing had ever happened.

I didn't believe it.

If someone in my life had been responsible for locking me in my house for three months, I would never speak to him or her again. But Jason said that while he thought that what she did was wrong, she was in such a fragile state at the time, he didn't hold a grudge.

I wasn't buying it. Was she trying to find a way to hurt him? I told him not to tell her where we lived.

"Chill out, Natal," he said. "She said she wanted to apologize."

I said fine, but don't bring her to our house.

He met her at Cipriani Downtown while I went off shopping. And when I say shopping, I mean a major retail-therapy binge: dresses at D&G, leopard-print undies and bras at Patricia Field's Hotel Venus. Oh, and some shiny things: a Tiffany-style chunky silver chain bracelet with a deep magenta crystal heart hanging off it, earrings and a necklace to match and some giant white gold hoops.

After a few hours, I figured he'd be ready to give me a full report about what exactly Mona wanted.

I walked into the loft, fumbling with my multiple shopping bags. As I walked into the main area, I could hear what I figured was a porno playing on the TV. But there, on the massage table in the middle of the room, was Mona. And there was Jason—on top of her.

I guess she found out where we lived.

It wasn't just some girl he was randomly having sex with, which I'd seen before. This was something else. But I didn't say anything; I just walked into the other room.

They stopped, walked in and said "hi," and we all acted like nothing had happened.

*   *   *

Over the next two weeks, she'd stop by, and believe it or not, we'd hang out. I told her what was happening with the agency, and she actually seemed impressed.

Every time Jason asked if she wanted to come back, she'd say no. But I could see she was caving. She couldn't stay away.

"How could you trust this person to bring her back into your life?" I would ask him. It was like he was deaf. He was desperate for an operations manager. He couldn't handle the logistics of our rapidly expanding business. His hands were full recruiting and closing appointments. Where do you recruit for someone to run an escort agency? There wasn't a big labor pool to draw on.

Finally, the inevitable happened, and the bitch who had falsely accused her ex-boyfriend of throwing her down a flight of stairs, was back—running his business. She came in like a tornado in reverse, creating a whole new organizational flow chart and booking-sheet system, putting up whiteboards and pictures of girls on the walls and setting about undermining everything I had built up.

If you think your office is a sexual battlefield, ours was Fallujah.

*   *   *

Being top girl was like being the most popular girl in school. I had the money, the clothes, the $1,000 handbags. I lived in the loft's master suite. I had a full-time maid who made me breakfast, washed and ironed my clothes, and even organized my drugs for me.

Below me were some of the hottest women I had ever seen. Most of them were like me: innocent-looking, North American, young, fresh and enthralled with their newfound career. At least seventy-five percent of them had better bodies than I did. Some were taller, or had bigger tits, or faces worthy of the cover of *Maxim*. But a lot of them had worked as strippers before. They had that stripper gaze that looked right through guys. I was different. I hadn't been damaged. *Yet*.

Mona didn't care about any of that. New York Confidential made its name on new, fresh girls. When Mona's New Order began, she started hiring girls who'd obviously been strippers before. She didn't get, or didn't care, about the ethos of the brand Jason and I believed in so strongly.

Before she arrived, if a big client called, I was the one who got booked, unless they wanted an Asian or a blonde. I had earned it. I had gotten Jason out of Jersey and helped him set up this new fabulous life. I actually overheard her telling a new booker, "I don't even think Natalia is that pretty. I have girls who look like models."

Another time, I heard her calling a girl a lying, stealing bitch. The girl had finished a booking at 4:00 a.m. and had gone home rather than to the office to hand in her money. She was calling to apologize and let Mona know she'd be there before noon. Mona said, "You'd better be or you won't ever get another booking here or with any other agency in the city."

I thought that we were doing something unique. There was this sense of good karma. People walked away feeling happy, not depressed and guilty. We genuinely believed we were changing the industry

But Mona was a ball of toxic negativity.

I found out later Jason offered her a bigger commission, which of course meant a smaller cut for the girls, but not for him.

That said, she knew how to run an office. Thanks to her, we had multiple phone lines, a streamlined booking system, a super-talented web guy who updated our site daily with photos and profiles of new girls and a payroll system that appeared to be actually paying girls what they were owed. Because we only accepted cash, at the end of each night stacks of bills would be doled out proportionally like at the end of a high-stakes poker game.

When you think about it, it should be a cash business. You don't write a check to your pot dealer. But many clients liked to use their credit card. Escorts are usually an impulse buy, and few ATMs dispensed enough cash for even one hour of our girls' time. We desperately needed to set up a merchant account with a bank to handle electronic transactions.

So Jason walked to a branch of a nearby bank and asked for a meeting with a manager. He explained that he ran a modeling agency and needed merchant services and invited her over to the loft to take a look around.

He arrived home and warned me that the manager, a woman named Yolanda, was coming. I was to play the role of his girlfriend and sometimes model. I went more with girlfriend. I'm five-foot-four—way too short to be a model.

Yolanda arrived. We chatted for a minute and then I briefly showed her the loft. She seemed impressed by the photography equipment. We had lights and a backdrop to shoot girls for their web pages.

"Yeah," I said. "We get wannabe models coming through here all day. We snap their picture and keep a file for each one on the computers in the office."

White lie. We did get girls coming through all day and some of them did want to be models, but we were not going to book them for *Vogue* covers, that was for sure. Yolanda accepted a glass of wine and talked with Jason for about half an hour. She was in her mid-thirties and was very attractive, although, by New York standards, she would probably have just blended into a crowd. She had a pretty face but looked a little worn, as if she were a single mom or had some extra baggage in her life.

She left, and Jason was happy, "She's coming over with the guy who handles merchant services for the bank tomorrow night."

As promised when I arrived home the next day, the loft was buzzing. Yolanda and a young male banker were on the couch drinking wine and were laughing and talking with Mona and Jason.

Jason took me aside, "Natalia, we are going to be huge. Clark here is going to deal with us directly...we'll never turn down a client again."

I smiled through my fear. I didn't know if I could work more hours.

Clark was likeable. He was good-looking and confident, without being too arrogant, and built like a tank. That was my first impression. Apparently it was Mona's, too. They were clearly flirting with each other. It was the first time since she'd become the agency manager that I saw her relaxed and smiling.

Mona looked down on all the girls who worked for the agency as if she were disgusted by them. She was originally from Las Vegas—maybe that had something to do with it. Perhaps her mom had been an escort, or maybe she had been one herself and was ashamed about it so she took it out on all of us. Who the hell knew? She was like a sober, hot version of Miss Hannigan from *Annie,* and we were all the orphans.

I guess that made me Annie. Fuck it, I always wanted to play Annie.

*   *   *

Jason pulled me into our bedroom, and we started making out. We had a quickie on the bed and then he said, "Do you have any more bookings tonight?"

I shook my head no. I was so relieved. I really wanted to snuggle up in our big bed and finally get some real sleep. But Jason had other plans. He pulled out a huge Ziploc freezer bag filled with magic mushrooms and popped a couple. I couldn't resist. I stuck my hand in the bag.

When we went back into the living room, Yolanda was sitting between two escorts, looking like she was having a great time, and Clark had his shirt off. Mona was giggling and ran up to us. She saw the bag of mushrooms, grabbed it and threw a couple in her mouth. Clark, the other escorts, and Yolanda each ate a few, and we threw on the disco lights—yes, we had disco lights— and a smoke machine. We laughed for about an hour, and I found a spot to chill, swinging lazily in our hammock.

The 'shrooms made everything seem like a cartoon version of itself. Jason was the perfect caricature, with his Cartier watch, big smile, and glass of Johnny Walker Blue in hand. Yolanda was sprawled on the couch, the banker gone wild, wearing one shoe and half her blouse, still drinking wine. The two escorts were dancing on the dining room table acting like they were in an Off-Broadway production of *Hair.* Clark was attempting to put his shirt back on, but Jason insisted he wear as little as possible—he was "great eye candy for the girls." Jason thought it was only fair that since any guy that visited the loft got to look at pretty girls, it was only fair we get the same treatment and have a perfectly ripped guy around us. Mona's jeans had come off, and she was in her undies. Clark couldn't keep his eyes off of her.

Finally, I walked over to Yolanda to make sure she was okay. We were a lot to handle for a mid-level bank manager. She was loving it all, but she was focused enough to mention something about having to work the next day. I made the executive decision that she was going to sleep over. I led her into the guest bedroom, handed her one of Jason's tee shirts to sleep in and tucked her in.

I set my alarm for 8:00 a.m. We couldn't be responsible for getting our new allies at the bank fired. I said a little prayer that the alarm would wake me up. I calculated how long I'd been awake: a little less than two days. I should be fine. Once you hit the three-day mark, when you fall asleep, nothing, nothing can wake you. It's called coma sleeping.

As I was falling asleep I heard the sounds of sex—really loud sex—coming from the main area. I crept to the doorway and peeked out. Jason was passed out on the couch with the two girls. I smiled; he looked happy. Mona and Clark were on the fire escape and, just as I'd predicted, they were naked and fucking. I said a little internal, sarcastic thank you to Mona for sealing the deal with our new merchant services guy. Even better, if this turned into something serious between the two of them, maybe she would focus less on Jason, be nicer to me, and the loft would become its former happy self again.

As I headed back to my sanctuary, I was still tripping hard. I looked up at the ceiling and caught sight of one of our twenty-six chandeliers. I rolled my eyes. I kept telling Jason I thought they were tacky—they gave the place a sort of B-movie version of *Masterpiece Theater* vibe. Then I looked again, and I saw a kaleidoscope of a million colors inside those huge crystal balls.

"Wow," I said to no one in particular, "Jason, I totally understand now."

That's what it was like: You know what you are doing is so decadent, so out of control, so *not quite exactly* legal. But then you're in this giant Tribeca loft with beautiful, barely clothed people everywhere, doing lines, drinking champagne, dancing to pumping music and having sex. All the while you're making money—cash, tens of thousands of dollars of it in thick envelopes from über-rich men who really want to give it to you for doing something you really, really like doing anyway.... All of a sudden you realize you're no longer a near-homeless, out-of-work, twenty-four-year-old actress with a boyfriend who hits you, and the twenty-six Swarovski chandeliers somehow make sense.

*   *   *

The next morning, I helped our friendly neighborhood bank manager wake up. I took out my professional steamer and made sure her clothes were in shape for her walk of shame. I kissed her on her cheek and sent her back to her office from where hundreds of thousands of dollars would soon be flowing through our accounts.

The next week, her colleague, Clark, came in after banking hours to oversee our electronic billing operation. By day, he was the buttoned-up banker; by night, he became an underworld financial kingpin. We called him Clark Kent, or Superman, when he took his shirt off. I can only assume he was better at his day job. He set up a system that would eventually get us all charged with money laundering. We billed as "Gotham Steak," a non-existent restaurant that served very expensive, imaginary prime rib. A good chunk of the guys charged their appointments to their corporate AmEx.

Below, Clark and Mona were the bookers, often there twenty-four hours a day setting up appointments. Within a month, we had a staff of ten and a roster of fifty girls. Jason even stole one of the top bookers in the city from another big agency. She accepted Jason's offer reluctantly. She had been a booker for a couple of years and was as cool as ice. Eventually, Jason convinced her to become an escort herself. He was that good.

We found our top booker, Hulbert, selling his paintings on West Broadway. It was Sunday, and we were cruising up West Broadway. The sun was out, and SoHo was full of tall, beautiful people with skinny jeans and oversized attitudes. We both stopped short when we saw Hulbert's paintings. Many New York artists sell their work on the street, and most of it isn't worth the canvas it's painted on, but Hulbert's was different. His paintings were sexy and vibrant. He had maybe a dozen pieces, all various representations of the naked female form, on display. Those were just his female series. We later found out he was known in the 'hood for doing politically conscious murals, like one in honor of Amadou Diallo, an African immigrant gunned down by the NYPD.

Jason told him he wanted to commission an original piece for our "home." Hulbert agreed to stop by later that afternoon to check out the space.

Jason commissioned a painting that afternoon. He also found himself a new booker. As always, his intuition was right on. Hulbert turned out to be a natural born salesman: a handsome, chiseled black guy from the south side of Chicago. He embodied all the attributes you wanted in a booker—smooth talker, deal-closer, charmer extraordinaire.

At first I didn't know what to make of him. He was almost too slick by half. I had invested part of my soul into this company and wasn't about to see it fucked with. But all my concerns regarding Hulbert disappeared in one moment. The first booking he closed for me, I was in my closet, alone, in my underwear, listening to Supertramp and downing some champagne when I heard a knock. I turned and looked toward the doorway and saw Hulbert standing there with his back toward me. He started to speak, explaining the details of the booking he'd just secured—the whole time with his back toward me.

I didn't even know what to say. It took me a minute, but I told him I'd get ready right away.

He paused for a minute, then said, "Cool," and walked away.

He managed to demonstrate what he was about with that one show of respect. He wasn't there to check out the girls and get laid. I loved him in that moment and the feeling never left. He became my rock from then on, through to the bitter end when it all came crashing down.

Hulbert idolized Jason. Through Hulbert's starving artist's eyes, Jason had it all. He was the American Dream personified. Hulbert asked Jason, "Aren't you afraid [about getting busted]?" Jason answered, "The only thing I'm afraid of is not being the best."

For most people, that would sound like some kind of C-grade Tony Robbins garbage, but within weeks, Hulbert was making more money than he'd ever seen before. Jason expected the same drive and focus that he prided himself on from everyone at the agency. It was a lesson in motivation and productivity that business schools could take a lesson from.

Unfortunately, Jason ignored some of the most basic fundamentals for a happy, drama-free workplace—like don't steal from your top earner who happens to be your girlfriend. And don't provoke the cops.

*   *   *

As the weeks went on, my days and nights got more and more frenetic. I'd fly to Florida for a four-day appointment, come back and immediately do a ten-hour appointment, followed by another two-hour job. I'd then sleep five hours and start all over again.

I worked like that for a good three months straight. For most of this time my fee was $1,200 an hour. Here's how it broke down: an average date was four hours (or $4,800), ten percent off the top went to the booker, leaving $4,320, which was split 50/50 with the agency (a.k.a. Jason). So I'd net $2,160 per date, $540 per hour—or the hourly rate for a top New York City attorney. I averaged between six and eight hours a day, with usually only one or two clients. Just as Jason had predicted, I was pulling in ten grand a week, easy. Sometimes nearly double that.

Not that I could hold on to it. I was so new to having such ridiculous amounts of cash, I didn't know what to do with it. I loved being able to give it away. I'd take six friends out for dinner at the Cipriani Downtown and not even sweat a thousand-dollar check. Two thousand dollars paid off my mom's credit card. Another stop at Western Union, and she was able to go back to college.

My mom appreciated it, but the gifts were making her suspicious. I tried keeping the lies to a minimum.

She knew that I had made really good money bartending in the past, so I told her I was working at the exclusive SoHo House in the Meatpacking District and the tips were enormous. I could tell she was skeptical. She couldn't stop giving me that mom voice, a mix of worry and fear, unsure of whether to believe me. But in the end, I think she believed what she wanted to believe; just like in high school when I'd show up with brand news clothes I'd bought with my drug proceeds. It was so important to her that I was happy, she ignored the red flags.

I didn't need to justify anything to myself. I walked around with at least $1,500 in my purse at all times. I kept at least two eight balls (3.5 grams) of blow in my safe at all times. I restocked every week. I was doing a lot of it, but sharing most of it with the bookers and other girls and all the new friends (I use that word loosely) Jason and I were making. No one was at the point of going to rehab, so it felt harmless somehow. My personal expenses weren't that high, considering my take-home pay. I paid $1,500 per month rent. My phone bill was about $400. Manicures, pedicures, tanning, and massages cost another $500 per week. I spent about a hundred dollars a day on cabs. When I was bartending I had no problem taking the subway everywhere, but there's nothing sexy about arriving to an appointment smelling like the Canal Street subway station. Oh, and those fuck-me shoes are definitely not made for walking.

Despite all my best efforts to keep a bit of positive structure in my life, the only healthy part was how much exercise I was getting. I was in amazing shape and didn't have an ounce of fat on me. My body was all lean muscle from copious sex and lack of food.

On the flipside, I was increasingly feeling lost and adrift. When you leave a client with thousands of dollars of cash in your purse, you don't know what to do with yourself. Since I was required to be on call around the clock, I couldn't make any long-term commitments. No auditioning for plays that would take up all my evenings and weekends, and I couldn't even take a vacation or make dinner plans with friends. Living in the moment meant everything else fell by the wayside.

Shopping was my therapy, which I usually did high as a kite. Living in Tribeca was great. I would walk north on Broadway to SoHo and hit my favorite stores: Atrium for jeans and jackets; Big Drop for hipster tees; and Lounge for handbags and dresses. Men love cute little summer dresses—they are so innocent looking and easy to get off.

When I really had money to drop, I went to Jeffrey on 14th Street as it had the best of everything: Yves St. Laurent, Dior, Galliano.... Before long, my closet was filled with a who's who of downtown fashion: D&G, Nicole Miller, Diesel, Miss Sixty and Marc Jacobs clothes; Gucci, Dior, Louis Vuitton and Yves St. Laurent accessories; Manolo Blahnik, Jimmy Choo and Via Spiga Shoes; True Religon, Seven, Citizens of Humanity jeans; La Perla and Agent Provocateur lingerie; Oliver Peoples sunglasses; and tons of stuff from Patricia Field's Hotel Venus and all the other little boutiques in SoHo.

* * *

It was a warm mid-week afternoon, and my New York Confidential confidant, Joelle, and I decided to hit the Alexander McQueen store on 14th Street in the Meatpacking District. It's the type of store I would have wistfully walked by in my former life. I found it painful to see beautiful things I couldn't buy, almost like self-imposed torture. Even when I saved up enough to actually purchase something, I'd be too intimated by the cooler-than-thou staff to go in.

The store had just opened, and I had a purse full of cash and new-found confidence—a dangerous combination. Joelle and I were drooling. The fabrics were so velvety, the colors so smoky and rich. Then I found "the dress." The grey top was like a corset, strapless with boning designed to squeeze in your waist and make your tits pop out the top a little. The outfit resembled a tutu, except the pink skirt didn't poof out, it fell in all these soft folds a few inches above the knee; just short enough.

I looked at Joelle, and she looked at me. I didn't look at the price, I just really wanted to try it on. I almost hoped that it wouldn't fit well so that I could walk away. Then I remembered the money in my purse.

I asked the salesgirl if I could try the dress in my size, and she asked me my size.

"Zero?" I offered, displaying my total ignorance of couture-dom by giving my American size.

The salesgirl graciously tried to educate me.

"Do you mean thirty-eight?" she asked, translating into the European equivalent.

"I don't know if we have one. Here," she handed the dress in her hands back to me, "this is a forty, why don't you try this, and I'll look and see about a thirty-eight." She led me through the shoe section and my eyes lingered on them, causing me to almost walk into her when she slowed down to pull aside a curtain for a changing room.

I was so excited. I pulled off my dress and unzipped the McQueen. I took it off the hanger and pulled it over my head, then I threw back the curtain and turned around for Joelle to zip me up. The dress was too big. I looked in the mirror anyway, and I felt like a princess. For the first time in my life I felt like a beautiful, pure princess. But it was too big. Joelle unzipped me, I went back into the changing room, and I pulled the dress over my head.

As I was hanging the dress back up, I checked out the tag. The original price made my jaw drop a little. Almost three grand. Then I saw another number below it in pen. In pen? The dress was on sale? Almost half off. I thought they didn't do that. Especially at the designer's own store.

This was a sign. I was supposed to have this dress. If only they had it in my size.

"Natalia!"

It was Joelle. I peeked out from behind the curtain. The salesgirl was standing there holding my dress. She smiled and handed it to me. I was giddy. It was the thirty-eight.

Then she asked me my shoe size. This one I knew in European sizes: "Thirty-six."

I was rushing to get the dress on. Joelle zipped me up again, and I turned around. The salesgirl was standing with a pair of silver-heeled stilettos that matched the dress perfectly. I put them on and stood up. The whole princess thing I felt when I first put the dress on? *Now* it was real. I looked at myself, and I was happy. Happy I'd left Paul, happy I was earning money, happy I was free...and young...and beautiful.

I bought the dress. It was a little under $2,500 for the dress and the shoes. Or about five hours of my time. We walked out of the store, and Joelle said she was proud of me. Even the shopping bag was gorgeous.

As I left the store, I felt like I was high. I turned to Joelle and said, "Let's get a room."

The obvious choice was the Gansevoort Hotel, less than a block away. Why would we get a hotel room in the middle of day? Part of it was I just wanted a nice, private place to do blow and have a drink that wasn't the loft. Part of me just wanted to rebel against being controlled, and to do something on my own time for once.

The manager saw my shopping bag and winked. I smiled—my aura must have been radiating pink stretch satin.

He asked me what I did, and I told him I was an actress.

"Are you visiting?"

"No, I live here. Sometimes I like to take a vacation from my life."

He liked my answer. He upgraded us to a suite and comped us a bottle of champagne.

We hurriedly threw on our new duds and jumped on the beds like ten-year-old girls. We were ecstatic. I couldn't control myself.

I was making more money than I had ever dreamed. I was wearing clothes straight out of *Vogue*. I had all the drugs I wanted, and more. We were walking clichés, and we loved it. It was a fantasy world that couldn't last. But at that moment, high as the sky, slurping Veuve Clicquot and giggling like we were at a slumber party, everything felt perfect.

Of course, nothing ever lasts. Our cell phones started ringing like crazy. First mine. Then Joelle's. Every three minutes. It went on like this for half an hour. We put them on vibrate and tried to ignore them, but they just buzzed around in circles like dying bees on the bed stand.

We looked at each other.

"Let's go on the roof and watch the sunset," I said finally.

"Totally," Joelle answered.

"I want to wear my dress!"

As we were leaving the room, I threw my phone on the bed in a final act of defiance.

The Gansevoort's roof deck is *the* place downtown to catch the sunset over Jersey. There are comfy lounge chairs, a pool, a 360-degree view and always a lively, sexy crowd.

We grabbed a little bench next to a particularly raucous group, which included Steve-O from *Jackass*, who was downing drinks like he was on some kind of dare.

It was one of those classic New York sunsets when the sky goes from cotton-candy pink to deep orange. I lived in awe of those sunsets—we didn't have them in Canada. I later found out that it's Jersey's poor air quality that makes the colors so vibrant. Whatever, still pretty to look at, right?

Joelle and I ordered Cosmos and continued with our fantasy date.

Until reality barged in.

Jason burst onto the deck. He was clearly angry. Being in fashionista mode, my first reaction was, *wow, he looks good.* His style had become a little more downtown, and I liked it. He'd developed his own relationship with the salespeople at Jeffrey, and it was paying off.

He was with Bill, his account guy. Not his accountant. His account guy. Jason was an ex-con with horrendous credit, so he could barely get a 29.9% interest credit card, let alone a cell phone or a lease or a merchant bank account. So, Bill was the man who signed the contracts. Jason gave him and his pregnant wife an all-expense paid trip to Vegas as a thank-you. Nice guy, if maybe not the brightest bulb.

Jason was on the warpath. I could tell he was about to go into a tirade like I'd heard him do on the phone that first day in Jersey. He saw my dress and paused for a second. He seemed confused by it. Bill tried to preempt any ugliness by acting as intermediary. Of course, he was just protecting his investment, really. His name was on our lease, and if I wasn't earning money, the rent didn't get paid.

I told Jason to fuck off before Bill could get out a complete sentence. I was the one making the money that was paying the rent and his massive salary. He should show me some respect.

If I wanted to take a break and chill out on a deck with my friend, I could take a fucking break and chill out on a deck with my friend.

I was a little hot under the satin ruffle, I admit.

Jason wasn't having it. He starting raising his voice, telling me that I needed to get back to work and that he was my boss.

Then words like "client" and "bookings" started coming out of his mouth, and people started to look at us. I got up and walked away without saying anything. He was totally out of line. I was still guarding my double life closely. It was the one thing I had to hold onto.

I called the elevator and held back my tears. I couldn't believe the disaster that was unfolding. Everything had been so perfect.

Jason, Joelle and Bill all showed up just as the doors were opening. We rode the elevator in silence, and I swiped the room key and pushed open the door.

Once we got into the room, Jason admitted he didn't have any bookings for us. He just couldn't stand that I was having such a good time with someone other than him. He called me a "cunt" and screamed that Joelle was a bad influence on me.

She was a bad influence?

Pimps have never been known for their sense of irony.

"So you're going to be just like Paul?" I screamed. "Why don't you just hit me, too?"

I started crying. Bill and Joelle went into the other room and gave us some space. Jason tried to hug me, and I pushed him away. He suggested we go back to the loft. I said I didn't want to. I needed some space.

After a couple of minutes, I realized my play time was over. The mood was ruined. What was the point?

I agreed to go back.

It was no better there. Jason sent Joelle home, but she wasn't happy about it. I wasn't either. It only made me more upset with him. He fired Joelle and told me I was banned from ever seeing her again. I chose money over my friendship with her. I had only known her for a couple of days, but I felt bad about it. I cast her aside in order to make things right with Jason, but I was a girl with a goal—and independent life and walking away from my source of income with a girl I'd known for just a few days was not going to get me there. Was this job already changing me? I didn't know. I do know that we did manage to get good use out of the suite at the Gansevoort later that night. Jason booked me for a three-girl, $15,000 date that paid for my dress a few times over.

CHAPTER FIVE
MEET THE CLIENTS

My attention increasingly shifted to my clients: bankers, record producers, entrepreneurs, trust fund kids, and even a sports icon. They flew me to the playlands of the rich and debauched. I stayed in $5,000-a-night suites at the Waldorf and ordered room service for three days straight. I drank Dom Perignon in Miami Beach like it was Sprite. I ate filet mignon in a penthouse at the Bellagio. Tens of thousands of dollars were wired to the New York Confidential account for the pleasure of my company.

After having to rely on boyfriend after boyfriend for rent and spending money, now I knew how Steve Rubell and Ian Schrager must have felt with all of that cash stuffed in the ceilings of Studio 54.

I got into the escort world with a clear plan. I was going to apply the Wall Street Rule: set an amount of time and an amount of money, and then get out. I set the goal at $100,000 by the end of August. I later learned that the Wall Street Rule never really works for bankers either. What was designed to be a quick fix, turned into a permanent lifestyle before I could blink.

Rent, salaries, drugs, magnums of champagne, Dolce & Gabbana suits, advertising—running a house of ill repute—isn't cheap. To keep the whole operation humming, Jason increasingly needed me to work eighteen hours a day, three to four days at a stretch. I'd sleep for twelve hours before starting all over again. It was grueling, and it didn't take long before I needed serious amounts of chemical assistance just to make it to the next appointment.

If this were a *Behind the Music* episode, this would be the part where our first album goes platinum overnight, and the party never seems to end.

Cue the guitar riff.

*   *   *

One night, I arrived home at around ten o'clock. The loft was empty, which was extremely rare. There was always at least one of the girls or managers milling around on the $10,000 leather couches smoking, doing their nails, or snorting a line the size of Cuba off of an ornate Baroque mirror.

The first thing you do when you arrive at the loft is check the booking sheets. The booking sheets list all the women, their appointments, and Jason's notes on the clients. The notes included the client's occupation, favorite movies or books, their height, weight, a note about how hooker-y they wanted the girl to look (some guys want a slutty Christina Aguilera, others want you to be able to pass for a bridesmaid at their sister's wedding). None of Jason's notes were sexual. He wanted to know what the guy was really like: his personality, his quirks and his interests. He built detailed profiles, which helped us deliver exactly what the client was looking for.

I believed in what we were selling. It got to the point where I was actually advocating "choosing an escort" as a lifestyle. Choose an escort over your secretary and minimize your guilt and the potential for ruining your marriage/life, while maximizing your pleasure and happiness. Inspire the rest of your life by having the best sex of your life with me. I thought it all made sense.

Even the top girl had to man the phones if no one else was around. I never liked booking my own appointments. It felt weird. As ridiculous as it sounds coming from someone who did what I did, I hated mixing business with pleasure. It affected the dynamics of the appointment if I had to first haggle with the guy over the phone before we met.

As I was perusing my booking sheets, I noticed that one guy had booked three girls over the course of the weekend. Booking two girls for a big weekend was not uncommon. But booking three was rare. In addition, the guy had told Jason that he was an agent. He named the agency. I knew it well, as did every aspiring actor, director, and screenwriter. It was by far the most powerful agency in L.A., and probably the world. Every once in a while, a client would be forthcoming with his identity, but it was rare, especially if he worked in a high profile industry such as entertainment.

The phone rang and I answered. It was the agent. He wanted to confirm his appointments. I felt a lead weight drop to the pit of my stomach.

I used to joke with Jason that one day I would win an Oscar for playing an escort in a remake of *Pretty Woman*. But deep down I knew what I was doing was probably not the best move if I wanted a shot at a legit film career, let alone an Academy Award. But the naïve Canadian in me blocked all that out when I picked up the phone. I asked the agent why he hadn't booked an appointment with me. I told him my name and, feeling especially confident, interjected, "I'm an actress," seductively adding that I would love to see him.

We made an appointment for the next day at seven.

No matter what, I was reliably late for all of my bookings. Most of the time, it wasn't my fault. I was so overbooked that I'd end up with appointments fifteen minutes apart at opposite ends of midtown, or even overlapping appointments. Or something would come up, like Jason would find some woman walking down the street and want my help to convince her to try escorting. Or I was just late.

It was a warm night, and I took my time getting ready. I put on one of my favorite outfits, a green Dolce & Gabbana summer dress and a pair of Manolo Blahniks with three-inch heels. One cool perk about the business was that when you see someone only once, you can wear the same thing over and over again. The Dolce dress was perfect. During the day or early evening, you want to look casual and cute, but not too trashy or you'll stand out. I jumped in a cab, all nerves, and headed up to the St. Regis, the majestic old hotel on Central Park South.

As we got closer to the park, the traffic got horrendous. It was already past seven, and we were fifteen blocks of gridlocked traffic away. I started to freak out. I pleaded with the cabbie to do something, anything, to get me to the hotel quicker, but we were locked in a classic midtown scrum. The puny air conditioner's whiff of cool, dusty air on my ankles was the only thing keeping me from blowing a gasket. I started to sweat— nervous sweat—profusely, which is never good for business. Finally, I snapped. I threw a handful of bills at the driver, jumped out two blocks from the St. Regis, and started running. Well, not quite running, but hustling like a crazy streetwalker as fast as one can through an apocalyptic traffic jam in $600 Manolos.

What had I been thinking? What could possibly come out of this? The starry-eyed actress in me, with dreams of a Hollywood fairy tale, fantasized I was Lana

Turner heading to the soda fountain—not an escort going to an expensive hotel room.

By the time I made it to Central Park South and turned toward the hotel, I was already almost an hour late. I started having one of my panic attacks. The chaos of midtown Manhattan started to swirl around me. People were rushing by, going about their normal lives completely oblivious to this secret other world I was part of. I felt so far removed from everything.

Out of breath, but nearly at the hotel's gilded revolving doors, I called my girlfriend Andrea, the only person from my regular life who knew about my new career. A former escort herself, she had encouraged me to jump into the profession.

"Andrea, what do I do? The guy's a big time agent!"

She said, "Do you know how many actresses would kill for a chance to have five minutes with someone from [that agency]? You get to spend two hours with him."

That made sense, or enough sense at the time.

The doorman gave me a warm smile as I slid calmly through the large, ornate revolving doors.

I always liked the St. Regis. It's got class. The staff never made me feel uncomfortable. The security guards, doormen and clerks at the big hotels know exactly who the escorts are and what you're up to. Some treat you like shit. Most don't seem to care as long as you're discreet. Some are actually really nice to the escorts. Each hotel has its own preference about how they want you to go about your business. Some prefer that you check in at the desk and call up like a regular guest. Sometimes that can get awkward. During the Republican National Convention, the security was so tight they actually made me sign in with my I.D. at the front desk before calling up to the client's room. Fortunately, I used my real name so it matched my I.D., but most hotels, knowing that their high-roller clients want their nocturnal hijinks kept on the DL, prefer you to keep a low profile. Keep your head down and head straight for the elevator. However I did it, I always hated lobbies. I felt so vulnerable walking through them with a purse full of credit card imprint slips, condoms, lube, and thousands of dollars in cash in $100 bills stuffed into envelopes. I had this reoccurring nightmare that as I'd be walking through this super-swanky lobby full of rich and famous people, I would trip and fall, and as I skidded across the hotel lobby, my purse would spill open, spilling all of my illicit accessories all over the hard, marble floor.

I slid past hotel security without looking up and pushed the button for the sixth floor.

The agent opened the door. He looked a little peeved that I was so late, but he didn't say anything.

I gave him a quick hug and got down to business.

"Hi, I'm Natalia. Do you mind if we handle the financial stuff now? It's easier this way."

"Sure," he said.

The first thing you do when you walk in the client's door is take care of business. It's an awkward way to start a "romantic" encounter, but it's absolutely necessary. I had my own special way of greeting the guy so that it would be as comfortable as possible. It made it better, but I was always happy to be over that part of the appointment.

If they paid me in cash, which they mostly did, I never counted it in front of them, though the rules are you're supposed to. If they used a credit card, I had to place the card under the double layer slip, line it up correctly and rub an imprint with a pen or lipstick, like a Chinese food delivery guy. I always hated that. It felt so tacky.

As the agent handed me an overstuffed envelope I tried to break the ice.

"I told you I'm an actress, but don't worry, I won't pull out my headshot and resume. But if you like me and there is anything you could do for me that would be cool, but if not I won't, like, start crying or be devastated or anything," I said awkwardly, adding, "I want us to just be able to hang out and not feel like I have an agenda."

Sometimes I don't know when to shut up.

He quipped, "It might already be too late" under his breath as he walked to the mini-bar to pour himself a drink.

The agent cracked a bottle of red wine and told me to take off my clothes. He was no Ari Gold, but he was obviously a guy used to ordering minions around without wasting any time on Ps and Qs. He was surprisingly well built and had some very expensive shoes on—which I appreciated. I took off my dress slowly, slipping my panties down over my shaved pussy. All the while, he showed no emotion. He was as cold as ice.

There are basically two types of clients—men who would like to go out on a date with you and those who just want to fuck. I could tell right off the bat the agent wasn't interested in the girlfriend experience.

It was the first time I felt awkward and unsexy. My confidence evaporated, and a million questions raced through my head. When I became an escort, I developed this almost overwhelming desire, a need even, to please people—my clients' enjoyment became my entire focus. Now, I had done something to throw the agent off. By hoping to get something out of him, I had totally destroyed the mood.

Nevertheless, that didn't stop him from getting hard immediately and getting on top of me. As he started to pound away, I couldn't relax. I was trying to suppress what was really going on in my head—trying not to think about the power this person had to fulfill all the dreams I had originally come to this country to pursue. I tried to pretend he was someone random to help defuse my anxiety, but that wasn't helping, so I decided to live the fantasy. Every woman has created the fairy tale in her head at some point when having sex—*This is the guy for me, he really loves me*—even when she knows he's not and probably doesn't.

So I shrugged it all off and started fucking him like I was Julia Roberts, and he was Richard Gere. I told myself that he was going to look down at me and decide I was the most beautiful, talented women he'd ever experienced. He'd hook me up with the best manager, get me cast in the next Leo vehicle and give me the life I had always dreamed of. I didn't know what he was thinking about or feeling, but I was living a superstar life in L.A. as he pounded away. I came. Hard. Then I gave him a blowjob like his cock was my Academy Award.

I hung around and tried to strike up some conversation with him. But he wasn't buying the GFE act. In fact, he wasn't that into me at all.

When the hour was up, I slid out the door. He barely grunted a good-bye.

I would always get so mad at Jason when he'd try to lure young innocent girls right in front of me, or enlist me to help him. I was like the angel on his shoulder, trying to keep him from becoming evil. Some women were dying for a shot at the money. But there were others who were just not emotionally equipped to do what we did, and they were easy to spot. All you had to do was look into their eyes. I thought I was immune, that

I was the ultimate actress who could go into character four times a day and walk away untouched. But as I made my way down Fifth Avenue, trying to hail a cab as buses and cars zipped by, I asked myself for the first time, *"Was I in over my head?"*

*   *   *

A prominent British Lord called the agency one day. He said he liked to watch. He explained that he had a male escort whom he wanted me, and only me, to fuck while he watched. When I called him to coordinate the time and place, he warned me that this escort, Taylor, was so handsome that every girl who met him fell in love with him. When he told me about Taylor in his almost comical, posh English accent, he made him out to be some sort mythical hero out of *X-Men*.

I told him I was up for the challenge.

By the time I showed up, the suite at the Waldorf Astoria was already trashed: empty bottles of champagne, coke everywhere, porn on the TV. When I took the credit card imprint and read "Lord" it was only because my jaw was so clenched from the huge line of coke I'd just done that it didn't hit the floor.

Taylor was as beautiful as the Lord had said. He had dark hair and dark eyes—picture a smoldering Brad Pitt, but taller. He must have been six-four with long, lean muscles, like an Olympic swimmer. He could pick me up with one hand. And he did. We went straight to the bedroom. I was a little nervous, but more turned on by this new person. He knew the Lord well—they exchanged a hug. When Taylor looked around the room he said, "We're going to have a little talk later. You can't keep going like this. But for now," he fixed his eyes on me and smiled this warm, genuine smile, "let's have some fun."

He sat on the bed, and I sat on his lap, facing him. We started kissing—that great kissing: deep and slow, hard and in synch. I hesitated and looked toward the living room of the suite, not sure if I was behaving as per the Lord's wishes.

"Shh." Taylor turned my face back to his. "You pay attention to me, I pay attention to you, and he'll love every minute of it."

I smiled a little. The better our sex was, the happier our client would be.

And we began. We went for almost two hours. I got lost in space giving him a blowjob that I think I felt and loved just as much as he did. His penis was strong and big. The only awareness I had of the Lord was our positioning, the angle of our bodies. Other than that I have no idea what he was doing besides watching.

In his *Brideshead Revisited* accent, he'd make the occasional comment like, "Taylor, why don't you turn her around? I'd like to see you fuck her from behind." But not so often that it broke our rhythm, and his voice was so pristine I felt like Lord Olivier himself was directing us.

He would bring a silver tray over with a bump for me every once in a while. Taylor never took any. I guessed it was because it would mess with his hard-on. He came over and over again. I was on top when I felt my mind and body connecting and a really intense orgasm starting. I made it last. He felt so good inside of me, once I'd come I thought my orgasm was over, but then it started again. I was confused but let it take over again. I think it was the closest thing to Tantric I'd ever experienced.

Afterwards, Taylor took me out for a coffee at a nearby diner. He said he was worried about me. He told me I would never get ahead if I kept hurting myself with drugs. He said that he was living proof that you could develop a clientele and lead a wonderful, healthy life as a professional escort.

Taylor was one of the only people who cared enough to offer me solid advice. And though I didn't heed any of it, he and I formed a friendship that would last through my darkest moments. After our coffee, he dropped me off at the loft, and it was back to New York Confidential.

*   *   *

Taylor was the exception. At least eighty percent of the escorts I knew got high on pot, coke, heroin, ecstasy, crystal meth, Special K, Valium, Vicodin, Oxycotin, Percocet, Xanax, Ritalin, Adderall, Dexidrine... the list goes on. Many New York agencies specialize in party girls. They are in the $300-400 per hour range, and they also deal coke to the clients. There is a lot of money to be made in that racket. These bookings go on for hours, sometimes days. In theory, if you're a girl who likes her drugs, these are dream appointments—you get paid to get high and have sex—but it can be exhausting, and it sometimes got ugly. Girls told me stories about guys freaking out as the drugs wore off because they couldn't get it up, or the flipside, because they had a four-hour Viagra and coke hard-on and couldn't come at all, or because they'd just blown thousands of dollars, and the party was over, and they were due at the trading desk in a couple of hours and hadn't slept in days.

In the first couple of months even I had a few of those types of dates. They weren't as bad as you might think. But once our prices shot up from $800 to $1,200 an hour, everything changed. The Hyatt, W and Marriot upgraded to the St. Regis, Four Seasons and The Peninsula. Soon, almost none of the clients partied. It was a much better and healthier vibe.

*   *   *

Financially speaking, my best client was Neil. He was from old money, the CEO of his family's company. He ran one of those unsexy, behind-the-scene businesses no one ever thinks about.

The appointment had been booked for over a month with another girl. As the date got closer, Jason got on the phone and spoke to Neil about me, suggesting we change it up, and I go see him instead. Neil hesitated; he didn't like last minute changes. We spoke on the phone for a few minutes, and he asked me about myself. I told him I was an actress from Canada and that I'd only been escorting for a few weeks. I asked him what he was looking for, so that we could see if we really were compatible.

"I want someone to have a really nice evening with. I'm looking for a beautiful girl, outside and in."

His slow, deliberate Midwestern accent was curious to me; I hadn't heard anything quite like it before, especially not in New York.

I smiled and said, not to brag, but I considered myself beautiful, but on the inside where it's really important.

"Although, I've been told I'm nice to look at, too."

He laughed, and I put him back on the phone with Jason. They talked for a few more minutes, and Jason gave me a thumbs-up sign.

I was going to Chicago.

The first time we met, Neil fell in love with me. His marriage was 100% about family. He was deeply committed to his child, but his relationship with his wife wasn't sexual or passionate in any way. I gave him a blowjob, and then we had sex. It was really generic, but apparently as far as he was concerned I was the best thing since sliced bread. He was so satisfied I couldn't help but feel something approaching compassion and empathy for him. He was the client I saw the most. Our first appointment was in Chicago. We spent four hours together awake, and then the next morning I flew back to New York with six thousand dollars. I kept in touch with him via email, and he booked me for the weekend. He wired $26,000 to the New York Confidential account, and we spent three days together on a private island in the Florida Keys.

We saw each other about a dozen times over the next ten months or so. He paid $6,000 a day, and we would spend two to three days together. He wasn't very tall, or handsome, really. He was from Ohio, thin, pasty and very conservative. He was romantic in a traditional kind of way, but if there was one client I had to act with, it was him. He would never have been into threesomes, and if I'd have introduced him to Jordan, my crazy, party girl, new best friend, I think he would have been on the next plane back to Cincinnati. But of all my clients, he cared for me the most. He always listened, and I was honest with him. Except when I wasn't.

Our New York "dates" were always the same. Neil and I would go out for dinner together, share a bottle of wine and go back to his hotel on Central Park South. One night, his driver had just dropped us off after an elegant dinner at Le Cirque. I had had some wine and was feeling good. I took a nice bath, removed the tags from my new floor-length, black silk La Perla robe and slipped it on. I had never felt anything else like it. I opened the bathroom door and stood in the doorway. He looked at me and sort of half smiled.

"Do you like it?" I asked.

I knew he did. He'd bought it for me.

"Just don't wear it for anyone else."

"Okay," I promised, but, of course, it was a lie. It's not like I had a closet full of $600 robes, a new one for each client. I did think of him every time I wore it, but I'm pretty sure that's not what he had in mind.

I walked over to him. He untied the robe and started kissing my tits and my stomach. I lay back on the enormous bed and pulled him into me. We kissed, and he asked if he could go down on me. I had to bite my tongue. I hate it when guys ask, but I smiled instead. He started to lick my pussy, and my good mood returned. It felt good, but it was hard to focus. Like a lot of clients, he could be deathly boring. And after a bottle of wine or three at dinner, I was ready to go out and have some fun. As his tongue started circling my nipples, and he worked down to my pussy, I tried not to think about my friends partying sixty blocks downtown.

I tried to get into his vibe, his pace, to become the other half of this guy who thought I was Aphrodite reincarnated. It worked. I started to enjoy myself, my pussy got wetter, dripping down to my ass. He wasn't so boring after all.

I decided to reward him with a really good blowjob. I knew what he liked. Gentle and soft, but not too intense, or he would come before we had a chance to fuck.

I pulled out a condom and put it on him. He loved being on top of me and looking into my eyes. I let him look. He fell asleep almost right after he came. I went downstairs, smoked a cigarette outside the canopied entrance to the hotel and watched the cars turn into the park. I was looking forward to the $12,000 Neil would be paying me for our two days together. God, could it really be this easy?

When I woke up the next morning, Neil was sitting in the living room of our suite. He seemed removed and upset.

I thought he was pissed it was eleven, and I was just rolling out of bed. He wasn't paying me to sleep. Did he think I was doing drugs? Neil is the kind of guy who's probably never seen a joint, let alone smoked one.

"Don't worry about it. I ordered breakfast, but it was getting cold so I ate it."

"What's up?" I asked.

"Natalia, I'm not happy," he said.

Wow, this was a first. I'd had many clients open up to me, but no one had come right out and said it so plainly. I listened, waiting for him to reveal what the source of his unhappiness was. I was kind of nervous—I wanted to be a good friend and help him in some way, but I was totally caught off guard.

"I want more from our relationship."

Whoa? What did he mean?

"I don't see where our relationship is going," he said.

He said he wasn't happy our relationship wasn't progressing. He wanted more. He wanted me to move to Cincinnati where he'd get me an apartment. I'd become his full-time mistress.

I was knocked off guard. Maybe I should have seen it coming, with all of the romantic dinners and gifts. I mean he lavished me with gifts: an incredible, burnt red John Galliano gown (which I'd never worn), Gucci gloves, Christian Dior boots, a couple of dresses, the black La Perla robe....

At first, I was dumbfounded. What do you say to a guy like that? "Dude, you've seen *Pretty Woman* one too many times."

But I recovered and gave a flawless performance.

"But Neil, we've had the best time together," I said. "This has been amazing."

I told him what we had was perfect—a simple relationship with clear boundaries. I was exploring my acting career, and I needed to be in New York to do that. I knew he loved me and wanted the best for me, and wanted me to be happy.

"You have your family in Cincinnati to think about."

He was crushed, and I felt horrible. As much as I wasn't interested in him, I felt something that resembled love. I connected emotionally with all of my clients, even though that's probably hard to understand.

It's incredible how much power I had over guys like Neil. I could have led them on, told them I loved them and then bled their accounts dry. Even worse, I could have blackmailed them by threatening to make that dreaded call to their house that would destroy their lives. (It happens more than you might think.) What separates escorts who manipulate and destroy men from those who don't is a soul thing. There were women who would squeeze everything they could out of a guy without feeling even an ounce of remorse. For them, this was what you were supposed to do. This was the unwritten code of the business: get whatever you can, when you can. The hardcore escorts will probably read this and think I'm a fool. But I never took advantage of guys, and on some intuitive level, all of my clients knew that. I never lost track of who I was. That's one reason I was the best.

My little talk with Neil worked like a charm. He didn't leave his wife, I didn't move into a condo in beautiful downtown Cincinnati, and he kept wiring copious amounts of money into the agency for the pleasure of my company.

The fact was this guy was my bread and butter. He paid my rent, kept my drug habit going and fueled my

Manolo addiction. I had to help him see that the fantasy in his head could continue, if he just didn't let reality sneak its insidious way in.

*   *   *

He is a scion of one of the richest families in North America. He has dark hair, bright cobalt blue eyes and a perfect tan. He's six feet tall and built like a beach volleyball player. Think JFK Jr., if JFK Jr. were a coke-snorting, up-and-coming Republican who could fuck all night.

He was my favorite client, for reasons I think will become obvious.

He called New York Confidential out of the blue one night and asked for me by name. I was sitting right there as Jason made the booking. As he was closing, they started to haggle over the fee. Jason actually put down the phone and asked if I'd be willing to work for $1,000 an hour.

"Depends," I said.

First things first: "How old is he?" I had had a run of old guys and needed some young blood.

Jason: "Twenty-eight and hot. And he's got a super-hot girlfriend, who will be there, too."

Me: "Where is he from?" Russians freaked me out.

Jason: "He lives in California, but he's originally from New York."

Me: "Where is he staying?" A cool hotel is always a good final indicator of a guy's style.

Jason: "The W."

Good enough.

Deciding what to wear was pretty easy. Most of what I had in my closet was hot and expensive and made me look sexy, and I was going straight to their room (it was 2:00 a.m.) so I didn't have to worry about looking too trampy for dinner at Le Bernardin. However, I did take the time to pack my Louis Vuitton duffel bag with all my favorite sex toys (double-sided dildo, restraints—you know, the basics) and was on my way.

When the girlfriend opened the door, I blushed. She looked just like me, well not exactly, but she was hot, petite, with brown curlyish hair. Add it to my long list of sexual quirks: I'm attracted to girls that look like me. Sue me.

She introduced herself as Amanda and showed me in. She suggested we sit down and have a glass of champagne. She was dressed like they had been out, so I asked them where they had gone. She said they were at Marquee and Pink Elephant, two super-hip spots of the moment.

These people couldn't be cooler, I thought to myself.

Since she seemed particularly chatty, I asked her what she did. She told me she was an actress. She and Scott had been dating for about a year. They lived in L.A. They were visiting for most of the summer, and she was nervous because he was taking her to meet his parents the following week. I told her she was beautiful and seemed really nice and that I was sure they'd love her.

Scott appeared out of the back room with his credit card. When I saw the name on it I had to bite my tongue. It was his dad's; a very well-known, very, very, very rich man. That I recognized him is saying a lot—I'm not exactly a subscriber to the *Wall Street Journal*. It seemed a little crazy for Scott to be exposing his dad like that. I didn't even know his real name at this point.

I just had to ask: why not pay in cash?

I figured he'd give me the standard answer that he couldn't pull that much cash that late at night.

Whenever guys couldn't or didn't want to spend a lot of money, they would use the excuse that they couldn't get that kind of cash from the ATM.

But he didn't. He apologized, explaining that he didn't have access to his money right then and there. He was on an allowance and had gone through all his cash. He said this in a shy, embarrassed tone, like he was ashamed of having a trust fund.

I surmised that the credit card bill must go directly to his dad's accountant. The way his old man rolled, Scott must have known the bean counter would never look twice at a Gotham Steak charge for three grand.

He asked me if he could put a tip on his card, and I told him sure, even though I'd have to split that additional money with Jason, if I saw it at all. Cash would have been mine to keep.

Amanda brought me into the bathroom and said, "Let's get changed."

I didn't know what this meant exactly, but they'd already won my running "hottest client" contest I had going on inside my head so I was game for whatever they wanted of me. Her request was pretty tame. She pulled out a garter belt and fishnets, "Scott loves garter belts."

"So do I," I said.

So we got bordello-ed up and went into the bedroom. Out of the corner of my eye, I saw an ornate silver tray with a pile of blow the size of Mt. Kilimanjaro. I was confused. Did they travel with that? The tray, not the blow. I don't remember those coming standard with the rooms at the W. Then I remembered the W Hotel franchise mantra, "Whatever, whenever." I had heard rumors that included drugs, and I wouldn't be surprised if a few of the doormen had a great side business selling to all the VIP clients, but an empty silver tray was a pretty funny thing to order from room service with a straight face.

Scott did a long, fat line and offered me the straw. I usually liked to use my own straw, but I was in the presence of the equivalent of North American royalty and didn't want to be gauche. He didn't look like he was carrying hepatitis—if anyone can not look like they have an invisible disease.

So I did my own humongous line and thought to myself, "Okay, so it's going to be that kind of party."

We tied Scott up. We were tied up. He watched us. He did more blow. We talked. Scott oozed charisma. Amanda radiated sex.

At one point, I sat back on the couch watching her suck his perfect, hard cock, sipping from a chilled bottle of champagne, and thought to myself, *I cannot believe I am getting paid for this.*

Over the course of the night, he came five times, so did Amanda and I. When I left, I kissed them both on the cheeks. He gave me some coke and a few hundred dollars in cash as a tip. A nice gesture, I thought. And then I said goodbye.

*   *   *

The Quarterback's booking was scheduled for nine o'clock. I heard someone mention he was really famous, but the booking sheet didn't give many details. I was as excited as I was intrigued.

I arrived in the lobby of the W Union Square, looked around, and was approached right away by a short, overweight and not at all sexy guy dressed in ill-fitting Dockers and a pink polo shirt. Could this be the Quarterback? How could he let himself go this much? I didn't know much about American football, but I didn't think quarterbacks could be that short, or ugly.

As we got into the elevator, the man told me that he was actually taking me to someone. He was his agent. I tried not to look too relieved. I was nervous as we walked down the long, dimly lit hallway. There was a part of me that always hoped I would meet the love of my life and that he might be someone like the man I thought I was meeting: a famous sports legend.

The suite was big and nice, but still just the W— nothing mind-blowing. Or maybe I'd just seen it all before.

The agent left me alone for a second and went in the other room. He came back, and I panicked that the client didn't like me, that maybe he was looking for Gisele rather than Natalie Portman. Despite my reviews and status, my ego was still as delicate as any girl's, so when he handed me my envelope, I smiled with relief. I loved it when they just paid me, and I didn't have to ask.

The agent disappeared without saying a word, and my quarterback walked into the room. He was older and obviously retired, but he looked as fit as ever and had a warm, friendly face. He poured me a glass of champagne from the bottle that was sitting on ice and casually lay back on the bed where he'd been chilling when we arrived.

He turned on the large flat-screen and selected a Keanu Reeves movie on pay-per-view. No one's ever accused pro athletes of having great taste in art.

We lay together and watched the laughably bad flick. He still had the toned and muscular body of a jock, despite having been retired for many years. I touched his skin, which was tanned and moist, and we compared scars. He won, easily. His shoulder, hip and knees were covered in them, souvenirs from a decade of pounding in the NFL. Mine ran down my stomach from just below my belly button to just above my pussy. I always worried that guys would be turned off, or that someone would complain about it in on TER, and my career would be over, but it never happened. That's something else I learned from this job. Women think men want perfection. They're wrong. Men want to be appreciated. They want to be adored. Perfection intimidates them.

He had hired a call girl, of course, but I sensed he wasn't so much turned on by sex as he was in recapturing the glory days: crazy post-Super Bowl parties full of drinking, strippers and hot female fans throwing themselves at him. Some guys want you to dominate, even if they don't say it. Not the quarterback. When I kissed and sucked his dick I did it with an intensity almost bordering on worship. I could tell he needed to know that I knew how lucky I was to be with him.

Whether it was because of his tired athlete's body or because he wanted me to earn my money, at first he let me do all the work. I gave his gorgeous cock one last lick with my tongue, then reached for a condom. I climbed on top of him and put him inside me. This was at the peak of my career. I was in phenomenal shape and could stay on top for forty-five minutes and not ache. I looked directly into his eyes. He lifted me up and flipped me onto my back. I could tell he wanted to show me what he could do—old athletes never lose the drive to win. He went down on me forever and though I really wanted him to fuck me again, I knew not to stop him. When I complimented him on how good he was, he said, "I was always more of a giver than a receiver."

I laughed.

Finally, he was ready to fuck me some more. He turned me over on my stomach and gave it me hard. All I wanted was for him to come. Feeling a guy about to explode is usually all it takes to get me there. I came and so did he.

We lay down together. As I lay across his chest, he confided that he ached all the time. I stroked his body as we laughed at Keanu's acting. I became an expert in telling time. Without the aid of a watch or clock, I was able to tell exactly when the appointment was up. Two hours had passed.

He smiled his million-dollar smile, and we said goodnight. I told him how much fun I had had and thanked him for having me over.

Back at the loft, I went straight to one of the computers. I'm from Canada and can name every hockey icon, but up north we just don't do football. I wasn't quite sure whom I had just slept with. The agent had told me his first name when we were in the elevator on the way up. I Googled famous NFL quarterbacks with his first name. My jaw dropped.

I went downstairs with a big smile on my face and told Jason. Jason was a serious star-fucker, so I figured he'd be impressed.

"Guess who my last client was?"

He stared blankly at me. He didn't understand anything I had just said. He was blitzed out of his gourd on Special K. He wouldn't have cared if I'd said I just fucked Bill Clinton.

Sometimes Jason would drift off into a K-Hole. I knew that in those strange distant moments he was thinking about his time in jail. I would lie with him, looking into his face—with his pupils dilated and his memory shot—and try to guide his mind to help him see that he could shape his destiny.

"Jason, you do not have to go back to jail. Jason, you do not have to go back to jail," I would say over and over again like a mantra. I believed if he knew that in his soul he could prevent it from happening. His choices would keep him safe. If you believe a sting will kill you, you stay away from bees.

But Jason had built a beehive, and his recklessness would get us stung.

CHAPTER SIX
THE PERFECT FLOWER

With business booming at New York Confidential, we were in constant need of fresh talent, and Jason would go on scouting tears in order to meet the demand. Like a hawk, he'd observe his prey, circle, then swoop in for the kill, or in his case, to make the vague, enticing promise of easy money. He'd introduce himself, engage in idle chitchat, flash his giant white smile, and then, almost like it was an afterthought, he'd slip the girl his metal business card, seductively whispering that if she wanted to have fun and make some serious cash, she should call him. There was no place he couldn't find a potential new girl. Of course, nightclubs—where the music was pumping, the girls were most likely drunk and/or high, and the promise of sex was everywhere— were his most successful recruiting grounds. His other trusty locale was the Gansevoort, the trendy Meatpacking District hotel where Joelle and I had our girls' day out that ended in tears.

It was during a recruiting spree at our favorite haunt that Jason discovered my latest BFF Ashley. He caught her by the hook and then made damn sure he wasn't going to let his new find get away.

After Jason's newfound treasure gave him a little naked "audition," she put back on her pair of Seven jeans, tank top and heels (almost identical to what I'd worn to my first meeting with Jason in Hoboken). Just hours after he'd laid eyes on Ashley, Jason wanted to send us straight to work, but she wanted to go home and change first. Instead, I loaned her a top and dressed down a little, too, so that we would match. I gave her a razor so she could shower and shave her legs and pussy. She borrowed some of my makeup and my D&G purse. I gave her some condoms and showed her the credit card imprint slips and how to fill one out. We were going together, but I wanted to walk her through everything.

Jason had a great client lined up for us: a TER regular. He wanted Ashley's reviews up and working for her right away. He wanted her first guy to be a winner. The truth is, most of the clients were pretty amazing—the types of guys I would be happy to go out with under normal circumstances, that is, if they didn't cheat on me with escorts.

Ashley and I were amazing together. I loved her body. She wasn't skinny at all, you'd never feel like you could break her, but she didn't have any fat on her body. She wasn't noticeably muscular either—she had a naturally gorgeous frame and shape. The only thing I didn't love were her breasts. She had implants, and I didn't think they were the greatest. She told me she got them when she was sixteen. That shocked me. I felt like such a foreigner. What's more American than fake tits at sixteen?

When I saw Ashley's pussy, I was overcome with the need to lick it, to devour it. And when I did, I didn't want to stop—she tasted so sweet. Ashley was at that point when girl meets woman, and it's spectacular. I had to stop before I wanted to. I couldn't be selfish as there was a client in the room. I must have inspired him. He laid Ashley and I side by side on our backs. While he went down on her, Ashley and I started making out, kissing really slowly and softly. He switched to my pussy and then back to her and then back to me. I was observing Ashley as much I was participating in the moment because I was going to have to deliver my report to Jason. He wasn't going to get *all* the details—he was after all, still my boyfriend—but I was definitely going to deliver my opinion: this girl could be our next superstar.

When she came, I tried not to judge. It was believable, for a civilian, but I could tell she was faking it. You can't come every time. I came most of the time, but when I didn't, I had paid enough attention to my own orgasms to know how to fake 'em and sell 'em. There are certain things my body would always do when I came that I duplicated when I was faking: the way my eyes rolled back just a little; the speed at which my body moved; the way my legs would shake a little after, as though I'd just run a marathon. It was all part of the show.

When Ashley and I arrived back at the loft, I took Jason aside immediately. I said, "You've got to book this girl. She has the most beautiful coochie I've ever seen."

Jason wanted details. I struggled to find the words. Pink, small, pretty? How do you describe a perfect pussy? It's the great existential question. How do you describe the perfect flower or sunset?

I just said, "Don't you trust that I know something beautiful when I see it?"

He cracked up.

So Ashley officially became Victoria, and we all drank a champagne toast.

* * *

It was around seven o'clock on a Wednesday night. The loft was not over-crowded, which meant there were at least eight or nine people milling around. Thank God for my closet, otherwise I would never have had any privacy. It bothered Jason that I always locked myself away in our room, but I needed my down time or I would have gone crazy. I saved my energy for my clients.

Ashley knocked on the entrance to my closet and peeked her head through the curtain. She totally got why I needed refuge from the chaos of the loft.

"You want some sushi?" I asked.

She shook her head no. I dialed up my favorite sushi joint and ordered some tempura and a bunch of sashimi, keeping my fingers crossed that I wouldn't get a booking before I had a chance to eat. *This is what being a firefighter must be like*, I thought to myself.

I never felt hungry, but around that time I was always bordering on being too thin. I loved my close-to-zero body fat, but I hadn't had my period in months— great for business, but a little scary health-wise. Most girls have to take at least a few days a month off.

Among all my other roles at the loft, I had also become the period expert, teaching girls the industry secrets, like how to stop bleeding for a few hours. I'd send them to Duane Reade where they could find a natural sea sponge in the makeup aisle. Then I'd show them how to put it in like a tampon. It would stop the flow of blood for a few hours, and the client wouldn't feel anything different. CVS, Duane Reade's main competition in Manhattan, carried something called "Instead." It looks like a disposable diaphragm, a little disk that you push up inside of yourself that acts in a similar way to the sponge. I preferred the sea sponge method as I thought clients would be able to feel the plastic of the "Instead" thingy and wonder what was up.

I looked at Ashley, "How are you?"

I poured her a glass of champagne.

"Where are you from again?" I asked her before she had a chance to answer.

"New Jersey."

I was always confused about New Jersey. The image I had was that it is was sort of ghetto. Newark. Jersey City. Trenton. But I'd also seen *The Sopranos* and knew there were parts of New Jersey that were desirable in a nouveau-riche-suburban sort of way. My guess was that if Ashley could afford breast implants at sixteen, her family had at least some disposable income. But I knew nothing about her at this point and was dying to get the full story.

*   *   *

Ashley was lying on my bed. I was on my laptop, with TER open, checking to see if I had any new reviews posted. Regular people have Facebook, we had TER. I scrolled down and saw the name Victoria. I clicked on it and pulled up a new review for Ashley.

She jumped up and read it over my shoulder. It was a 10/10; I gave her a big hug. The review started by talking about Ashley's personality (sweet) and her goals in life (aspiring singer).

"Wait, you're a singer?"

"Yeah, you didn't know that? I thought I told you."

I thought, for a second, maybe I should introduce her to Peter, my record producer client. He was behind some of the biggest names in the then super-hot, pop punk scene. Then I rewound. Did I really want to send this bright, young thing to see one of my best clients?

I'd have to think about that one.

"That's so cool," I said.

I was about to ask her about her family, but I didn't. That was one question that didn't come up around the loft. The girls never talked about their families, and I always assumed the worst.

Right on cue, my cell phone rang. It was my mom. I hit the mute button—now was not the time. My mom's phone calls required a few things: patience, privacy, and at least twenty minutes. I breathed out and shook my head, trying to let the emotion go. A nice cocktail of guilt, frustration, annoyance and sadness.

"My mom," I said to Ashley, gesturing toward my phone. She didn't say anything. It was almost like she hadn't heard me. I guess we weren't going to be sharing family secrets.

She never did tell me much about her past. Like the rest of the world, I read about her back story after she found herself embroiled in one of the biggest political scandals in recent memory. By the time that happened, we'd drifted apart for a number of reasons.

Once the agency was shut down, I stopped answering my phone when anyone "escort-related" called. I got a new number that I only gave to certain clients, and everyone else got cut out of my social network. Ashley and I had some mutual friends, but generally we ran in different circles. She was career-driven, and as a result, most of her circle consisted of the music industry—or wannabe music-industry—crowd. My circle was more acting/entertainment-industry types and native New Yorkers/hardcore party-people. After New York Confidential, our separate worlds hardly ever collided.

When we hung out I thought I knew everything about Ashley, even though she kept her family history so secret, but when I, like millions of others, read her MySpace page, I realized I didn't know her as well as I thought I did. Although we shared the same life for a while, and I feel like I know her better than most people, there's a lot we never got to and a lot we hid from each other.

I read about her screwed up childhood, where she alluded to childhood abuse and her drug addiction. She grew up in a rich suburb of northern New Jersey with her mom and her oral-surgeon stepfather. In the middle of high school, she moved to North Carolina to live with her real dad and showed up in New York not along after graduating. Her family may have had a lot more money than we did, but like me, she was a wild child who'd split town to seek something better.

I worried that that our shared spirit might mean she was reckless. And in this business, you need to be careful with every move you make.

"Ash, do you know how to stay safe?"

She picked a condom up off my dressing table and held it in the air with a "duh!" expression on her face.

I laughed, "That's not what I mean. Like, legally?"

She shook her head no.

I explained to her the way it had been told to me. As escorts in New York, we existed in a legal grey zone. We weren't prostitutes soliciting clients on street corners, charging $50 for a blowjob or $75 to go "around the world." The way it had been explained to me is that we would be hired and paid legally for our time and companionship. Whatever happened between two consenting adults would be their decision. As long as it wasn't explicitly stated that you were exchanging money for sex, you'd be okay.

"Think of it like this," I said. "If you go to your hairdresser, you get a haircut, and then decide to have sex with your stylist, that's not illegal, right?"

She nodded.

"Here's where you have to watch out: If a client ever mentions or even alludes to sex, or tries to get physical before the financial transaction has taken place, there's a chance he's a cop, and you need to get the fuck out of there immediately. If a client tries to offer you more money to have anal sex or sex without a condom, you should leave because cops supposedly are under orders to bust unsafe escorts. And you should never have sex without a condom, or in my opinion, have anal sex with clients. That's just crazy. You can get really hurt."

She just nodded.

"Any questions?"

She shook her head.

"I've never met any of your friends. Do they know what you're doing?" I asked.

Now that we had gotten through the legal stuff, I was curious to see if she was like me, building a life full of secrets. I was desperate for someone to talk to about it. Part of me hated the double life. But another part of me felt like I had tapped into some secret fast-track to happiness and success—a loophole in system that I wanted to share with someone who was doing the same thing. Everything I was doing was illicit and counter to the mainstream's norms. But it all came so naturally, and I was having so much fun, I was beginning to think that maybe the whole of western society had it wrong, and we were the ones who had it right.

"No, they don't," Ashley said. "And I'm planning on keeping it that way. It might really fuck me when I get my record deal."

"That's totally cool. I understand," I said. "So who's your favorite client so far?"

"There's this hedge-fund guy. He's like twenty-five or something. And he has this sick apartment on the park. The other night he took me out to Quo, and he fucked me in the bathroom. It was incredible. I have no idea what the fuck a hedge fund is, but hedge-fund guys are, like, hot," she said, in her best mock-Paris Hilton.

"Totally," I said, giving her my best skinny, drugged-up Nicole Richie.

"Are you going to see the guy again? I asked.

She knew exactly what I was getting at.

"If he books me again, yeah. I mean, I hope so."

As much as Ashley was growing on me, I tried to keep an eye out for girls who were stealing clients from the agency. It happened a lot. I was, after all, Jason's girlfriend. But this girl knew how to play the game. She knew the better she was to the agency, the more money she would make. I knew part of the reason she was hanging out with me so much was exactly for that reason, and I was okay with that. I think we would have been friends anyway.

* * *

After a civilized brunch at Balthazar—heavy on the mimosas—I found myself in a chauffeured Escalade with Jason and Isabella on our way to the loft. All morning, Jason had been dealing with a Russian girl who used to work for him and Bruce, his former business partner, with whom he'd had that blowout fight over the phone. The split with Bruce created a mess: a bunch of girls didn't get paid for past appointments. Neither Jason nor Bruce wanted to take responsibility and pay up. This girl in particular was freaking out and screaming into the phone that Jason had to take her pictures down off the New York Confidential Web site. He had been telling her for days that he would take care of it. Just as we were turning onto Worth Street, his cell rang and on the other end was an attorney calling on behalf of the girl. Whatever he said, it must have been effective because Jason went pale for a second, and for the first time I'd ever seen, he went speechless. But he quickly recovered and did what he did best: charm people into his world. Jason turned the tables and starting asking the guy a series of questions and discovered that the lawyer, whose name was Mel Sachs, had been an old friend of his mother.

Jason flipped out. His mom was everything to him, and anyone who had known her was instantly like family to him.

The original purpose of the call was forgotten, and Mel agreed to stop by the loft later that day. As an afterthought, Jason reassured him he'd take down the Russian girl's pics.

When we got to the loft, Hulbert told me Ashley was on her way over. She knew if she were around, she'd score more work.

Jason made it known that if you hung out, preferably naked or in lingerie, he was more likely to book you. He liked—check that—loved having beautiful girls around him at all times. It inspired him—motivated him. It's an instinct as old as the first harem. It was part of Jason's personal philosophy, which basically boiled down to an obsession with beauty. You could say he was sort of a beauty-Nazi. He would actually argue that beautiful people were smarter and more trustworthy than ugly people. Sometimes it seemed that all he thought about or cared about was making sure he was surrounded by hot chicks. In some ways, it was sort of pathetic. Like he was making up for a personality or physical defect. But on the other hand, you could argue he was just an old-fashioned aesthete. The history of Western culture is full of great artists, thinkers and leaders who wanted to be surrounded by beauty at all times. I'm not saying he was a Degas or Gauguin. Caligula maybe, without the legions.

Jason's personal philosophy was an integral part of how he sold the New York Confidential brand to prospective clients: "Splurge on one of my girls, and your whole life will get better—their beauty and sexual energy will make you happier and more productive. Think of it like an investment in your general well-being."

I think there's actually a grain of truth to it. Sex is the ultimate release, and the attention of a beautiful girl lifts any guy's sense of self, even if it's temporary and paid for. The thing that Jason didn't understand is that most people have a conscience. He was so far gone, he couldn't see that what he sold created a lot of guilt and regret, especially for clients who were married or in a relationship. And, in a second, those negative thoughts could destroy all the happy ones that were supposedly making them so carefree and focused. On the extreme end of the spectrum, many of our clients were as addicted to escorts as they were to drugs or gambling. For them, the "happiness" that Jason was peddling was part and parcel of their road to ruin.

*   *   *

It was one of the rare New York summer nights when the air is warm and clear. Ashley and I both had bookings: hers was an hour long, mine was two. We both managed to extend them for an extra hour, and when I got back to the loft, Jason was on top of the world. He worked hard to book us the best appointments he could, and when we managed to improve on what he had already done and earn more money that was magic in his eyes.

Mel Sachs, who I later learned was something of a legal legend—he had represented everyone from Mike Tyson to David Copperfield to Derek Jeter—had come by the loft while we were out. Jason couldn't stop raving

about him. Jason loved the fact that Mel had been a
friend of his mother's and knew of his family's wealth
and status—two things that meant everything to Jason.

Jason's real name is Jason Sylk. His "sperm"
father, as he called him, is a guy named Leonard Sylk,
the son of a drug-store magnate who once owned part of
the Philadelphia Eagles. Jason's dad did well with his
inheritance, becoming a well-known businessman in his
own right. According to Jason, he was famous in the
Jewish community for being down with everyone from
the bookies to the bagel makers. When Jason was little,
he was the only Jew for miles in Philadelphia's super-
WASPy 'burbs. His family had had an eighteen-car
garage and a heliport pad. Jason told me that the prime
minister of Israel had once stayed at their house.

As a kid, Jason summered in the Catskills and
became part of the Jewish rich-kid mafia. He hiked,
swam and ate gefilte fish with guys like Jason Binn, who
went on to start the high net-worth targeted magazines,
Hamptons and *Los Angeles Confidential*. Jason
worshiped Binn. Although Binn's dad was a billionaire,
he went out and created a booming publishing empire on
his own. The New York Confidential name was a sort of
homage to Binn's chutzpah.

When his parents got divorced, Jason lost
connection with his real dad and became almost
claustrophobically close to his mom. He talked all the
time about how beautiful she was, how she was the
original MILF. She married well again—this time to Ron
Itzler, a big-time lawyer who lived in a posh part of
Jersey. When she died of cancer, Jason was crushed.
Jason was still in his twenties, and for all intents and
purposes, Ron became his dad.

Jason always talked about how everything he did was to make his mom proud. *New York* magazine later summed it up perfectly: his life was "a mini-epic of Jewish-American class longing, a psycho-socio-sexual drama crammed with equal parts genius (occasionally vicious) boychick hustle, heartfelt neo-hippie idealism, and dead-set will to self-destruction."

*   *   *

Mel had invited us to the opening of über-promoter Noel Ashman's new club, NA, so Jason called for our stretch Escalade, his chariot of choice. Jason was toying with the idea of having one on call 24/7. He said it would be cool for the girls and make them feel like movie stars, but I secretly feared he just wanted a floating hotel room to book even more clients. Rooms in Manhattan's best hotels can be expensive and hard to come by during peak seasons. And there was nothing Jason hated more than having us worker bees not making him money because we couldn't get a nice room.

I was so excited to be going out as a regular social person, I couldn't contain myself. I was bouncing off the walls. I had been working nonstop for weeks. I downed a glass of champagne, did an enormous line and offered one to Ashley. She shook her head, and I offered it to her again. She leaned forward and did it. I realized Ashley probably hadn't been partying that long. She was only nineteen and couldn't even drink legally! I felt a twinge of guilt that I was leading her down a dangerous path, but the truth was I was selfish. I desperately wanted a girlfriend who could keep up with me.

Her faced scrunched up as the powder shot through her sinuses. When your body isn't used to it,

coke can feel like Drano. I had been doing so much, it felt
as normal as drinking an espresso. It was my fuel.

Jason and Isabella were already in the limo. So
we dashed out the door, giggling as we burst onto the
sidewalk. We jumped in, and Ashley screamed, "Pump
this bitch up!"

Jason told the driver to turn on Hot 97's
Funkmaster Flex. The limo thumped with a heavy hip-
hop beat. I could feel my heart flutter from the
combination of the bass, the excitement and the coke. I
gave everyone a knowing smile. They all smiled back. I
felt invincible.

We pulled up, and the doormen showed us right
through. The club was cool, but it had the energy of a
party just getting started. Mel greeted us as we walked
in and told us to wait as he brought the owner, Noel. He
immediately set us up at the first booth, right where
everyone could see us. I assumed the New York club
stance: I jumped up on the banquette and started
dancing, helping Ashley do the same. I could tell she was
a little edgy. Edgy feels like this: you aren't comfortable
in your skin, almost to the point where you don't have
total control over your body. The remedy is a drink, or
ten. So I played bartender with the bottle of Grey Goose
that had magically appeared on our table. She shook her
head, again. I put it in her hand, and we drank up. She
was beginning to learn the drill.

We settled in, and I took a look around. As far as
club openings go, it was average. It didn't have the usual
crowd of underage models, and, as a result, we were the
main attraction.

Ashley was glowing. I mean literally. I loaned her
some shimmery lotion, which we rubbed all over her
arms, legs, cleavage, you name it. It went perfectly with
her tan. Remember the Versace dress J.Lo wore to the

Grammys a few years ago? Green, flowy and cut down to her belly button and up to her cootchie? Ashley's dress was kind of like that but sleeveless. She looked stunning. For a second, I looked down at my own tits and thought maybe I should reevaluate my feelings about implants. I tried to imagine what they would feel like and that's when my "what if" fantasy dissolved. I liked being small in a Kate Moss way. I'd leave the Carmen Electra look to Ashley.

Although she wasn't my type, Isabella looked hot in an all-white outfit right out of Miami or Caracas. I never liked her super-long, French-manicured nails and flashy, South American look. Jason and I were big on the New York Confidential image. Remember how he made me stop and buy Manolos the day I got my first review? I didn't buy it then. But over the weeks, I'd become a believer: clients were paying so much to see me, I made sure I delivered the whole package.

Isabella's style was definitely on my radar. I complimented her when she got it right and loaned her stuff when she didn't. She didn't mind, but she also didn't seem to get it, which made her an ongoing project. There was more than just the agency's image at stake. I was worried her skin-baring Latin look would draw too much attention, specifically the law enforcement kind. I loaned her a dress and helped her tone down her makeup, but I couldn't do anything about her long, French-manicured acrylic nails.

I decided to go a little extreme myself, Carrie Bradshaw-style, and wore a dark, silver metal, backless top, a super-soft, black leather skirt and my new present from Jason: the most expensive Manolos ever made. They were full of Swarovski crystals and made me feel like a rock star. Beyonce wore them that year when she performed at the Grammys. Between my sparkling

Beyonce shoes and million-dollar strut, Ashley's cleavage and J.Lo dress, Isabella's Colombian accent and oscillating ass, the Escalade limo and our "manager" Jason with his diamond Cartier watch and 10K in cash folded in his pocket, we were on fire—the sex industry's version of *Charlie's Angels.* The whole vibe made me really horny. I was secretly praying for a late-night booking.

I looked over at Jason. He was beaming. Mel brought over a well-dressed guy in his early thirties and introduced him as Andrew, a designer and owner of a high-end boutique on Madison in the Seventies. Well, that's what Jason told me when I asked him later that night. I couldn't hear a thing between the music blasting through my head and the coke flowing through my veins.

Ashley started dancing with me, and I pulled her in close, and we started making out. I was making Jason proud, and I was having fun. Jason had become the most important person in my life, and I liked making him smile. Ashley knew how to play the part just as well as I did. Our session started to draw a crowd, entirely male, eager to become part of our circle. Jason stepped in like P. T. Barnum , introducing each of us to the throng as he helped us down off the banquette. The guys swarmed around Ashley. She really knew how to get guys into a frenzy. She definitely made me feel a little threatened, but I liked the challenge. She was exactly what I had hoped she would be.

Soon, though, the club got boring. You can only dance on a banquette for so long before it gets old. Without anything to look at, or anyone else to meet or talk to, we lost interest. We made a move to our waiting chariot with Mel and Andrew in tow, and Jason told the driver to take us back down to Worth Street. I looked Mel over. He was wearing a custom-tailored suit, shirt and a bow tie—apparently his signature look. Andrew wasn't the best-looking guy, but he was super well-groomed and immaculately dressed. I jumped onto Jason's lap, and Mel focused in on me, complimenting me on my beauty and energy. His voice was like raspy velvet. Jason whispered the name of Mel's most recent client.

"Whoa! You represent Lil' Kim!" I'd had quite a bit to drink and couldn't hold back.

"Natalia, you have to come meet her Thursday night. She's performing at Marquee. I'll introduce you. It'll be fabulous."

I'd never heard a straight man say fabulous and make it sound so good. We arrived at the loft, and Ashley, Isabella and I floated into my closet and checked ourselves out in the mirror. We each did a line, and I thought to myself: *Okay, maybe that's enough for tonight. I need to sleep sometime.*

"NATALIA!" Jason's familiar call for me drifted into the closet.

Ashley and Isabella went back to the men, leaving me alone in my closet.

"NATALIA! Get out here! I have a booking for you!"

My smile dropped, and I looked into my eyes in the mirror, then squeezed them shut. I touched up my make-up, grabbed some condoms and a credit card imprint form and slipped them in my purse. I stood up tall and put my smile back on. I went into the living room and waited for Jason to give me the details.

"This sounds like the coolest guy in the world. He's at the Mercer. His name is Alex. He's an actor, thirty-two. You're going to love him. An hour and a half, $1,800, cash. Take the limo—it's still outside. Call me when you get there."

Wow, okay, I had gotten my wish. I skipped out of the loft.

I could hear Jason say to Mel, Andrew and the girls, "Watch this, she's going to get another 10/10 review."

As the limo pulled away, I made it my mission to come back with another perfect score.

*   *   *

Weeks went by and Ashley and I became closer with each passing sexcapade. She went from being my protégé, to being a friend and a partner in cri...I mean legally dubious, nocturnal activities. But I found that she still needed me to look out for her sometimes like a big sister.

Ashley and I had done the post-club stretch at a loft near Union Square. She wasn't used to what I called "activities," or the more extreme "adventures," so she looked a little worse for wear by the time we rolled back to the agency at around nine in the morning. She crawled into my bed and crashed out immediately.

You can only sit around doing lines, listening to random, almost-strangers ramble on in never-ending coke-fueled diatribes so many times before it gets tiresome. I was over that. When I partied, which was usually everyday, I liked to do stuff. Nothing too stressful, nothing that required too much concentration or brainpower. Shopping was my favorite. Armed with sunglasses, flip-flops, a grand or two in my purse, I'd do a bump and be on my way.

When we finally woke up, Ashley was not feeling so hot. She looked at me like I was insane when I suggested we go to D&G on West Broadway.

I was used to that reaction by this point.

"Ashley, trust me, once you get outside it's fun."

She didn't look impressed and needed some more convincing.

"It's an adventure," I added.

She reluctantly put on her oversized black Dior shades, and I grabbed her arm. We walked, and I chatted, trying to keep her mind occupied. I thought once we got to the store, she would feel better.

I found a few things for her to try on, passed her a baggie and a straw, and let her go to the fitting rooms. I found the cutest shoes, asked for them in my size, and sat down and waited. What is taking her so long? I slipped my flip-flops back on and knocked on her door, "Where are you?"

She opened the door a crack, and I peeked in. She was sitting on the little bench, the clothes still on their hangers, and a miserable expression on her face. I needed to get her out of there and back to the loft, quick. My shoes! Shit, they were beautiful, but I guess it would have been insensitive of me to make the poor girl wait while I tried on a pair of shoes when she obviously wasn't well. We walked out onto West Broadway and luckily grabbed a cab immediately. SoHo can be tricky for cabs. She flopped over and laid her head on my shoulder.

Lesson learned: shop solo.

"We'll be home in two minutes."

Shit, we were passing by Toys in Babeland, a great little sex store, and I was running dangerously low on condoms—never a good thing for an escort.

Ashley's exhaustion was contagious, and by the time we stumbled into the loft, I was ready to crash. We ripped our clothes off down to our undies and climbed into my enormous, super-soft bed, still wearing our sunglasses, and snuggled up for a nice nap. I kissed her forehead and thought, *I'm going to have to take care of this girl a little better.*

A few hours later, Jason woke us up by snuggling with us on the bed. Somehow, I wasn't the usual bitch I am when I'm woken up, and I actually smiled. Ashley rolled over, and Jason looked at me.

"We partied a little too hard last night...I mean, this morning," I said.

"You're crazy, Natalia," Jason said. "Nobody can do as much coke as you. How is she going to work?"

"She'll be fine."

I jumped out of bed, went to my makeup table and saw my mirror with a nice little line waiting for me. I felt Jason's eyes on me. I kept walking into the bathroom, turned on the shower and sat down to pee. I was going to have to slow down. I wasn't stupid. I'd seen *Scarface*.

CHAPTER SEVEN
BIRTHDAY BOY

Ashley and I were right at the height of our mutual success. I'd been with New York Confidential for five action-packed months and had attained an impossible seventeen consecutive 10/10 reviews on TheEroticReview.com. Ashley was right behind me with many 10/10 and some 10/9 or 9/10 reviews and we were earning a minimum of $1,200 an hour.

We were inseparable. We even found that we had a lot of friends in common. I could feel a lot of them start to wonder where our newfound riches were coming from. The fruits of our shopping sprees didn't go unnoticed, especially by our girlfriends in the nightlife scene. No one had the guts to come straight out and ask Ashley and me, but it brought up two problems for our friendship.

I'd become a little more comfortable with people learning I was an escort, specifically for Jason and New York Confidential. It was sort of a gradual thing. There wasn't one moment when I actually came out of the closet. You could say I didn't really have much of a choice considering Jason told everyone he met that he was the biggest pimp in New York, and I was his star. This reached a new level when he started running a weekly half-page ad for the agency with my face in the back of *New York* magazine shot by a really well-known fashion photographer.

I actually thought it was all a waste of time and money. None of our clients were looking in the back of *New York* magazine. They were coming in through referrals from friends or the underground rep we'd earned over the last six months. Even with the money we were making, which was pretty insane at this point, the ads were a significant expense. They cost thousands of dollars per week. Jason knew the ad didn't pay for itself, but that wasn't the point. For him, it was about getting our name, and my face, out there in the world.

Whatever. I drew the line when he suggested I should pay for half since it was my face and my name in the ad. I countered he should pay me for the same reasons.

Ashley's dreams of being the next diva meant she was not at all into anyone knowing how she was paying her rent. I messed up a few times and called her Victoria in front of her friends. I would always recover by joking it was my nickname for her, *because she was posh like Victoria Beckham.* Everyone bought it, but I could tell it still unnerved her.

*   *   *

One night, Victoria, sorry *Ashley*, and I found ourselves alone in the loft. It was a minor miracle. The phone lines at the agency forwarded to Jason's cell. Hulbert had the night off—the first I'd ever seen him take. Mona and Clark were nowhere to be seen. The office was, for a brief moment in time, magically transformed from brothel into play den.

"Yay! My sushi is here!"

We went into the living room and had a little sushi party. I poured soy sauce in her belly button and dunked a big piece of tuna sashimi in it. She put wasabi on her nipples and dared me to lick it off. Of course I did and then ran around the loft with my sinuses on fire for the next five minutes. Wasabi and irritated sinuses due to prolonged cocaine use do not mix.

Ashley popped in a custom house and hip-hop CD that our friend, the DJ Lee Kalt, had made especially for me. We were both so sick of Jason's Frank Sinatra fixation, we could have puked. Ashley jumped up on the couch with the empty bottle of Tattinger we'd just polished off in two minutes flat and started singing along to Mary J. Blige's "No More Drama." I flopped on the floor and rolled with laughter as I watched her shake her ass like a hoochie girl from a rap video.

All of a sudden she froze, "Oh, my God, it's Nas' birthday! I almost forgot!"

I shrugged. I mean, I like Nas as much as the next club-hopping white girl, but not enough to get broken up about not remembering (or knowing) it's his birthday. Did she want to send him a card or something?

She grabbed my hand and pulled me into my closet, "Come on, get dressed. We have to go to Select."

Ashley was on one of her missions, and I was riding shotgun. She believed she could magically jump-start her music career if only she could be in the right place at the right time when the right producer could meet her and be blown away by her mere presence. She always talked about how Mariah Carey had swept hair at a salon and checked coats before Tommy Motolla discovered her working as a waitress in a cheesy Upper East Side bar. Ashley, then just a year younger than Mariah when she was catapulted into super-stardom, had way more connections than a random waitress, and she sure as hell had the drive.

She pulled out her phone and dialed, "Hey, is he still there? Cool, I'll be there in fifteen minutes."

She hung up and looked at me, "Nas is still there, we have to hurry."

I grabbed a tiny Miss Sixty dress, a pair of Manolos and my purse, tossing in a full baggie of blow. We jumped in a cab and were at Select in two minutes. One nice thing about living most of your life in the wee hours of the night is you miss the cross-town traffic.

Ashley gave the magic word to the 500-pound doorman, and the velvet ropes parted like the Red Sea. But when we walked in, it was sort of anti-climatic. It was around 1:00 a.m. and the place was almost empty. Not what I was expecting considering he was one of the most famous rappers on the planet. I counted thirty guests in a club that could probably hold twenty or more times that.

The first hip-hop industry party I'd ever been to, just a few months after I moved to New York, was a Wu-Tang Clan release party. It was mayhem. I was the only white girl that I could see there and had to escape to the kitchen a few times. The guys were getting a little crazy, and I was too green to know how to fend them off.

So when I saw an empty dance floor and a small group of people lounging around Nas and his then-girlfriend (now wife), the singer Kelis, I was sort of relieved. Both of them were tearing up the charts. Kelis' "Milkshake" song was the anthem of the summer, and Nas was, well, Nas. If you're not into hip-hop, you won't understand.

The owner came over and set us up at the table next to them. It hit me. *Wow, so there was Nas.* I used to dance my ass off to his tracks, like "One Mic." I was never that into rappers, but he was definitely one of my favorites. He's strong and smart at the same time, and he's never succumbed to all the hip-hop clichés about busting caps in people's asses or calling women bitches every other line. He's an innovator and seeing him sitting right across from us was a thrill. He exuded that fame-glow I came to recognize from people who had ascended the heights. There is an intangible aura famous people have—a certain quality that lights up rooms and makes people turn their heads. Maybe it's their skin products.

I was excited, but Ashley was absolutely giddy. She could barely contain herself. For her, this was how I would feel sitting next to DiCaprio or De Niro.

I had a cool idea.

"Ash, let's buy Nas a bottle of champagne for his birthday."

She looked at me a little confused. Then like I was crazy. Then she gave me a big smile, and nodded.

"I'll go find out what they have," I said.

I skipped over to the owner and asked what kind of champagne they had. Veuve Clicquot and Dom Perignon. I asked how much they were. Three-fifty for the Veuve, four-fifty for the Dom. We decided to go for the Dom. So much cooler. Five hundred clams between the two of us was nothing.

I put in the order, and both of us sat there feeling a little gangster, a little hip-hop, and very rich.

While we waited for the waitress to bring the bottle, Ashley explained how we were able to crash Nas' apparently super-private party. The owner had given invites only to people Nas personally approved, but Ashley had told him about her dreams of making it as a recording artist, and I'm sure flirted her ass off, and he gave her two invites without bothering to check in with the birthday boy. She was like Charlie getting the gold-wrapped candy bar.

The waitress delivered our birthday present to Nas' table with our best wishes. Nas looked up confused, and then motioned for us to come over to his table. Ashley put on her game face.

We introduced ourselves. I made sure to give Kelis the vibe that we weren't groupies on the prowl, and it was just an innocent birthday toast. We hung out with them for a while. Two of his boys zeroed in on us, and it took some polite maneuvering on our part to keep our distance. Our time was money, and we were here to rub shoulders with Nas, not some of his boys.

It was getting late, but I was fresh off a bathroom (code word for coke) break and enjoying a little surge in energy, when I came up with another brilliant idea.

"Why doesn't everyone come back to my place?" I chirped.

Nas looked to Kelis uncertainly. She shrugged. We all piled into two Escalades, and I gave directions as we barreled downtown toward Tribeca.

They all, including Nas, did a double take when they walked into the loft. I'd bought them a bottle of champagne, but this was another story. Just the height of the ceilings was enough to blow most people's minds.

"You live here?" one of the guys asked.

"Yes, she does. All by herself," Ashley answered for me.

I put on the killer house CD we'd been listening to before and made everyone drinks—some of Jason's Johnnie Walker Blue for the boys and more champagne for the girls. I felt a little guilty about serving Jason's scotch to these guys, but we hadn't had many mega-platinum recording artists come by (okay, none), so I figured I should represent. We mingled for a minute, but then as quick as it started, the party was over. Nas and Kelis rounded up their entourage, said their thanks, and were gone. Unfortunately, two of the posse stayed.

They were the biggest and least friendly of the bunch. And that was saying a lot. They paced around the loft, checking out everything from the flat-screen, to the stereo, to the chandeliers.

My phone rang, and I walked over to the coffee table with one eye on our guests. I winced. Right next to my purse was this week's *New York* magazine, conveniently opened to the page with our ad with my airbrushed face staring out. I quickly turned it over, wondering if they'd seen it. I looked at my missed calls. Shit, five, all Jason. I dialed him and headed across the loft and into my bedroom, closing the door behind me.

"Where have you been?" he asked me. "I have a booking for you."

Oh no, not now. It was late.

"Jason, I'm so tired."

"C'mon Natal, it's only an hour."

"I don't do one-hour bookings, Jason!"

"Fifteen hundred, hun, for one hour. Write down the info."

I sighed and picked up a pen, scribbled down 60 Thompson, the guy's name and room number, and hung up the phone. It was at one of the hippest hotels in the city, so it might not be too bad, I thought.

I called out to Ashley, and she came into my bedroom.

"I have a booking," I said.

Her mouth dropped.

"We have to get them out of here," she said.

I didn't know what to do. We couldn't just kick them out. Or could we? I had to do something. There was no way I was going to leave Ashley alone in my house with two thugs.

I went into the loft and told them that I was really tired, but maybe we'd see them again sometime. I put their numbers in my phone (then deleted them) and walked them to the door. I said Ashley was already lying down, she was exhausted, too. I waited a few minutes and made sure I had everything I needed for my appointment, including a credit card imprint slip. The appointment was $1,500 cash, but my past experiences at 60 Thompson at this time of night involved copious amounts of drugs and lasted for hours. I slipped out the door and into a cab.

A few weeks later, the loft door buzzed. When Hulbert went down to check it out, four massive black guys rushed the door. Luckily, Hulbert was able to push them back. As he struggled, he could see that they were carrying metal pipes and bats. He was just able to push the door closed and lock the bolt. They jumped into an SUV and peeled off.

Jason, his lawyers, and everyone else around, freaked out. They all had their own theory about who was behind it. The Russians, the Armenians, the Mob, a rival agency, dirty cops. Ashley and I had the best guess, but we never told anyone. If we had, we'd have had to explain why we'd thought it was a good idea to invite a bunch of thugs into a loft full of tens of thousands of dollars worth of electronic equipment, piles of cash, enough drugs to keep Amy Winehouse high for a month, and a closet full of designer duds to keep Carrie Bradshaw happy for a year.

CHAPTER EIGHT
THE $2,000-AN-HOUR WOMAN

As the months went by, the clients got more and more exclusive, and the piles of cash grew larger and larger. Everything Jason had envisioned was coming to fruition. It was eerie. There was an almost magical sense to everything that was happening. Our drug-fueled 3:00 a.m. fantasies were actually coming true.

Then Jason came up with another one of his brilliant ideas. He believed in the Grey Goose-marketing strategy. The more you charge, the more they'll think you're worth—even if you're basically selling the same formula of fermented grain or the same girl with the same ass, pussy and mouth.

"Natal, I'm going to up your rate to two grand. What do you think?"

This would mean my hourly rate would be more than double what most of the top high-end escorts in the city were charging, including ours. You could make the argument I had earned it. Thanks to the full-color ad with my face in *New York* magazine and an unprecedented run of seventeen perfect ten out of ten client reviews on the TheEroticReview.com, I had become something of an underground legend. Everyone wanted to know what was so special about "Natalia," New York's hottest escort.

Here's the crazy thing: I am not a supermodel— far from it. I'm cute, but nowhere close to drop-dead hot. I do have a great ass, and I enjoy sex like a true nymphomaniac,[3] but my secret was I made guys want to hang out with me. I listened to them when they bragged about how much money they made or went on and on about their favorite baseball team. We joked, we partied, and then I fucked their brains out.

"Uh, what do you think I think?" I said. "But will anyone pay that?"

"We'll find out. Next call that comes in, I'm going for it."

His thinking was we would not only be making that much more money, we could use the notoriety that came with me being the most expensive girl in the city as a marketing tool for the entire agency.

So we sat and waited. Twenty minutes went by. Nothing. Then the phone rang. It was a new client—Asian, in private equity. Perfect. Jason looked at me, smiled and took a chance. He asked the new client if he were looking at our Web site.

"Look at Natalia's page and click on the link to her reviews. Read a few and call me back."

He hung up the phone. We waited. A few minutes later, the phone rang, and we both smiled.

Jason spoke first, "So what do you think?"

He said something that made Jason laugh and respond, "She's sitting right beside me. Are you ready to have the best sexual experience of your life?"

Jason listened, then winked at me, "How much? Her rate is two thousand an hour, with a two-hour minimum."

I could almost see Jason's pulse quicken. I couldn't believe it—he was about to close this guy. Jason's technique on the phone had been evolving. It was almost like the clients were being interviewed to see if they were deserving enough to see me.

---

[3] I actually looked it up in the American Psychiatric Association's Diagnostic and Statistical Manual of Mental Disorders. I fit the profile to a T.

"So, tell me about yourself," Jason said. "Well, you sound like someone who knows the best things in life don't come cheap."

He had flipped the whole game around. It was absolutely fascinating to watch.

"Excellent.... Where am I sending her? Better yet, how about this? We have a gorgeous loft in Tribeca...why don't you come here?"

My excitement vanished, and I did a little inward groan. I really, really didn't like seeing clients at the loft. The energy of the place always interfered and made for a less than intimate experience.

"Get over it," I told myself. I didn't want to let anything bring down this moment. I could see the adrenaline flowing through Jason's veins as he reassured the guy I was going to be worth every penny.

He hung up the phone.

I squealed with delight.

I was now, by the only measuring stick that mattered, the top escort in New York City.

I looked up to see Mona's reaction. She had daggers in her eyes.

"Look at you, Natalia," she said with a smirk. "You'd better be worth it...you know how Jason hates refunding clients."

I felt the tears welling in my eyes, about to stream down my face. It took everything I had to hold them back. I had sacrificed so much to get to this moment. Just three months earlier, I had been a nearly homeless out-of-work actress with a boyfriend who hit me, now I was poised to become the city's most expensive date. Some of the richest men in the country were lining up to pay more than I had ever made in a month to be with me for a couple of hours. It had all become so unreal. When I started, I instantly became addicted to the pursuit of the ever elusive *more*: more sex, more fun, more money. Now my competitive nature had kicked into overdrive, and I was becoming addicted to the recognition—the idea that everyone would know me as the best. It seems so crazy in retrospect—who would want to be a famous escort? But I was so detached from the mores of the mainstream world, it had consumed my notion of self-worth. This moment. My Oscar. If only Mona would let me enjoy it.

I had vowed not to let her hurt me. It wasn't easy...her words were venomous. She wasn't just our office manager, she was Jason's ex-girlfriend, and she knew just how to get under my skin. Screw her, I told myself, they were just words. As Jason hung up, I challenged myself: turn this client into a regular and silence Mona. With this kind of money coming in, I could actually start to save, instead of blowing it all on drugs and clothes, and get out of the game and away from her for good.

Hulbert walked into the loft carrying some canvases and shopping bags with his paints and brushes. Jason was letting him use the loft to paint as it added to the vibe.

"Hey, Hulbert, I just booked Natalia a two-hour, four-thousand-dollar appointment. Am I the best or what?"

"That's what she should have been getting all along," said Hulbert, as he gave me a quick smile.

I loved Hulbert.

* * *

Despite my new-found underground celebrity, not all of my appointments ended with soul kisses and doggie bags of blow. Sometimes things would go seriously FUBAR, and it always seemed like it was up to me to keep the train from flying off the tracks.

Ashley and I were lounging around the loft. It was past midnight. We hadn't had a booking, and we were losing our energy. Then the phone rang. We could hear Jason answer it in the office upstairs, but we couldn't catch what he was saying. We looked at each other in anticipation, hoping it would be a winner.

Jason came down the stairs with the details: Me, Ash, plus a third girl to Finn's pad on Wooster Street. Finn was the skin-mag publisher who had booked me in the early days. He had become one of my favorites. He knew how to treat a girl right. We'd be able to party, drink, and have a fun little sex-party in his massive designer loft for the next two hours and each walk away with $1,000 plus.

Just what we needed to salvage our night.

Then Jason threw in the monkey wrench.

"And oh, I forgot to tell you. Brigit is the third girl."

I gave him the look. The *you've-got-to-be-kidding-me* look. Brigit is a pill-popping ex-stripper with way too much plastic surgery and a volatile ex-boyfriend who used to run a competing agency known for its party girls: escorts who doubled as drug dealers. The agency was busted, and he was residing under the care of the New York State Department of Correctional Services somewhere upstate. Brigit was an emotional time bomb waiting to explode. She was infamous for getting totally hammered and regaling her clients with tales about how she'd been raped multiple times, survived cervical cancer and was on the verge of getting kicked out of her apartment. Every guy's fantasy, right?

She was the polar opposite of a New York Confidential girl.

Jason and I had had the Brigit discussion before. But I gave it another shot. I laid out why he should

NEVER, under any circumstances, send her to a client. I didn't want to deprive the girl of a living. But the ex-boyfriend was reason enough to stay clear, I argued. The guy was public enemy number one in the sex industry with law enforcement, which meant she was probably on their radar as well. I tried to explain to Jason that, if she were ever arrested, she would rat us out in a heartbeat to avoid going to jail. Hell, she might even be able to buy her man some time off in exchange for info on the city's hottest agency. I'd watched enough cop shows to know how it worked. Furthermore, I explained, she was *killing* our rep. I detailed the numerous occasions she melted down in front of clients in my presence. Who knows what happened when I wasn't around?

Jason listened, but was having none of it.

"Guys don't care what comes out of a girl's mouth if she's got a hot body."

First off, she did *not* have a hot body. Most of it wasn't even hers. And even if she did, his argument ran totally counter to the whole philosophy behind our little enterprise. We were selling healthy, positive encounters where everyone parts happy.

She was poison in a push-up.

Maybe he felt sorry for her and wanted to give her a break. Maybe he was a better man than I gave him credit for. Or maybe he was just a greedy bastard and wanted as many girls who liked money and sex as he could get his hands on, even if they were certifiable. To this day, why he kept her around is a riddle wrapped in a mystery inside a Trojan.

Ashley looked on quizzically. She had not had the honor of meeting Brigit.

"You'll see," I told her, admitting defeat.

As Ashley and I arrived at the street entrance to Finn's loft on Wooster, I tried to suppress my dread at seeing Brigit again.

Finn opened the door with his arms spread open wide and grabbed me into a hug.

"Where have you been? I've fuckin' missed you."

His eyes drifted to Ashley.

"And who is this? Holy shit, Jason is not fucking around."

He was so obviously at home in his enormous SoHo loft. It fit him like a glove. The last time I'd been at Finn's, we'd spent the last half hour of our appointment lying naked on the carpet in his living room, draped over each other. He pointed to each piece of art one by one and gave me a mini-art lesson.

"That painting over there is a Damien Hirst."

One by one he listed their names: Kenny Scharf, Kostabi....

"I'm waiting for a Warhol to be delivered. I don't know what I'm going to get next, maybe a Keith Haring," his deep, scratchy voice saying their names like they were guys he went to high school with.

"This is Victoria," I said, using Ashley's professional name. I was as proud of my little protégé as he was to meet her. "Jason is stepping it up a notch, you know?"

I giggled and jumped into his arms, wrapping my legs around his waist. He spun me around, and I grabbed Ashley and pulled her into the apartment. I was going to show her how good this job could be.

We each did two shots of Grey Goose, sniffed from the three-foot line of coke on the black marble countertop, and then I unzipped my Louis Vuitton duffel bag. Finn gave me his best bad-boy smirk.

"Did you bring toys?"

I smirked. Of course I'd brought toys. I'd brought toys *and* lingerie. I told Finn to turn up the music and soon the place was thumping with a killer house beat.

I pulled Ashley into Finn's bedroom and gave her a garter and some fishnets.

"Put this on."

I went back out to see Finn right away. He was paying to feel like a king, and we were going to make him feel more regal than the Sultan of Brunei. I straddled him, and we started kissing. He squeezed his hands around my waist and then picked me up, flipped me onto my back and was about to climb on top of me when something caught his eye. I looked over and saw Ashley walking toward us. She was wearing the garter belt, thigh-high fishnets and stilettos, and she'd taken one of Finn's ribbed wife beater tees and tied the front in a knot. I pushed Finn away from me, and he reached for Ashley, who leaned over him on the couch and gave him a nice long kiss. Then she turned her attention to me, and we starting kissing, slowly, then more intensely. I felt like I was in a trance. My mind was clear and empty of all thoughts other than how good this felt. The electricity between the two of us transfixed Finn. We were both such naturals. We were able to connect and focus huge amounts of energy on another person, so when we both turned that skill on each other, I'd never felt anything like it.

She pulled my dress over my head and bit one of my nipples. I grabbed one of the cushions from the couch and tossed it on the floor as she slid to the carpet and lay back, resting her head on the padding. We were giving Finn the best, hottest sight ever. I pulled her panties to the side and licked her clit. I looked up at her, and we smiled at each other. I kept going and, as I felt Finn's hand move up my leg, I moaned and couldn't wait for him to touch me, to put his fingers inside me.

Ashley's top came off, then Finn's. I knew exactly what to do next. I kissed Ashley one more time, and then we crawled toward Finn, who was kneeling a few feet away, his hand on his cock. We pulled down his underwear, and I licked the head of his penis. He sighed and leaned his head back. Ashley's tongue joined mine and we slowly started giving him a blowjob together.

After a few minutes, I got up to get some condoms and came back to the living room. Finn took Ashley's hand and mine, and we all walked to the bedroom. Finn unwrapped a condom, and I got down on my knees, put him all the way in my mouth, sucking until I felt there was no way he could get any harder and then let Ashley put the condom on for him. I lay back on Finn's bed. The sheets felt like butter on my skin. He pushed my legs open and slipped inside me. Ashley disappeared for a second and came back with a small glass dildo.

She lay down beside us and, as I closed my eyes and arched my head back, I saw her slide it inside her.

"I've got to see your ass," he said as he flipped me over. I loved how good it felt. I came and let Finn shift his attention to Ashley. She straddled him, and I could tell he was about to come. I leaned down and licked his balls a little, and he came super hard and so did Ashley. I smiled, so happy, and let myself fall back against the mountain of pillows to chill for a bit.

I lit a cigarette, took a few drags and then passed it to Ashley. She took a small puff as she didn't smoke that much. The doorbell rang.

Who the fuck is that? I wondered. Ashley looked at me and shrugged.

BRIGIT!

The human needle scratching across the record. Shit, I'd totally forgotten about her.

"A little late, isn't she?" Finn joked.

She was almost two hours late. I had a bad feeling about this.

She walked in like she owned the place, but didn't much like it. She looked disapprovingly at the art on the walls. "Oh, hi, Natalia," she said, and then made a beeline for the bottle of Grey Goose on the kitchen counter.

"Brigit, this is Finn, and do you know Victoria? She's new."

"Oh yeah? Is Jason giving her all the bookings? Is she why he hasn't been calling me?"

No, it's because you're fucking crazy, the voice in my head answered.

She turned to Finn, "This is your place? How the fuck do you afford this?"

Finn did not miss a beat, "How the fuck did you afford your tits?"

Then he turned to me and asked, "Natalia, you want a roofie?"

Dude was hardcore. Who pops roofies on purpose? Roofie is the nickname for Rohypnol, a.k.a. "the date-rape drug." Finn swore by them. He preferred them to Valium or Xanax as a comedown from coke. I knew what Finn really meant was, "I'm ready to call it a night."

I followed him into the bedroom. He handed me a few pills.

"I don't even know what to say. I'll get her out of here," I said.

We heard a loud pop!

"She just opened my champagne," Finn said, dejectedly.

I went into damage control mode. Brigit was flailing around the living room in her underwear, waving the bottle around.

Oh God, fucking Cristal! Who pops a $500 bottle of someone else's champagne at four in the morning— and drinks out of the bottle?

She flopped on the sofa, her dirty feet flying up in the air. She fumbled through her purse with one hand, nearly spilling the champagne on the carpet with the other.

Ashley looked like a deer in headlights.

I did a quick line of coke for courage and motioned for Ashley to come over to me. I handed her the straw and said, "Do a line and then get all our stuff together. We gotta get out of here before all hell breaks loose."

I started sorting though everyone's clothes, which were scattered all over the loft's giant main area. Finn was nowhere to be seen, but my first guess was that he was on the phone with Jason. *Not good.*

Luckily, Ashley was gripping her situation. She'd located her skirt and shirt and was ready to walk out the door. I was now dressed and holding the loco bitch's clothes.

"Brigit? We're gonna go."

"Okay, have fun, bye!"

She popped what looked like three Vicodins.

"No, we all have to go."

"Well, I just got here. Am I going to get paid? Jason told me this was a three-hour booking!"

"Brigit, you were two hours late."

"Motherfucker!" she swore and stomped toward the bedroom.

"You had better pay me!" she screamed in Finn's direction.

This was going from bad to worse.

"Of course you'll get paid. Come on, let's go to the loft," I pleaded.

She disappeared into the bathroom. We followed with her clothes and made her look presentable. I dug around in my duffel until I found my sunglasses and went to find Finn. He was sitting on his bed, his head in his hands. When you lay down the kind of money he did, this is not how you imagine the night is going to end. I felt for him.

He looked up at me, and I was relieved. He seemed annoyed, but it looked like he'd get over it.

He stood and asked, "You going to be okay?"

"What do you think?" I chuckled.

I'm indestructible...didn't he know?

He smiled and kissed my forehead. We were cool, at least.

When we burst through the front door to the street, the sun was just coming up. The cover of darkness was gone. I had to get our sideshow act off the streets, and quick.

Brigit stumbled and almost took a nosedive off the curb. She caught herself and took a big swig of champagne. Holy shit! What was she doing with the champagne?

This was so not good. Three escorts with a duffel bag full of sex toys, condoms, lube, a wad of hundreds and a credit card imprint slip with all Finn's info on it. Plus, I had a non-negligible bag of blow in my purse. If a cop drove by, Courtney Love here would take us all down.

I'd never been more happy to see a cab barrel down Broadway. I waved my arms like I was on a deserted island, and it was my rescue plane. The cab swooped over to pick us up.

I wouldn't have stopped if I were him, but I'm not a man.

I held off calling Jason while we were in the cab. The driver was already way too interested in us. Jason would see for himself soon enough what he had wrought for ignoring my sage advice.

Now at this point, you're saying to yourself, *It's impossible that every client was a mega-rich, art-collecting, party-animal stud,* and you're right. I didn't mind if the guy was packing a couple of extra pounds or had less than a full head of hair. If he was a nice guy and had a good heart, I liked being with him. What I couldn't stand were the Type A assholes, and as you can imagine, at my price point I got more than my fair share. At the top of that list was my high-ranking government official. He seemed to be some kind of head honcho at a powerful federal agency. We met during my early days at New York Confidential, and about once a month he called to see me.

I had a "don't ask, don't tell" policy. A client's personal details—everything I didn't need to know—was none of my business. But most of the time, clients wanted to talk about themselves, and I didn't stop them.

William was married and lived in the suburbs. Our first meeting was actually perfectly pleasant. He booked a room at the Pierre Hotel, and I was a little late (as usual)—okay, very late. He wasn't impressed and let me know it. But I must have won him over because over the next two months, he kept calling back again and again and wouldn't take anyone else at the agency but me.

He was one of several of my regulars who would try to help me "reform." He would tell me I should start auditioning again and find some other way to make money, that Jason was using me, that I could do so much better with my life. I laughed. Having sex with me was a funny way of getting me to stop having sex. I told him if he was intent on getting me out of the game, he should give me a job.

"My bosses are big on background checks," he responded flatly.

I explained to him I was happy. This was a short-term thing. Jason knew I wasn't going to be working forever.

One day I wasn't available, and he booked Isabella. She returned to the loft within a half hour. He had sent her back. The smoking Colombian!

Jason made each client a promise that if they weren't happy with the girl for any reason, the agency would give the client a credit or send another girl as soon as he could. I respected him for that, and it made sense. It kept clients coming back. We never baited and switched, like a lot of agencies. Our Web site had full-body pictures of each girl, most of which showed their faces. So the only variables left were personality and chemistry—subjective but important. William apparently didn't vibe with Isabella, so he sent her back, like an undercooked steak. He waited in his hotel room until I was available two hours later.

When I arrived, he looked happy to finally see me. But he seemed put off. When I tried to make some light conversation, he wasn't having it. Like most clients, I don't think he liked the idea that he had to wait his turn while I serviced another man. No client, especially guys like William, likes to be reminded of that aspect of the arrangement.

The sex was rough...not his usual style. He held my wrists over my head, which I normally really liked, but it didn't feel right this time. He was holding them too tight. There was anger in his face. It was hurting me a little. I pulled away, and he stopped and asked me what was wrong. I didn't know what to do. I had a responsibility to my client to provide whatever he was into, right? It wasn't so much he was physically hurting me; it was more his attitude that was freaking me out.

Wasn't he paying for the right to be in whatever mood he wanted to be in?

Now isn't the right time to deal with these questions, I told myself. I smiled at William and kissed him, "Nothing's wrong, I moved my wrist weird...my fault."

We got back into our rhythm. Even though I was still out of sorts, he didn't seem to notice. As we lay on the bed afterwards, he turned to me, and apropos of nothing, said, "You know, Jason is going to get busted."

My eyes flew open, "What do you mean?"

My mind reeled. Did he have some inside info?

"When he does, you will get arrested. Is that what you want?"

The answer seemed pretty obvious.

"Um, no," I replied.

I waited for him to keep talking, to tell me what he meant, what he knew, but he just stopped.

As we lay there, I started to freak.

Finally, he broke the silence, "Natalia, if that is your real name."

"It is!" I interrupted, eager to hear more. "Well, almost. It's Natalie."

"Can I call you Natalie, since you know my real name?"

He was fucking with me at this point. He didn't care what my name was. He didn't want to call me by it to feel closer to me, the real me. He just wanted to be on an even playing ground.

"Of course," I said, forcing a smile.

"Let me fill you in on how things work, Natalie. The authorities know every agency in New York. One by one they shut them down. It's very easy. They send in a client, someone who looks a lot like me, and they single out a girl, someone high profile, who has her pictures and reviews and identity all over the Internet. Someone like you. The 'client' meets with the prostitute regularly, has sex with her each time, establishing a pattern. Then they move in and shut down the agency, sending everyone to prison for a very long time. It's that simple. It's just a matter of time."

He looked at me with eyes cold as ice.

I stared back. Was he trying to play games with me? Or was this something else? All sorts of scenarios went through my head. Did he know about an imminent crackdown and actually care enough about me to help me out? *That doesn't really make any sense*, I thought to myself. *If he does know of something specific, wouldn't he be begging me to keep his name out of it? Then again*, I thought, *maybe he's so connected he's already cleared himself from any connection. Or maybe it's just what it appears to be: a not-so-friendly warning.*

My mind was reeling as we continued to lie there in silence.

Finally, our time was up. I said I had to take a shower and went into the bathroom.

Okay, new rules, I thought to myself: *No more bringing any Class A offenses to appointments.*

If I were arrested, having drugs on me would definitely not help my case, but that was a side issue. The larger question hung out there like a dark cloud. What was I thinking? What was going on with me that I would do something so risky? Believe it or not, I had never really honestly thought through the logical conclusion of what getting busted meant. I had totally blocked out the idea of prison altogether. Now it all came crashing down on me. I would never survive in prison. You had to be hard. I was the opposite of hard. I was soft jelly.

I thought I had it all figured out, especially when Jason introduced me to Mel Sachs, the legal eagle who assured me we had all of our bases covered. I thought that if I didn't sell drugs or make stupid mistakes, I could go on doing this forever. It's amazing what stacks of hundred-dollar bills will do to your powers of self-deception.

Instead of gripping all of this, I focused my anger at William. What was his problem? Why did he want to make me feel so bad? I slammed my purse down on the vanity and pulled out my baggie and straw, did a quick bump, put my hair in a ponytail and jumped in the shower. I got lathered up with some fruity-smelling shower gel and let the warm water drench my body. By the time I had dried off and put my black La Perla G-string back on and pulled my dress over my head, I had pushed all of his negativity out of my mind.

William pulled me close and gave me a kiss goodbye and made no more additions to his cryptic warning. As I walked down the ornate hallway of the Pierre to the elevator, the anger came back. Tears started flowing down my face. Instead of taking his sobering warning to heart, all I could think about was what an asshole he was. If only I were working independently, I thought to myself, and not for Jason, I could refuse clients I didn't want, like William. And I wouldn't have to deal with any of this mind-game bullshit.

By the time I got to the lobby, my eyes were dry, and I was already wondering what new adventure I was going to go on that night.

*   *   *

Before there was Samantha, Natalia or Victoria, there was Cheryl.

She was spoken about in legendary terms. She was New York Confidential's first girl. If I helped build the agency from the ground up, she laid down the foundation. She was actually the one who invented the New York Confidential "This is my boyfriend of six months" mantra Jason made all girls say before they hooked up with a client. She was also the first girl to go from $800 to $1,200 an hour, and she had had her own streak of 10/10 reviews on TER.

But she retired before I showed up. Quit while she was ahead, I presumed. I always wondered what made her so special. I used her as a sort of benchmark to keep me motivated. It worked pretty well. Then one day the phone rang. Cheryl wanted back in the game.

Jason was on top of the world. He was actually careful to make sure I didn't feel put out, but I could see the excitement on his face. He felt like the Gods were on his side, giving him back Cheryl.

"With you and Cheryl, I can take over the world," he said.

I have to give it to Cheryl, she was smooth. She treated me with respect. She didn't patronize me or any of the other girls. But you could tell she knew she was the shit.

I liked the way she dealt with Jason. She laid some ground rules. Unlike the other girls, she was to be paid in cash after each booking, regardless of the client's method of payment. The other girls (except for me) received a weekly check for their credit card bookings and cash for cash bookings. Cheryl wasn't having any of that.

We got along really well. She was sweet and beautiful and pristine. She was a contemporary dancer and a former ballerina. She was twenty-five with dark blond hair, sapphire blue eyes, a smooth, angular face and a taut body. She was extremely flexible and moved like a lioness. She was intelligent and sultry at the same time. Like a lot of people, she didn't approve of my drug use, but she tolerated it. She lived with her boyfriend, a shoe designer (you can imagine her shoe collection), and didn't like to talk about how she felt about lying to him. I came to learn through the loft gossip mill that she was torn about the whole thing. She loved the guy, but either loved or was addicted to escorting. Whether it was the money or the sex, or both, I never found out. But she couldn't stop.

She had been retired for almost a year. But once news spread online that Cheryl was back, she was booked solid. This was actually great for me. I was burnt out. I had been working since May 17th, the date of my first ever appointment, for seven nonstop months, at an average of six hours a day, seven days a week—and that was just my bookable hours. On top of that, add in the travel, which was taking me all over the country at least twice a month. I didn't mind working every day, but it was nice not to feel pressure from Jason to be working every single minute. Now, because one of us was always with a client, he was always making top rates, and he was happy.

It got even better when Cheryl and I started working together—we were so in sync that clients were flipping out. Jason set our rate at $4,800 for two hours, and we had a waiting list ten deep.

It was late on a Friday night and Cheryl and I were sitting in my closet, hanging out. We had an eleven o'clock appointment together booked—the client had asked for midnight, but Cheryl had a curfew, so eleven it was. In very uncharacteristic Cheryl style, she'd had more than one glass of champagne, and I even think she got a little drunk. I still knew better than to offer her any blow, and I'm glad I didn't because as we were sitting

there in front of my mirror she turned to me and said,
"Natalia, I know you're a big girl, and I don't mean to nag
you about the drugs. You know it's because I really care
about you, right?"

She didn't need to say anything else.

"I know it is. Thank you. I really love you," I told
her.

She hugged me and whispered in my ear, "If you
need anything, let me know."

I pulled away and quickly changed the subject.

"So. What's going on with Craig?"

She hesitated.

"He proposed."

"Oh, my God!"

"Yeah, on our roof. It was so romantic."

They lived in an amazing Upper West Side
townhouse, full of books, a spiral staircase and a lived-in
kitchen, with a spectacular private roof—a perfect pad to
start a family.

Something was going on inside her. I could see it
in her eyes. Her lip was shaking a little. She was even
more beautiful than I had remembered.

"I think I have to tell him."

I stopped mid-sip. I couldn't even put down my
glass.

I started to speak and then stopped myself.

Whoa. This was big.

"I get it." I told her. You can't build a life together
that's full of secrets and walls. In my opinion, she had to
either break up or tell him. She really believed this was
the guy, so she had no choice.

She was totally surprised.

"Oh, my God, everyone else thinks I'm crazy."

"You have to," I said.

She looked relieved, like she knew she'd been right all along.

We decided to walk to the hotel. Damien, the client, was at the Ritz Carlton in Battery Park, a twenty-minute walk from the loft. We both wore really short skirts, made of the same torn-up silk in different colors, heels designed by her fiancé (was that wrong?) and slinky off-the-shoulder tops. We held hands and turned down Church Street, with the Chrysler Building shining like a beacon behind us. Somewhere around Fulton Street, we heard a crack of thunder and the sky just opened up. We ducked into a doorway as it started pouring. We hoped we'd see a taxi, but there are never any taxis in that part of the city late on a Friday night.

"What do we do?" she asked.

I looked at her. We were already a little wet.

"Keep walking, I guess."

We arrived at the Ritz, soaked through to our skin. We giggled and ran to the elevator. It opened, and we went in. Cheryl pushed me to the wall and started kissing me. I kissed her back, our tongues moving together. She kissed my neck, and the doors opened.

We arrived at the client's door draped over each other, soaking wet in every way. Our client had high expectations. We were the famous Cheryl and Natalia, and he had made the trip from L.A. to New York especially to see us, but nothing prepared him for the sight of the two of us.

He smiled and laughed a nervous laugh, then recovered and said, "I can't believe I expected anything less from the two of you."

He invited us in. There was a bit of a dilemma: we were booked for two hours. I didn't think we should take our clothes off *right* away, but we were soaking wet and while we had made the best entrance ever, once we were in the room, we were just wet. Our client came to the rescue.

He pulled two small bags out of the closet: La Perla. Cheryl and I unwrapped identical slips and g-strings—mine in black, hers in light pink. We smiled at our client and slipped into the bathroom, out of our clothes and into our presents. I looked at the two of us in the mirror. "Wait," I said. I pulled off my undies and gestured for her to do the same. We traded and put them back on. Now I had on a black slip and pink undies and Cheryl the opposite. Perfect.

We left the bathroom, and Damien, an entertainment lawyer, handed us some champagne, and we all clinked glasses. I kissed Cheryl and smiled at Damien, and we all sat on the bed. It was kind of funny. I could tell he really wanted to hang with us, but he couldn't focus on conversation and really wanted to have both of us immediately. Cheryl and I made him wait a little longer. She lay back on the big bed, and I kissed her and got on top of her. I pulled down the strap of her slip and sucked on her nipple a little, then covered her back up again. She lifted my slip up over my ass and pulled me closer to her so that I could feel how wet she was. We slowly turned our attention to Damien. She kissed him slowly on the mouth, and I started to undo his shirt. I lay back on the bed for a minute and watched them, then got up again and started to rub Cheryl's pussy through her panties. She moaned, and we took off Damien's shirt. We undid his pants and started giving him a blowjob together. It only got better from there.

For the next hour and a half, we had really deep, really intense sex. I came a few times, and I know Cheryl did, too. Damien came twice.

We all lay in bed together. Cheryl and I were both warm and glowing and snuggling into each other.

Damien was laying on his side looking at us. He talked about L.A., and we told him about our lives in New York. Cheryl left out the part about her fiancé. We were so similar. She was herself but knew what to talk about when. She told him about her horse that she kept in Long Island. She'd bought it with the money she'd made before her "retirement." Now she wanted to save and invest some money over the next few months.

I slipped away to the bathroom to do a bump and check on our clothes. They were dry enough to wear. Our time was almost up, and Cheryl had to get home to her fiancé before she turned into a pumpkin.

We told Damien how much fun we'd had.

He said, "You girls don't even know."

He promised to write us a review. I had a feeling we were going to earn another 10/10.

*   *   *

A week went by, and no one had heard from Cheryl. I was worried, so I texted her proposing coffee in the Tribeca Grand Hotel lobby.

She looked horrible.

She had told him, and her world had collapsed in on itself. She thought the depth of his love for her would enable him to work through the reality of what she had been doing behind his back, and they would live happily ever after. I guess he couldn't see past the betrayal. He flipped out and rescinded his marriage proposal, which maybe wasn't so surprising in retrospect. After a week of crying and talking and sleeping in separate beds, he cut her out of his life forever.

I was just happy to see she wasn't suicidal or anything. As we sipped our cappuccinos in the atrium of the trendy hotel, where between the two of us we had probably been with more than twenty guys, she changed the subject and asked me how everyone was doing: Jason, Mona, Clark.

I told her fine. "Forget us," I said, "How are you?"

She teared up right away, "I just miss him so much."

"I'm so sorry," I said.

I felt for her, but I didn't feel guilty for giving her the advice that I did. I don't think she had a choice. If her escorting had been in her past, before she met the guy, it might have been a different story. But she had been doing it through most of the time they had been dating. She'd taken time off, but then she'd come back for more. If she really loved him, he deserved the truth. Furthermore, if this was his reaction, it was better to make the break now than to start a life together, have kids, get older and lose some of her killer looks, and then have him find out and have it all ripped out from under her.

I asked her, "Do you think if you'd told him it was something in the past, he might have been okay with it?"

"There was just too much," she answered. "He couldn't get over all the lies I'd told him. We never even got to all the guys I'd slept with while I was with him."

She said she was moving back to Connecticut to mend things with her family. To make matters worse, her fiancé, thinking she needed help from a larger support group, had taken it upon himself to fill them in on the awful truth right before he'd dumped her.

"Nat, look at me," she said. "You need to stop. I don't want you to end up like me."

She went on about how what we did was destroying us.

I listened and tried to take it in.

As she was leaving, I asked her where she was going.

She paused, and then said, "I...I'm going up to the W."

I mean, puh-leeze. Don't tell me about how fucked your life is and tell me how I need to change my ways, and then tell me that.

We kissed goodbye on the cheeks. I knew I probably would never see her again. As I headed back down through Tribeca to the loft, I couldn't help but tear up. I felt so bad. I really did feel something like love for her, and even though she was a total hypocrite, as I walked through the empty streets, her warning started to get to me.

Then, as I turned onto Worth Street and approached our little den of sin, the rationalizing part of my brain put her predicament into perspective. *I am not Cheryl*, I reassured myself. *I don't have a man who wants to marry me and thinks I'm something I'm not. I might be lying to my mom, but I've been doing that all my life. I'm living on my terms, and no one else is getting hurt.*

I knew I'd have to figure what I want to do with my life eventually, but I was twenty-four. *Isn't this the age when everything in our culture is telling us we're supposed to be free-spirited and carefree? Shouldn't I just focus on what I want now and live every minute as it comes? Wouldn't that be the Zen thing?*

I only heard from Cheryl once more. A few weeks later, she called and wanted to know if I had any clients I could refer to her. I knew just the guy. I gave her William's number.

CHAPTER NINE
THE JASON SHOW

I was dreaming. My ex, Paul, and I were in the shower. I could feel the water. I could feel the warmth of Paul's body, but I couldn't see anything, and I wasn't breathing. Then I tasted water. It was going up my nose. I felt myself being pulled out of the shower, into the tiny bathroom, and I heard screaming...my own and Paul's voice.

"Stay with me, stay with me," over and over again.

I started taking deep breaths in and out, trying to do what Paul was telling me to do. I looked around and saw my bedroom, the loft. I was awake. I had just relived one of my many overdoses. One of the numerous times Paul saved my life before I left him.

Everyone has nightmares, but these were different. They were more like flashbacks. These felt real, like I was reliving my overdoses over and over again in my sleep. It was actually worse than the actual event. One of the things about an overdose, the ones you survive, is they usually have a profound effect on the people who witness them, but usually have little or no effect on the person who actually takes the drugs. Even though the drug users are the ones most in need of a wake-up call because they've lost consciousness, they wake up as though nothing happened and go right back to whatever they were doing.

It was like those dreams had a purpose. Like my subconscious was reaching out trying to remind me of just how dangerous I could be to my own well-being.

I felt myself changing. My ego would like to argue that I was evolving, but that's not what was happening. Evolution implies some type of progress and, while there were aspects of my life (notably the financial) that were so much better than before when I was with Paul, I was surely regressing in my connection to myself and who I was as a human being. I was lying more and more to my mother and ignoring the advice of well-meaning people like Taylor and Cheryl who were reaching out to me and trying to get me to look at how I was living. I wasn't auditioning for any acting roles. I was doing more drugs than ever. The trauma of what I went through with Paul left me so wounded I was eager for a new identity and a new life. Now I was telling the normal world to fuck off and was being lavishly rewarded and praised for it. But it was turning me into a ruthless little girl who didn't care about anything but having fun, making money and getting really, really high.

*   *   *

I rolled over and opened the bedside table drawer, which was always full of chocolate and candy. It was one of the little ways Jason tried to show me that he loved me. I was addicted to sugar—well, pretty much all white substances—and needed it to get out of bed.

I starting popping peanut M&Ms as I stared at the ceiling, trying to let my white room blot out the darkness of my dream.

We had a California king-size bed. It was so big, and I was so small that I could sprawl out into a star shape, and I still couldn't touch the sides. We had

Egyptian cotton linens with a 1,500 thread count and a huge fluffy duvet filled with the down of 10,000 virgin Canadian geese (okay, I made up that last part).

Our cleaning lady, Valeria, changed our sheets every day (for obvious reasons), and they always smelled fabric-softener fresh. We had this really beautiful antique-style Asian wood table that was exceptionally high and long. Above it was one of my favorite things: a print of a photo by another artist we'd found on West Broadway. He sold his stuff across the street from where we met Hulbert. It was the richest, deepest blue color, and if you looked really close, you could see that it was a photo of water blown up. I love that color blue, and it worked like magic, taking me right out of the edgy, unsettled mood the nightmare had left me in.

I finally got up, and I walked up to the office. I was wearing a super-cozy, short, black and pink nightie. I didn't sleep naked so much anymore now that there were almost always people around in the mornings. I had a whole section in my wardrobe for things like little booty shorts and silk nighties.

Jason was sitting at our enormous mahogany dining room table, dozens of booking sheets laid out in front of him, talking on the phone. I sat on his knee and looked over them. It was an impressive testament to my work ethic. There were scores of entries each representing one of my recent bookings—the lowest was for $4,000 and the highest for $15,000.

I took out my little black Moleskine book and started jotting down my upcoming appointments. I kept immaculate records of my schedule. I recorded the client's first name and last initial, the number of hours and payment breakdown. I also did some quick checks on my outstanding payments. I was the only one who paid any attention to my earnings. Ever since I started, Jason had never paid me for my electronic billings. I was still making more cash than I could spend, but I wasn't seeing the payouts from my big clients who paid with credit cards or wire transfers. So, ironically, the more I was earning, the less I actually got. At first, I thought I was protecting myself. I was wary of my "Canadian situation," as I called it. I wasn't about to get busted by the IRS, ICE or some other three-lettered bogeyman for cashing huge checks when I didn't have a work visa, let alone a legit job. When Jason and I were on good terms, I felt safest keeping my money with him in the main agency account, which was basically his to do with as he pleased. But now, with things rocky between us, I was getting nervous. A quick calculation showed that I was owed somewhere north of $150,000.

Even with all my Manolos and McQueens and sleepovers at the Mandarin, I had ended up in the same lousy situation as the hoochie on Bensonhurst Avenue: my pimp wasn't paying me. I had once again let myself be forced into the victim role, first with my ex-boyfriend bullying and bruising me, and now with Jason booking me 24/7 and holding my money over my head. If I demanded he pay up, what leverage did I have? If I threatened to go on strike or walk away, I risked losing it all if he called my bluff. If I asked him nicely, he still could see it as a signal that I didn't trust him or that I was thinking about retiring, or even worse, defecting. If I forced the issue, it would throw off our already shaky dynamic—a dynamic that was so integral to the success of the business and my general happiness.

I was so obsessed with keeping everything in our world positive and drama-free, I did what any ever-hopeful girl who wanted to work things out with her man would do, I sucked it up. Deep inside I really believed Jason loved me and that he would eventually pay me what I had earned. So I told myself that I'd bring it up later, at a better time.

What happened next would only confirm in my mind I was making the right choice.

* * *

Jason hung up the phone, quickly shuffled the booking sheets into a pile, and turned to me.

"Natalia, this guy keeps calling. He says he's some TV producer, and he read about you on TER and wants to meet you."

My heart skipped a beat, "So?"

"So, I told him he had to book an appointment with you if he wants to meet you."

Under any other circumstances, I would have laughed at Jason's attitude, but he touched a nerve. The old Nat came flooding to the surface, and I felt a surge of adrenaline mixed with desperation. All the original reasons why I came to New York came rushing back.

"He hasn't stopped calling, and now he says he wants to meet me, too, and that he can turn us into superstars. He sounds like he knows what he's talking about."

"You want to talk to him?"

He pulled down a Post-It from the board filled with names, numbers and amounts of money owed, or credited. It read: "Joe Dinki," along with a cell phone number.

"His name is Joe Dinki? You've got to be kidding me."

Jason didn't even blink. I mean that literally. He was famous for not blinking. It helped fuel his rep for being unfazed by whatever was falling apart around him.

"So what? The guy's got a funny name."

"If you worked in entertainment, or business, or anything except maybe the circus, and your name was Joe Dinki, wouldn't you change it?"

Jason ignored me and dialed his number. It was already ringing when he handed me the phone.

"Hello?"

"Hi, is this Joe?"

"Yes, and who's this?"

"Natalia."

I lived in a one-name world by this point, like Madonna. Or Bozo.

"Well, hello, Natalia. You're not an easy girl to get in touch with."

"Yeah, my agent Jason screens all my calls," I joked.

He laughed.

"I don't know how much Jason told you, but I know all about you. I'm a producer, and I'd really like to meet with you to tell you about a concept I have for a show."

I looked over at Jason.

"Well, I'm going to have to pass you over to Jason, but I think that should be okay. We should definitely meet."

I handed the cordless to Jason, keeping my fingers crossed.

"What are you doing right now?" Jason is a "right now" kind of person.

He gave Joe the address to the loft, and I skipped to my closet. What do you wear when you are meeting the man who's going to make you a star? The daydreams were already running through my head.

Mister Dinki arrived within the hour. I played it cool and waited in the wings in my closet. I could hear him and Jason talking. Finally, Jason called for me.

I waited a minute, for dramatic purposes, gathered my confidence and made my entrance.

Joe looked more like a grip than a director or producer. Then he opened his mouth, and it went downhill from there.

"Natalia, I came here to meet you, but at this point I'm way more interested in Jason. This guy is amazing. Where did you find him?"

I gave a fake laugh and wandered over to the kitchen. Then I made a beeline back to my sanctuary. I had to regroup. *What an idiot! Who says that? He's either really smart, or really stupid,* I thought. He might have realized that he would have to win over Jason in order to get to me to make this TV thing happen. That would make him smart. But he didn't seem that sharp; he seemed like just another sucker eating up Jason's bullshit.

I would have to make him fall in love with me. It felt strange. I wasn't used to being in competition with Jason for people's attention, but these were not normal circumstances. This was our future at stake.

I composed myself and went back out to see Jason and Joe. Jason welcomed me onto his lap, and I looked Joe in the eyes.

"I've read all your reviews, Natalia. Do you know how famous you are on the Internet?"

"Sort of," I said. "So what's the deal, are you going to make me really famous?"

"If Jason will let me, I'll make you both huge stars."

"And how will you do that?"

"I want to shoot a reality show about you and Jason. All he can talk about is how amazing you are and how in love with you he is. I just watched him book a client over the phone, and I was going nuts that I don't have a camera here right now. I want to shoot a pilot. I know you guys are busy...two, maybe three days of filming and then sell the show to a network. I know a lot of people at VH1, and they would freak over you two."

"You haven't seen anything yet," I responded.

*   *   *

The next day, I found Jason laid out on the couch, a huge L-shaped chocolate brown leather sectional with a view of almost the entire loft. I happily lay down on his lap.

He was finishing up a call with his step-dad.

"Dad, I'm so happy we've talked about this," he said. "Mel Sachs is calling me back any minute. I'll keep you up to date."

He hung up the phone and said, "My father thinks we should do the show."

Wow, that was a surprise. Jason called his step-dad "dad." He was really the only family he had left, aside from an estranged sister. His step-dad had distanced himself from Jason after a brouhaha over a loan for one of Jason's borderline-legal start-ups. In his twenties, Jason had made millions on his phone-sex business in Miami. He'd hung out with guys like Chris Paciello, the notorious club owner who dated Madonna and was later convicted of murder, at the height of the Miami club craze. But that business tanked, and he ended up owing creditors more than four million dollars at thirty-six-percent interest and was forced to declare bankruptcy in 1997. He lost everything, including an Aston Martin and probably his most savvy investment ever, ownership of the URL: *pussy.com*. Shortly after, he moved to New York and started his second doomed brainchild, SoHo Models. Then came the *Details* exposé and the feet dangling over the ledge. He tried to kill himself twice: once with a knife, the second time with "a milk shake," which he later told *New York* magazine contained "75 Valium, 75 Klonopin, and a couple bottles of Scotch."

I don't know which of Jason's sketchy career moves his step-dad had gotten caught up in, but whatever it was he had learned his lesson and kept his distance when it came to money. But they were somehow still close.

I was definitely surprised to hear the old man had given his blessing to Jason's latest and greatest big idea. Jason explained that his step-dad agreed this could help him finally make a move into the mainstream. I wasn't quite sure how his step-dad equated reality TV with respectability, but I guess when it came to Jason it was all relative. The important thing was Jason would now do everything he could to make his "dad" proud. That's all I cared about.

*   *   *

Jason called for Hulbert.

He sauntered down the stairs wearing his uniform: jeans, motorcycle boots, black bandana on his head and a lot of awesome chunky silver jewelry. His muscles rippled under his wife beater.

He stood in front of us, like a soldier standing at attention, ready to take orders from his commanding officer.

"No, no, sit down," Jason told him.

The ringing house phone cut him off.

"Mel!" Jason said, looking over at us excitedly. "So what's the verdict...are we shooting this show or what?"

Mel Sachs had been working his magic on Joe Dinki, getting him to agree to give Jason a cut of the show.

Jason reached into his back pocket to get his cell phone, which started to blare its Usher ringtone. I had to jump off his lap so I wouldn't fall off.

I sat beside Hulbert as we became spectators.

"Mel, hang on," Jason said, as he flipped open his cell. "Hello? ...Mr. Dinki!"

My eyes lit up. I started bouncing up and down on the couch. Could I be more excited?

"I'm just on the phone with my lawyer, Mel Sachs."

Namedropper!

"Can I call you back?"

He hung up his cell and went back to Mel.

"Mel, talk to me...how does the deal look?"

Jason got up, wandered over to our bedroom and closed the door. What could he have to talk about that Hulbert and I couldn't hear?

All right, there was plenty, but I was dying to know the details.

"What's up, Natalia?"

Hulbert broke me out of my thought.

"This producer wants to shoot a reality show about me and Jason and the agency."

"Whoa, cool," he said. "Do you think there's room for me in there? I would love to get my paintings on TV."

We were sitting underneath Hulbert's masterpiece, the commission that had brought him into this crazy world. Out of anyone else's mouth that question would seem blatantly opportunistic, but not from Hulbert.

"I think the genius painter/escort booker would make a fantastic character on the show. You have to be in it. Too bad Monster Mona and Clark Kent will probably be in it, too."

"I don't know about that, Natalia. I don't think they'll be too enthusiastic about this."

"What do you mean?"

"Well, Natalia, they don't care about life the way you and Jason do. They are here for the money, that's it. And Clark's got a day job...not sure he'd want his face up there."

Hulbert and I were discreet about our shared aversion to Mona and Clark. Hulbert witnessed Mona's wretched behavior towards me—the name-calling, the booking sabotage. He knew if she was treating me that way, it was only a matter of time before she turned her sights on him.

"And this TV show will do good things for you and Jason and hopefully me, too, but they won't get anything out of it."

I made a note to make sure Jason and I were solid and were at the top of our game. Maybe the heavens would align, and Clark and Mona would lose interest in the agency altogether and just leave?

Jason opened the door and spread his arms wide.

"Oh, Natalia," he sang. I flew across the room and into his arms, jumped up and wrapped my legs around his waist.

"We start filming tomorrow," he whispered in my ear.

The magic words.

"Hulbert, ready to become a TV star?"

"Damn straight," he confirmed.

*   *   *

It turns out VH1 was interested, but, not surprisingly, unnerved by the potential legal issues surrounding shooting a New York City house of ill repute. This wasn't the Bunny Ranch in Nevada, where it's all above board. And this wasn't HBO. This was basic cable. VH1's corporate parent, Viacom, had merged with CBS, home of *60 Minutes*, and it hadn't yet made its move down-market with Flavor Flav and his harem of hoochies. I could imagine the in-house lawyers' heads spinning.

So VH1 told Joe they wanted us to shoot a pilot before they would make a commitment. Whether this was just a polite blow-off, or legitimate interest, I'll never know. In our drug-addled brains, we believed we were one step away from becoming the next big reality superstars right up there with the bible-quoting bounty hunter, the wannabe top chefs and the money-grubbing apprentices.

I called Valeria to come by as soon as she could. The loft needed a facelift. I looked down at the huge mirror on my vanity and was stumped for a minute. What to do with it? I was pretty sure drug use wasn't an activity that was going to be highlighted on the reality show. Or was it? I knew just what my morning errand would be. I was off to the head shop on West Broadway, right next to the Soho Grand Hotel. I needed a bullet, an oval-shaped container that holds about a gram of coke with an inhaler mechanism that makes doing a bump in public possible. My mirror was going to have to go into hiding for a while, well, at least for the two to three days Mister Dinki said we would spend filming the pilot.

I vowed to myself that while my drug use was, for obvious reasons, going to have to be hidden, all other areas of my life would be open for the world to see. I would be candid and honest and insightful about everything from sex to relationships to happiness and money. And I would be beautiful and compelling and fun to watch. I was convinced that it was the honesty of my energy that had gotten me this far—I wasn't going to go bottling it up now.

The reality show became the vehicle on which we hitched all of our dreams and delusions.

I arrived back from my little errand, pulled Jason in the bedroom and pointed to his plate of Special K on our beautiful, antique, wood table.

"You have to get rid of that," I said.

I handed him a bullet and went in my closet to fill mine up. As soon as I finished, the buzzer rang. I checked myself in the mirror and ran out to meet Joe Dinki and the crew, immediately recognizing the director, Ron Sperling. I had actually met him months earlier at a party at Stephen Baldwin's club, Luahn. We had chatted most of the night like we were old friends. Now he'd be directing me in my big break. *What an awesome omen.*

He set down the cases he was carrying, and I jumped into his arms.

Jason quipped, "Natalia, do you know everyone in this city?"

"If I don't already, I will after a few more months working for you," I answered.

Everyone cracked up.

* * *

The excitement built as the loft was turned into a TV set.

But as they laid cables, struck lights and checked their equipment, Jason started drinking a lot. Some people love being on camera, like me, and some people are either terrified and freeze, or just aren't good at it. Jason was so terrified of not being good, he froze.

They wanted to start with some one-on-one interview-style stuff with him, asking him specific

questions about what type of girl worked for him, why
New York Confidential was better than other agencies,
and his philosophy behind the way he did business.

But from the get-go, it did not go well. Jason
would ramble on, or just stop, unable to finish a thought.
By late-afternoon they had to shift their focus to Hulbert
because Jason was too messed up. I kept waiting for my
turn, but then I got sent to see a client, and when I
returned, the loft was crazy busy, with girls everywhere
and the cameras getting it all on tape.

I felt like I hadn't been in a single shot. How could
Jason do this to me? This was *my* dream. I overheard
him on the phone booking me another client. It made him
look great, but it just made me look like an escort who
worked too much. I ran into in my closet and cried.

I heard the door open, and Ron poked his head
around the corner, "Babycakes, where are you? We're
missing you out there."

He hugged me. It felt good and safe and cozy in
his arms.

"I feel like this is *The Jason Show*," I said.

Little did I know, *The Jason Show* hadn't even
started.

"Is that what you're upset about? Have you seen
him? Sweetheart, we need you! You are going to blow the
people at VH1 away. At the end of the night, we're going
to do a big shoot with just you. Now go have fun."

I jumped up and said to myself, *You've finally
found the role you've been waiting for, Natalia. Every
guy's fantasy.*

And I was. Then Jason gave me the details of my
next appointment: "Natalia, this guy is a rock star.
You're really going to love him. He's at the Four Seasons.
Go make me proud."

I jumped up and down with delight. Then I looked down at the booking sheet and saw the client's name. Holy shit! This guy really was a rock star! Okay, so he's a retired, recently divorced rock star from the 80s, but still hot and still cool. Besides, guys from the 80s know how to party better than their younger counterparts.

I kissed Jason's cheek, waved bye to my fellow girls and smiled for the camera.

When I arrived back a few hours later, on the high I got from being with a high profile client, I was on top of the world. I walked into my bedroom and gasped. It was beautiful. The crew had bathed it in pink lighting and lit sweet-smelling candles. The cameras were set up facing the bed and the crew was waiting for me.

"All right, Natalia, how long do you need to get ready?" Joe asked me.

Ron's assistant Alexandra was waiting in my closet to help me pick what to wear and do my makeup.

I wore a really cute little black and hot pink nightie from Victoria's Secret with this awesome sparkly heart-shaped necklace from Paris. I had a moment alone and had a little brainstorm: we'd just gotten a few ounces of mushrooms delivered by a photographer friend, AJ, and I thought it would be funny if I ate some right then. My thinking was that they'd kick in and start to affect me in about an hour, toward the end of my interview, and they might add a little Andy Warhol-ish flavor to some of my answers. I needed something. For the first time in months, I didn't have any coke on hand and none of my dealers were calling me back.

I pulled down one of my big white hatboxes from their shelf, undid the wide satin ribbon and lifted the lid. These hatboxes did not hold hats: one held my La Perla and Agent Provocateur lingerie, another my smaller, more delicate sex toys and different types of condoms. The last held our mushroom stash.

I was nibbling a small handful just as Chloe, one of our most fun girls, popped into my closet to say hi. She stuck her hand in and ate a few as well. Then she skipped off to hang with Jason while Alexandra started doing my makeup.

She made me gorgeous! I looked in the mirror feeling like I had finally closed the circle. I had turned my new career into a launching pad for my true love: acting. Then my stomach started to grumble. Then it started to gurgle. Then it rumbled.

I ran to the bathroom, grabbing the lid to the toilet. I felt everything spin, and I threw up a little bit. Alexandra came in after me and asked if I was okay.

I threw my head back and smiled, pretending like I hadn't just puked up my last glass of champagne.

"Nervous?"

I'd never been less nervous, actually.

I covered. "Yeah, a little."

Fuck, fuck, fuck. 'Shrooms might not have been the smartest blow substitute in this particular situation. I'd only swallowed them five minutes earlier, how was this happening? They were hitting me hard. Now I got nervous for real. I picked up my heart necklace off the vanity and tried to do the clasp at the back of my neck, but my fingers weren't working.

Just then, Chloe reappeared. We locked eyes, her pupils were huge. She came behind me and took the necklace. She managed to fasten it with some effort, whispering in my ear, "Natalia."

There was desperation in her voice.

"I know," I answered.

It was a place I'd been before, many times. It's that moment when you've taken something, Ecstasy, mushrooms, acid, whatever, and it's just starting to hit you and you're not sure if it's going to take you right off a cliff. There's nothing you can do about it. All you can do is ride it out. So I pulled myself together and walked into my bedroom, which had been transformed into a soft porn set.

Steady, Natalia, steady.

They attached a wireless mic to my nightie, but there was nowhere to clip the transmitter. I was only wearing a G-string, so I sat in the middle of the bed and sort of tucked it under my ass. We did a sound check and then started shooting. Joe Dinki was standing to the right of the camera, asking me questions. Alexandra went out to the loft to tell Jason to turn down the fucking Frank Sinatra.

Finally, someone had some authority to tell him to put a cork in Old Blue Eyes.

Here's the thing about Joe Dinki: he's actually a pretty smart guy. He had some really interesting questions for me. It seemed like they were molding Jason's character to be the gears of the agency while I was the soul. But there was a problem: Dinki would drag each question on for like five minutes. By the time he got to the end of the question/monologue, because I was tripping my head off, I couldn't remember the beginning of the question.

I managed to get through it without melting down or cracking up laughing, and I actually think there were a few good moments. Maybe.

At some point Jason got bored and snuck into the bedroom and lay on the floor out of everybody's way. He kept saying in between takes how beautiful I looked and that I was going to be a star.

We finally wrapped. Our last shot was of me flopping back on the bed, then jumping to my feet and jumping up and down on the bed. I was ready to start the party that night.

And boy did we party....

*   *   *

So went the next three days: the cameras rolled as I did my thing—working, shopping, partying, repeat. We kept the stretch Escalade for the entire time. The cameras came in the limo with me and I was interviewed before and after bookings. It was a blast.

But on the second day of shooting, Jason's ego went off the charts. He actually started calling it "The Jason Show," just like I had joked. He sent me on as many bookings as he could, in what was so obviously an attempt to keep the cameras focused on him. He rarely spent any time with me except to flaunt some new woman he had found, suggesting that he was going to make her the new Natalia. Jealousy and insecurity is a part of any relationship. You would think that in mine, the insecure partner might be the one whose girlfriend is meeting and sleeping with rich men every day. It was a tribute to Jason's many talents that he could turn it around and make me the jealous one.

The irony was Jason continued to bomb on camera. He kept freezing up and getting lost in his answers. His interviews dragged on for hours.

He was so obsessed with becoming famous, but when the bright lights were finally turned on him, he couldn't deliver.

After three days, they packed up shop.

Two weeks later, Joe and Ron showed up at the loft with the first edit of the trailer they were going to take to VH1. It was awful, and Jason told them so. A week later, they came back with another cut. It was brilliant. The music was amazing, it told the story, and it was edgy. I looked beautiful; we loved it. We had thirty copies burned, and Jason started showing it to everyone that stopped by the loft.

Jason and Joe got a meeting at VH1 and presented the trailer. The suits allegedly liked it, but not enough to commission a show. They apparently told them to keep shooting. Who knows if they were just blowing us off. It wasn't like the network was putting up any money, but I turned a blind eye to any of the specifics. In fact, I ignored anything that could potentially bring me back down to reality and continued to snort away the day.

I avoided my mom's calls at all costs. I was doing a very good job of keeping any real feelings at bay and couldn't face dealing with her, or pretty much anyone outside of my escorting social circle. One of the only people I still spoke to on a regular basis was the exquisite escort Taylor, and even that was an effort.

He didn't understand why I was interested in filming a reality show, but he still listened to my problems, offered what advice he could and tried to bite his tongue regarding my drug use. If we'd been closer, or he'd known me longer, I could definitely see him pulling me into a different reality show altogether: *Intervention*.

He offered me all the bookings he could, even though he didn't want me to think he was trying to take over Jason's place in my life. I declined each one as I felt like I would be cheating on Jason and the agency, but a few times he was able to convince his client to call the agency and request me. After each one of those bookings, Taylor and I would go out for coffee, and I'd manage to refrain from slipping away to the bathroom for a little bump—long enough to land back on earth and get real with him for a minute.

No matter how much better I knew Taylor's lifestyle would be for me, I couldn't live without Jason. After our meetings ended, I'd go back to the loft and continue the nonstop party I was living.

And finally I came to terms with the truth; the reality (not the reality show). I was in love with Jason. I was in love with him. I dealt with all the bullshit, the drama, the pain and the arguments because I was in love with him.

Once I stopped resisting my feelings, Jason and I were on top of the world. He bought me presents, we snuggled at home, and watched our trailer over and over again. We even spent time with his step-dad. One day, he took us to lunch at the Friars' Club, the legendary private sanctuary for comics. Jason marveled at the huge photos of Sammy Davis Jr. and Frank Sinatra palling around. We were living the life he had always dreamed of.

CHAPTER TEN
DARK CLOUDS

Our love-fest continued for weeks. He'd even gone so far as to call Mona and cancel the booking I had scheduled one afternoon so we could hang out. We tooled around our usual shopping haunts, and then on the spur of the moment decided to get away from it all and spend the afternoon at the Hoboken apartment.

Crazy, I know, but we just wanted some mellow alone time together. The loft could be a bit wearing sometimes. I couldn't believe he had canceled one of my appointments. It was probably the most romantic thing he ever did for me, as pathetic as that sounds. Sure, he bought me stuff. But this was different. Maybe there was hope for us.

As we lay in bed in Jersey, Jason told me he had a drug test coming up and asked me to go with him. I told him of course I would. I had never gone with Jason to any of his bi-weekly check-ins and piss tests with his parole officer as he'd never asked me—it was something he did on his own. I came to learn firsthand that jail and being arrested and all things related to the criminal justice system are solitary and lonely events. It's like a doctor's appointment when you've got some particularly unpleasant disease.

We took a car service to the parole office, and I waited in the back seat as he went into the depressing grey building. He told me he wouldn't be long.

Cut to an hour later. I'm getting pissed. Where is he? I wanted to be supportive, but this was ridiculous. My phone was ringing. It was a number I didn't recognize. I flipped open my phone.

"Hello?"

"Natalia, Ron Itzler here."

"Hi, Mr. Itzler, are you looking for Jason?"

"No, I just spoke with him."

"Oh." I didn't get it.

"Natalia, they're taking Jason back to jail. He failed his drug test."

"That's impossible."

"He tested positive for cocaine."

"No, Mr. Itzler, that's impossible he hasn't done any cocaine. I would know. I can tell when he's done it."

"Well, Natalia, you are in a car service, right? Have them bring you back to Worth Street. I'll come by and see you later today."

I couldn't believe I was leaving the parking lot without him. It felt so surreal. I was stunned. What were they doing to my Jason?

Back at the loft, I closed the door to my room and threw myself on the bed, my face buried in the pillow, and let myself cry. There was no way he had done blow. He knew he was going to be tested. He would never have been that stupid. The last thing he ever wanted was to go back to prison. Something had to have gone wrong. Was he set up? Did Jersey finally get sick of him getting over for so long that they fabricated the results? Or was it just some kind of mistake at the lab? Or maybe it was my fault...some of my blow got mixed into his K? Who knows?

A million "what ifs" went through my mind. What if the judge decided to revoke his parole? He could go back to jail for at least a year. There's no way I could run the agency.

I'd spoken with Clark as soon as I got off the phone with Jason's dad. We decided that no one except our inner circle was to know about Jason's whereabouts. But what to tell everyone else? Jason's presence at the agency was all-encompassing. It didn't make sense that he would take a week off. Problem solved: Jason had a sister in California. We'd say she was sick, and Jason went out to be with her, although in reality she didn't want anything to do with him.

Clark came by later that night. We checked out the booking sheets for the next day, closed up the office early and retired to my bedroom. We sat around talking for a while. He told me he'd sleep over so I wouldn't be alone and come back after work the next day. Jason's dad was picking me up at noon to go see Jason and then Paul Bergrin, Jason's criminal lawyer.

The next morning, I made sure my purse was empty of all things illicit. I was freaking—I'd never seen the inside of a jail before. I got into Ron Itzler's big Mercedes, and we chatted a little about Jason. He summed up being his parent, "You have to be ready for anything when it comes to Jason. Nothing surprises me anymore."

Having Jason as a son must be quite the roller coaster. Ron asked me about my family, my life. I tried to stay away from talking about the agency. He was being so warm and nice to me, I didn't want to remind him that while I was Jason's girlfriend, I was also his star employee. As we pulled into the parking lot, Ron pulled a pill case out of his jacket pocket, opened it and popped a pill. He handed me a bottle of water and put a pill into my palm as well.

"Klonopin," he said. The Rolls-Royce of anti-anxiety meds. I guess it was necessary when you had a son like Jason.

We walked into the run-down corrections building. We showed our I.D.'s and were led into a bleak waiting room with posters warning us not to try and smuggle in any drugs.

They called out, "Visitor for Jason Itzler." I looked at Ron. He indicated for me to go ahead. I smiled weakly and walked toward a female officer.

"Oh no, no, no, honey. You cannot go in like that," she waved her hand over my top half. "Your shoulders have to be covered."

I had a feeling I was going to screw something up. I felt something go over my shoulders. I looked behind me. It was Jason's dad putting his suit jacket over me. He patted my cheek, and I walked down the hallway to see Jason.

He smiled when he saw me, and I smiled, too. I felt like I had seen this scene a million times before on TV. We said the typical stuff to each other: How was he, I was happy to see him, I miss you…. But it felt weird and stilted. I just wanted him to come home. I didn't want this life. He looked weak—his normal bravado deflated. He tried to give me some pointers about running the agency. He told me to trust Hulbert and Clark…they would make sure everything was okay. (He was half right.) I left and gave Ron his jacket. He slipped it on and went in to see Jason. He was back in less than five minutes. We drove to see Paul Bergrin, the lawyer.

Bergrin, a hard-as-nails, former federal prosecutor, was upbeat about the situation. It turns out Jason pulled off a crazy move. Knowing he hadn't done any coke, and the test was wrong, he took drastic action. When his parole officer informed him of the results and explained that meant he was going straight to jail, Jason fell to the floor, faking some sort of heart attack/stroke. As hard as it is for me to believe he had the acting chops to pull it off, he apparently was credible enough for them to rush him to a nearby hospital emergency room. In the ICU, he got the doctors to test his blood again. They did, and it came up negative for cocaine. Bergrin said he'd be able to get him out based on the new test, but it might take a little while.

*　*　*

Meanwhile, back at the bat cave, all hell was breaking loose. Mona was in Peru on vacation, so with the cameras rolling, I was forced to take over the operation. I can confirm the adage: Pimping is not easy. I would much rather be out working than handling all the bullshit that comes with running an office.

It was midnight, and Scott was on the other end of the phone. He wanted to hang out. The office was really busy, so I couldn't really leave. But he refused to see anyone else, and I really wanted to go. How could I say no to my favorite future senator?

I made him promise to book at least three hours, and then he told me that he was at his parents' place in Greenwich, Connecticut. This was something new. I'd partied at my friends' parents' houses in high school, but I'd never worked at one. He told me to start billing him from the time I left my house. I called our usual car service, gave them Scott's credit card number and told the driver not to worry—I knew how to get to where we were going. Then I kissed Ron and Alexandra goodnight.

We'd been filming for a few hours, but they knew I wouldn't be back before morning. They started to reset the lights for Hulbert, and I packed my Louis Vuitton again, this time including every possible garter/fishnet combination I had. My new favorites were some sparkly Roberto Cavalli garters and some lace fishnets I'd found at Hotel Venus, Patricia Field's store on West Broadway.

The car ride turned out to be torturous. I popped half a Valium as soon as we pulled away from the loft, but waited until we were on the highway to do a bump. I didn't want the driver to get pissed and leave me on a corner in the city. After about forty-five minutes, I passed out. I guess I really was that tired. I didn't wake up until we were in what looked like another country. I thought I was dreaming. There were trees and lawns everywhere. I got the most incredible waft of freshly cut grass.

The driver wasn't enjoying his nature ride. He told me he'd been driving around the same block for half an hour and hadn't been able to wake me up. We were on the right street, but he couldn't find the address. I got on my cell to Scott right away.

Scott explained you couldn't see the house from the street. He told me to tell the driver to take the private driveway right after the house with the white pillars. It was all private driveways with white pillars!

We eventually found it. I checked myself in the mirror. I had creases on my cheek from falling asleep against the seat. I began frantically rubbing my face. That never works.

I gave the driver a twenty-percent tip and got out of the car as quickly as I could.

Scott opened the front door and pulled me quickly inside. I guess he was a little nervous about partying at his parents' house. Though they probably weren't due back anytime soon, I guessed it was more the neighbors he was worried about. I followed Scott up the stairs to a sitting room that looked out over the backyard. It went on and on and on. The trees and plants and shrubs and lawn were all gorgeously manicured and sculpted. It was all very Versailles.

Scott kissed me on the cheek and invited me downstairs. He told me he'd missed me and seemed to genuinely mean it. I'd have to be careful. I could really fall for this guy.

With Jason in jail, the reality was sinking in, and it wasn't pretty. Take away the money, the clothes, the lifestyle, and Jason was, well, a criminal. My boyfriend was locked up. Even though things had been going really well between us, it was still in the back of my mind (and heart) that he wasn't paying me what I was owed. I didn't want to abandon him in his hour of need, but seeing him sitting in that decrepit Jersey jail, it all didn't feel like such a fairy tale anymore.

And there, standing in front of me, was Scott— tall, handsome, well-mannered, sweet, rich-beyond-belief Scott—telling me he'd missed me. Even when he was in bad-boy, coke-sniffing, porno-watching, fucking-me-doggy-style mode, I couldn't think of anyone more perfect for me. Throw in a little Amalfi Coast, beach houses in Malibu, the Hamptons, South Florida, a lodge in Aspen, the list went on.

I got off on Jason's particular brand of crazy, but Scott was like a real life Prince Charming. What girl wouldn't fall for him?

*　*　*

Paul Bergrin got his day in court to dispute the parole office's piss test. The judge accepted the hospital's test results, and Jason was released after spending two weeks behind bars. But there was a catch. He had some new terms to his parole. He had a curfew. He had to be in his Hoboken apartment every night by the stroke of midnight. If he was even one minute late, he would go right back to jail.

At Jason's request, Mona and Clark had stepped in after the first week he was locked up and had taken the bulk of the stress off my shoulders, but after he got out, things never really went back to the way they were. Jason was different, preoccupied. I think the ease with which his freedom was taken spooked him. He didn't have the drive or spark he'd had before, and he was doing enough K to, well, to knock out a horse.

So Mona and Clark became the new power couple. They made all the important decisions, collected all the money, hired the new girls. *Everything.*

At least once a day, Jason would do a quick survey of the boards, check out the daily totals and get a briefing on any issues that had come up: clients not paying, girls not performing, etc. It made me smile when he overturned their decisions. He seemed to be making sure they both got a good lecture at least once a day, but he wasn't the commander-in-chief he'd once been.

Jason and I tried to reconnect. In spite of the ongoing head games, at the end of the day, we shared a bond that I thought couldn't be broken. But we started to fight—a lot—screaming at each other in vicious verbal throw-downs. We could clear the loft in five minutes. Only Hulbert could handle it. He'd be upstairs in the office trying to cup his hand over the mouthpiece to prevent the client he was trying to close from getting a whiff of our ruthless insult-slinging.

I continued to be Public Enemy Number One to Mona, and since she was now pregnant—presumably with Clark's child, although it was everyone's favorite rumor that it might be Jason's—I now had her second-in-command gunning for me as well. Mona's the type to demand her partner's unconditional support, especially when she's on the warpath.

Her first move was to plant the seed in Jason's mind that I was a drug addict and would drag him down with me if he didn't cut me loose. Mona started the rumor that I had a secret heroin habit. The truth was, heroin was making cameo appearances at the loft, but never, ever with me. (That would come later.) She hired a batch of ex-models because she said they were every guy's fantasy, but they were jaded, snobby, boring junkies with eating disorders who'd never quite made it in the fashion industry. They were the ones who brought in the smack.

At the same time, things were deteriorating between Jason and me. Sometimes I felt like Jason was jealous of my relationships with my clients. Not in the typical boyfriend-who's-your-pimp way. He was jealous that I got to hang out with them. So many of our clients belonged to the legit world. They led the glamorous status-filled lives Jason had always dreamed of. I think if he could have come along to my appointments with me, he would have. I pictured him admiring the client's artwork and strolling from room to room while I was getting nailed silly. Then, as opposed to the usual girlfriend experience—affectionate, post-coital quality time—Jason would offer himself up, thereby getting to hang with the big boys. I even imagined him arguing that it was the perfect date: you sleep with the hottest girl, and then, instead of having to listen to her and act interested in what she has to say, you get a mini-boys' night out: scotch, maybe a cigar and some sports/politics/pussy talk.

As if to prove my point, a week after he got back from jail, he got a call from Scott. When Scott let it slip that it was his birthday, Jason insisted on going to the hotel to wish him a happy birthday personally.

I didn't know how Scott was going to feel about my bringing a chaperone. When we got to the hotel, I did a quick look around, noticing that Scott had cleaned up, big time. There was no coke on silver trays, and the TV, which would have normally screened some cool porn or erotica, played music videos. There were no sex toys, restraints (Scott had bought some of his own after our first meeting) or garters lying around. We all sat in the living room of the suite. I offered to make us drinks. I found a bottle of Grey Goose, ice and mixers in the bedroom. I called Scott into the bedroom to help me carry the drinks. I looked at him and said quietly, "It's 10, if he doesn't leave by 10:15, come into the bedroom. I'll take care of it."

At 10:10, Scott excused himself. I could tell he wanted Jason out of there, but Jason was blissfully sipping his drink as if he were at a swish cocktail party. My client was being cock-blocked by my pimp. Who else does this happen to?

"So, Jason, I have imprint slips, what did you guys work out?" He told me the hourly rate, and I stood up and told Jason I would call him when I was getting ready to leave. Jason took a last sip of his drink and left. Finally, we could get the party started.

The client issues started coming up when we were in bed, too. To be fair, I didn't always give Jason what a boyfriend deserves—what everyone deserves—their partner's love, body, enthusiasm, attention. It's like he felt cheated. All these clients had the time of their lives with me...why didn't he get that anymore? The answer was simple, but he didn't believe it.

I told him straight up, "Jason, when I get home, I'm drained."

Love? Check. Energy? Gone, spent. Body? Exhausted to the point of total disconnect—kind of a zombie feeling.

I would profess my love to him over and over and really mean it. But he didn't get it. He wanted me. He wanted what all the other guys got. He even went so far as to offer to pay me, kind of as a joke.

"Natalia, maybe that's it. You have become the world's greatest escort, and part of that means you are a little addicted to the money. You don't really get excited about it unless you're getting paid."

I had flashbacks of Samantha sitting next to me in Jason's Hoboken apartment, her hand on my knee, telling me with wide eyes (and a wet pussy, I'm sure) how she loved being handed a fat envelope and counting the hundreds in front of the client. Was this what I had become?

I didn't think so. I was just tired. I was even too tired to argue with him. I'd let him drop some hundreds on our bedside table, summon my inner-Energizer Bunny sex goddess, and then slip the hundreds back into his pocket when he wasn't looking.

When you combine the sex issues with the strain of Jason's new curfew restrictions (we rarely slept in the same bed anymore), our once unbreakable love affair was in danger. Maybe he could stop booking me on *so* many appointments? Get the hints I hurled his way that I really loved him and was pretty much ready to retire, invest the money I'd earned that was sitting in the agency account, become a successful actress, be his girlfriend forever, and live happily ever after.

It just got worse. In what seemed like a move designed solely to piss me off, he went on a recruiting spree, trying to turn out any beautiful young thing he could get his hands on. I couldn't stand it. He had gotten so good at it, it was almost disturbing. He'd force me to watch. I could tell in a flash which girls were emotionally equipped for it, like Ashley, and which ones would come back from their first appointment in a glassy-eyed daze and disappear forever. This job was not for the fragile or the naïve, as I was finding out. The fact was, I was excited about the TV show, but the reality behind the reality show was that I felt more and more like his partner in crime, rather than his girlfriend.

One night, we got into another one of our screaming matches. It was so bad I stormed out and went over to Ron's apartment. I pulled out a bag of coke, dumped out a few huge rails and asked, "What happens to our show if Jason and I break up?" I had gone over the ramifications in my mind. There was no show without the relationship. The hook of the show was that Jason and I were in love. The pitch was both scandalous and intriguing: how could two educated, intelligent, attractive people embrace this life—and actually be proud of it?

I already knew the answer to my question. Ron didn't even really bother responding, except to half-laugh. Ron had dropped everything in his life and invested his own money to produce the pilot episode of the series. If we broke up before the show had even gotten off the ground, he was toast.

* * *

Mona—observant, cunning Mona—sensed Jason and I were on the ropes and launched her second salvo: Jason and I needed to be divided in order to be conquered. She got Clark to swipe my Treo so they could find evidence I was stealing from the agency—meaning I was seeing a client directly and cutting the agency out of the profits. According to Hulbert, who'd witnessed the theft, they were convinced I was guilty but needed to prove it. At most agencies, girls steal every client they

Me with my Dad at my grandparents' summer pad in upstate New York. This is the only photo I have of us together before he left when I was 11 months old.

Me, age 4, so happy with my mom on a family vacation.

Me, age 4, with my brother, age 10, summer '84.

Me, age 5, at my Mom's house at Christmas.

Tap dancing at 5 to my recital routine, "On the Good Ship Lollipop."

Me, age 8, dolled up in my tap-dance costume for the end-of-year recital.

Me, age 16, the night I won the Canadian National Tap Dancing Championships.

Me, age 16, slightly star-struck after performing with Gregory Hines at Plaze des Arts.

BEATRICE NEUMANN, ORIGINALLY FROM GERMANY, IS AN AMAZING PHOTOGRAPHER I MET IN NEW YORK IN 2000, JUST A FEW MONTHS AFTER I MOVED TO THE CITY. WE USED TO DO SHOOTS TOGETHER IN HER EAST VILLAGE APARTMENT AND THEN LATER, WHEN SHE MOVED TO LOS ANGELES, AT HER FRIEND'S MALIBU MANSION. WHEN SHE WAS BACK IN NEW YORK WE WOULD SHOOT AT MY GRAMERCY PARK APARTMENT.

THE FOLLOWING PHOTOS ARE FROM A THREE-DAY SHOOT WE DID IN JUNE OF 2005.

On the windowsill in my living room, overlooking 23rd St., day one of our shoot. Beatrice and I were alone and used the time to catch up with each other. She's always been very protective of me, expressing her concern for me and asking me over and over again if I were really okay.

Photo © Beatrice Neumann

This was taken in the hallway of my building, right outside my apartment, day two of our shoot. We were interrupted when Mark Jacobson arrived to continue my interview for the *New York* magazine article he was writing about Jason Itzler and me.

Photo © Beatrice Neumann

Day three of our shoot, in my favorite broken-in jeans. My party friends had come and gone. When I was alone in my apartment, especially after I was arrested, the high ceilings made me feel less glamorous and the loneliness would creep in. Photo © Beatrice Neumann

This was one of the last pictures we took. We were both tired but not quite ready to quit. A few hours later, Beatrice packed up and flew back to Los Angeles.
Photo © Beatrice Neumann

From my first photo shoot with Beatrice Neumann in her East Village walkup apartment, October 2001, post 9/11. I was high, alone and scared in New York. Beatrice was one of my only friends at the time. Photo © Beatrice Neumann

Photos of me taken by a photographer friend in my bedroom at the loft, July '04.

The cover of *New York* magazine, July 18, 2005. Jason and I were featured in an article about our relationship and the business of high-end escorting. The notoriety from the article was one of the factors that alerted the authorities to NY Confidential's activities.

Jason Itzler, owner of NY Confidential, and my boyfriend. He was in his thirties when this photo was taken in our New York loft and already raking in hundreds of thousands of dollars per year with his high-end escort service.

THIS SERIES OF STILLS IS FROM FOOTAGE SHOT BY RON SPERLING, THE DIRECTOR OF THE VH1 REALITY SHOW SERIES THAT WE STARTED TO FILM IN '04 AT THE NY CONFIDENTIAL LOFT.

Jason and me enjoying the high life in our fabulous loft.
Photo © Ron Sperling

Jason and me having an "upfront and personal" moment.
Photo © Ron Sperling

Jason talking with an escort. His T-shirt says: "I am your girlfriend's pimp." It was everyone's favorite.
Photo © Ron Sperling

Jason and me
being "lovey-
dovey" and
kissing for the
camera.
Photo © Ron Sperling

Jason with some
of the girls as
they were about to
go out on calls.
Photo © Ron Sperling

Me in my
bedroom talking
on the phone with
a client.
Photo © Ron Sperling

Another still of me in a rare, quiet, reflective moment in the loft. Photo © Ron Sperling

This is a Polaroid picture that we took of Ashley for the files when she started working for NY Confidential. On it are her basic stats and some information regarding her personality. This was useful in matching potential clients with the right girl for their tastes.

My best friend and me in Paris, November 2007. This trip was a gift to celebrate how far we've come.

Faces of New York Confidential

The faces of NY Confidential represented on the bodies of animals:

Horse: Hulbert Waldroup (painter and booker)
Wolf: Paul Bergrin (lawyer)
Fox: Mel Sachs (lawyer)
Doe: Natalia (escort, Jason's girlfriend)
Ass: Jason Itzler (owner of NY Confidential)

Rooster: Clark (manager, accountant)
Vulture: Floyd Abrams (friend of Sachs, advised Jason on escort agency legality)
Cow: Mona (manager, Jason's ex-girlfriend)
Zebra: Marco Glaviano (photographer and friend)
Swine: David Elms (owner of TER)

Painting by Hulbert Waldroup · Photo © William Scott Sloan, www.scottsloan.net · Painting appears courtesy of Melanie A. Bonvicino

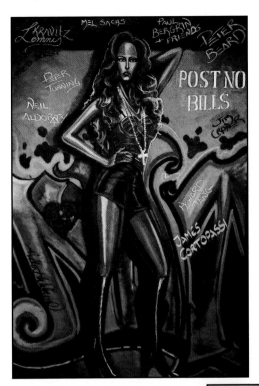

79 *Worth Street*

Me, outside the building where Jason ran his exclusive escort agency, NY Confidential. There was a rumor that the names on the wall were clients of NY Confidential. They were all popular people in New York City, but were they clients? I'll never tell.

Painting by Hulbert Waldroup · Photo © William Scott Sloan, www.scottsloan.net · Painting appears courtesy of Melanie A. Bonvicino

Natalia on the Edge

Hulbert used a photograph taken by my favorite photographer and close friend, Beatrice Neumann, as the inspiration for this painting. Both Hulbert and I signed it.

Painting by Hulbert Waldroup · Photo © William Scott Sloan, www.scottsloan.net · Painting appears courtesy of Melanie A. Bonvicino

Natalia Sleepwalks

Me, represented as sleepwalking (which I often did, especially when using drugs) among ravens, which symbolize the "johns." My personal favorite of Hulbert's paintings of me. It feels very intimate—Hulbert really understood me and my path in life.

Painting by Hulbert Waldroup · Photo © William Scott Sloan, www.scottsloan.net · Painting appears courtesy of Melanie A. Bonvicino

Natalia Stiletto High

I posed for this painting in the window of Ron's Broome Street loft. There was a film crew shooting a movie on Broadway—they admired our artistic process during their breaks.

Painting by Hulbert Waldroup · Photo © William Scott Sloan, www.scottsloan.net · Painting appears courtesy of Melanie A. Bonvicino

NATALIA'S PROFILE

| back | add to favorites | report a problem | link to this review |

general information

ad website: http://www.nyconfidential.com/girls/Natalia.asp
personal website: n/a
agency name: Unknown

agency: Agency   **service:** Escort/Massage
city: New York   **other city:** None
phone 1: (800) 692-6634   **phone type:** Other
phone 2: (212) 678-9000   **phone type:** None
in/out: Outcall   **email:** info@nyconfidential.com
delivered as promised: Yes   **smokes:** No
on time: Yes   **availability:** Daytime/Nighttime
porn star: No

appearance

real photo: Yes   **photo accurate:** Yes
build: Skinny   **height:** 5'3" - 5'5"
ethnicity: White   **transexual:** No
age: 21 - 25   **breast size:** 34-35
hair color: Brown   **breast cup:** B
hair type: Curly   **breast implants:** No
hair length: Below Shoulders   **breast appearance:** Youthful
piercings: None   **tattoos:** None
pussy: Partially Shaved

services offered

massage: Yes - Privates to Privates   **massage quality:** Don't know
sex: Yes   **s&m:** Don't Know
blow job: Yes without Condom   **cum in mouth:** Yes - Swallows
touch pussy: Yes - On the Inside   **lick pussy:** Yes
kiss: Yes - With Tongue   **anal:** Don't Know
two girl action: Yes - Really Bi   **will bring 2nd provider:** Don't know
more than one guy: Don't Know   **no rush session:** Yes
multiple pops: Yes   **rimming:** Don't Know

cost of services

SERVICE:	LENGTH:	PRICES:
Escort Outcall	2 hours	$2400
Escort Outcall	60 minutes	$2000

My profile on the Web site, TheEroticReview.com, commonly referred to as TER. Potential clients would use TER to select an escort, using both the profile and the reviews with numerical ratings given by men who had previously hired one.

MORSECODE'S REVIEW OF NATALIA

back	report a problem	see provider's profile	send mail

appearance: 10 - One in a Lifetime   **performance:** 10 - One in a lifetime
attitude: spectacular!!   **atmosphere:** supercharged!!

general details

used ny confidential 1nce before. jason really delivered 1st time with samantha, who was a dream come true. she was out of town this time; besides, he said, he had a new girl possibly even better. i thought, even better? can i even HANDLE evn better? i mean,how good does it need to be before i have a stroke!!... then i met natalia. i don't know where jason finds these beautiful, intelligent, purely sexual women, but the male world is better for it. read on, assholes ...

the juicy details

met her in an upscale hotel bar. caught in traffic, she was 1/2 hr late, but i didn't care; both she and jason called to apologize, and she was worth the wait. natalia's not only beautiful, but she's got the eyes of an old soul; you really feel connected to her instantly, at least i did. we hit it off big time at the bar, and lasted abt 10 minutes before we were both so hot we hightailed it up to my room. we ripped eachother apart like we'd been fucking for years... she has a perfect little body -incredible real perky tits that i couldnt stay away from, amazing ass,energy to burn; i mean, she was jumping all over the room .. at one point i was on my cell phone talking to a business contact while she stood over me on the window sill and i fucked her pussy and ass with my tongue between sentences!!and yet, as i say that i feel almost disrespectful to her, because i feel like what we shared was our own little private fanasy. she's crazy, affectionate, spontaneous, generous, creative and intelligent... everything you'd want in a girlfriend, instantly!! she made me feel like i was the best thing she's ever had (who knows, maybe she aint lying!). check the stats for particulars ... money?? what money? i thought i dreamed the whole thing ... anyway, don't call her -she's all minemine mine!!!

This is an early review of me. First reviews of new escorts were very important to Jason and NY Confidential and to the girls, too, as bad reviews could impact a girl's future in the business and the agency's revenues. My consistently high ratings eventually led me to be able to command $2000 an hour for my services.

PNEUMOCEPHALUS'S REVIEW OF NATALIA

back | report a problem | see provider's profile | send mail

appearance: 9 - Model Material   **performance:** 10 - One in a lifetime
attitude: Friendly   **atmosphere:** Charged

general details

When I was planning a business trip to NY, I ran across NY Confidential's website. So I thought I had to see what it is about the highest rated escort in the history of TER. I also liked that Greek goddess look about her. I booked my appointment about a week before my trip, and confirmed the date when I arrived at JFK. Natalia arrived at my hotel just as I was getting out of the shower. As I let her in I knew I had made the right choice.

the juicy details

Natalia is petite with curves at all the right places. She is also very pretty, in fact probably overall the hottest looking escort around. Any prettier, you would think she's crazy to make a living as an escort. Natalia is also down to earth and easy to talk to. Naturally we took care of business first. After some small talks, she leaned in and we shared a DFK that lasted forever. She's in my lap now, and my towel was nowhere to be found. I helped her undress as well. With me still sitting on the couch, she started a BBBJ. Within minutes I had to stop her because I didn't want to CIM. She finished me with a HJ that ended over her perfect natural chest. We cleaned up and chatted about things to do in NY. After a little while I was ready to go again. Again BBBJ followed by cover, then CG with her in my lap and rocking away. This was very enjoyable because we could DFK and my hands could stay busy. This lasted a while with my finishing inside her. Again we cleaned up and talked about my trip. With about 30 minutes left we went at it again in doggie, and let me tell you, you really have to have a lot of stamina not to lose it there right away. Overall the best session I ever had with a provider. It brought back some of the most memorable experiences in college. It was certainly worthy of the high price.

This reviewer responded to me being "the highest-rated escort in the history of TER" and wrote his descriptive review after having his experience with me—awarding me yet another "10."

can. It's the way the business works. Remember, agencies often take more than half of their girls' fees. Agencies can't stop the extraneous dates from happening, so most don't bother, and besides, a majority of the clients come to an agency looking for variety. They generally don't want to book the same girl over and over when there are so many different types of girls to choose from. That's a huge part of what drives the industry. It's like being a kid in a candy store.

At New York Confidential, we had a golden rule: You don't steal clients. Jason had an elaborate appeal, which went something like this: "Why would you want to hurt my feelings like that? If you steal a client, you're doing something really mean to me, and I know you're all good girls, that's why you're working here. We make people happy. Make me happy, stay with the agency, and I promise you'll make lots of money. Plus, clients never pay full price to the girl alone. Let the bookers do their jobs. You do it like this: if a client wants your phone number, you dangle a carrot. Tell him, 'We don't really know each other that well yet. Book me two or three more times through the agency, and I would love to give you my number.'"

I was the exception. I had most of my clients' phone numbers, and they had mine. When we were in Hoboken and things started getting busy, Jason would hand off my repeat clients' calls to me, and I would arrange the booking. They knew my rate. It was simple. That progressed to clients calling my cell directly or emailing me. It was because of this personal communication that I had so many high-paying regulars, like Neil at $6,000 a day for three days at a time. I always filled out a booking sheet and dealt with the financials the same way as all the regular appointments made by the bookers. In the beginning, Jason trusted me to the core and vice-versa. It was so relaxed and natural for us to be that way with each other.

When Mona saw all my clients' names and numbers on my Treo, she thought she'd hit the jackpot. She couldn't reveal that she'd had Clark steal my PDA, so she lied. She told Jason that one of the girls saw me with a client at a hotel bar when I didn't have a booking scheduled. I was either stealing clients or working for another agency, which brings us to another New York Confidential rule: we were New York Confidential girls and New York Confidential girls only. Again, the rest of the world doesn't care if you work for ten agencies, and the reality is owners and bookers aren't generally loyal to girls—they're interchangeable. If an escort wants to really earn, she has to work for multiple agencies. New York Confidential had made rock-star escorts with reps that spread across North America; it wasn't about to give them away.

Mona had just told a huge fat boldfaced lie. I laughed. This was ridiculous; she was losing her mind if she thought Jason would believe that.

I looked over at him. He looked uncertain. A wave of panic hit me.

"Jason, that's so not true," I pleaded. "I've never seen, nor would I ever see, a client without the agency."

I tried to play the logic card: What incentive did I have to see clients independently when I was overbooked as it was and earning one of, if not *the* highest rate of any girl in New York?

Mona was slick. She didn't argue—just left it like that and walked off.

The seed had been planted. I had been railroaded. A few days later, Mona floated the suggestion that I shouldn't be allowed in the office, and just like that, I was banned from the agency office—the agency I'd helped Jason build.

I was crushed by Jason's reaction. The trust we'd always had, that nothing and no one had ever cracked, was gone. I felt like Jason had vanished on me, literally. Ever since he got back from jail, he had been doing more and more K. He was a zombie—to the point I was constantly checking his breathing and pulse to see if he was still among the living. Then he'd come out of it and act like he'd just seen God, joyful and totally unaware that he'd been out cold for an hour.

It was tearing me apart to see him so zonked, even though *I* didn't have much ground to stand on. I was basically snorting lines from the minute I woke up to when I crashed, if I crashed at all.

With all of the potential drama over the money I was owed, ironically it was my drug use that became the focal point of our fights. I thought it was obscene that I was the only one being called out. I was ready to admit I needed to chill out with the nose candy, like indefinitely, but not if Jason was unwilling to go there with me and address the horse tranquilizer he seemed to love more than me—maybe more than anything, judging from the way he had checked out of running his business.

Our relationship was hanging by a thread. The only thing that was keeping me there was my pride. I wasn't going to be kicked out of my own house on my million-dollar ass, labeled a cokehead, a liar and a thief.

Then one day I came home higher than a space shuttle, having partied with all my old nightlife friends for the first time in months. I'd been up for days, working and then clubbing, continuing after hours at some loft, followed by a day on a boat sailing around Manhattan, and then a last hurrah at my friend Kenny's gorgeous Upper West Side apartment where we danced for two days straight. The apartment felt surreally decadent, especially in contrast to the dingy drug dens we'd familiarized ourselves with over the past few days. Instead, we walked in to find a modern, glass dining-room table adorned with a buffet of drugs. The usual menu of coke, MDMA, Special K and Crystal was laid out on fine bone-china plates in small white heaps, resembling a mini-mountain range, and there were little ornate dishes filled with a variety of pharmaceuticals, which we gorged on like children set loose in a candy store, until we finally reached the point at which we just physically couldn't ingest any more narcotics.

Mona took one look at me and declared, "Jason, she's on heroin! I told you she was secretly hooked on heroin. I bet you she's been giving it to all the girls."

So, instead of curling up on my bed and getting a solid eight hours, I had to sit in my own room while Hulbert, Jason, Mona and Clark hovered over me discussing what to do about me as if I weren't there.

"Rehab?" I heard Clark say, "Are you sure she's on heroin? I think she's just partied out."

Go Clark! I couldn't believe he stood up to her like that. Mona didn't scream at him. Instead, she pulled the pregnancy card: "Wow, so is this how it's going to be when the baby comes? My feelings won't matter...what I KNOW is true, won't matter?"

Hulbert and I locked eyes, *This chick's good.*

"You're not on heroin, are you, Natalia?" Hulbert's concern couldn't have been more genuine.

My exhaustion took over. I curled up in a fetal position, and I started to cry.

"No, I'm not."

I cried harder.

"Hulbert, why is this happening?" I protested.

"Sweetheart, it's simple. This is all Mona."

"No," I shook my head. I could barely hold it up. "Why is this happening?"

Hulbert helped me get up, and he started the shower for me. In classic Hulbert style, he held up a towel in front of me, giving me my privacy and making sure I didn't fall getting in the tub. He said he'd be back in two minutes. He was going to tell Jason that he was putting me to bed and that no one was to disturb me. When Hulbert got serious like that, it could be intense.

I shook my head awake and in doing so almost did a back flip onto my head in the shower. *Wow,* I thought, *this is how people die in showers.*

I turned off the water, grabbed a towel and almost passed out again, smacking my head against the mirror. I looked through my closet to our bedroom. It was only about twenty feet away. I stole a glance down at my vanity as I passed it, checking to see if I'd left a mark on my face.

Nope, no bump.

I kept walking, holding onto walls and furniture for balance. I felt myself trip on the leg of my favorite chair and pass out mid-air.

Then I woke up.

I was on the bed. Hulbert and Jason were beside me.

They looked freaked out. Jason was like a ghost. Even Hulbert looked a little pale, and he's black.

"Natalia, you hit your head really hard," Jason told me.

I looked at Jason and remembered everything and started crying, "Jason, I'm not doing heroin."

"I believe you, Natal. Crazy Mona!" he laughed, and my face crumpled again. The tears were stuck inside me somewhere.

I lifted my hand to reach up and touch my face.

Hulbert gently guided my hand back down and shook his head.

Jason continued, "Boy, does she ever get nuts when she's pregnant!"

Hulbert and I locked eyes for the second time that day. Jason didn't get it. This was serious. If she kept going like this, she'd end up doing something crazy, like calling the cops on one of us and inviting them in. It's not like she hadn't done it before.

It was determined that I almost definitely had a mild concussion and therefore shouldn't go to sleep. I ended up *having* to do more coke so I could stay awake. Un-fucking-believable. A few hours passed, and I was doing gram lines to keep my eyes open, and it was still so hard to stay awake.

Finally, Jason called Mel Sachs for help. Mel stopped by his doctor's office and gave him all of my details. I can just imagine the doctor's expression when Mel read him the grocery list of drugs I'd consumed in the last forty-eight hours.

Mel quickly explained that I had hit my head, hard. I had a huge, hideous bump above and below my left eye. After I'd tripped on the chair, I'd smacked my face on the six-foot fertility statue Jason had bought for our room. That's right, a fertility statue.

"Jason, do you think that's wise...a fertility statue in a brothel?" I asked him when he brought it home.

He just looked at me quizzically, not getting it.

Every time I walked past the statue, I gave it the evil eye.

Now the statue had finally got me back. My entire left eye and surrounding area was purple and black. Mel's doctor friend asked if I were coherent. Hmmm, define coherent. I was awake and knew my name. I knew where I was. The doctor said that I was allowed to sleep. Finally.

*   *   *

I couldn't work looking the way I did, so Jason and I finally got to spend some time together. We went out to Hoboken to decompress. I told him I had had enough of Mona forever, and the loft. Jason begged me not to move out. He said he felt so stupid for doubting me, and that he loved me, and I told him I loved him, too. I did love him. However, I wasn't happy anymore. In fact, I was miserable, and I needed to fix that. Furthermore, I tried to explain, I didn't feel safe at the loft anymore. Jason had started letting my room be used for in-calls by other girls when I was out. Sketchy guys were coming in and out of the loft (and my room) all day. Who were they? Mob guys? Undercovers? I made it a point not to know, but I definitely didn't want to be around. On more than one occasion, I'd found a condom in my bed.

I didn't tell him, but I sensed that something really bad was going to go down there soon. I didn't know what, but I had no intention of being around to find out. My life at the loft was over, as was the dream Jason and I'd had of transforming the industry—and ourselves.

*   *   *

I called Taylor, the one capable person I knew, and asked him to help me start over. Being the gentleman he is, he leaped into action, finding me a great sublet from a sweet lesbian couple in Chelsea.

I knew that if I left the loft, I would most likely never see the money I'd earned. That was hard. But I didn't have a choice. It was poisoned.

Mona was happy to see me go. I was packing my things, and she came in my room and asked me for my keys. I almost lost it.

"This was my house," I quipped back at her.

It was the first time I didn't hold back. Still, I couldn't let her see me break. I just laughed at her, but inside I was burning up. I couldn't believe that she was going to win. She'd managed to push me out and be Queen of the Castle once again.

* * *

I never did get my Treo back and was never able to defend my honor. I didn't blame Hulbert for not backing me up. If he'd confirmed that Clark had stolen it, they'd have figured out that he wasn't on their team and was keeping me up to date on everything they were doing. Hulbert was always there for me, he was my friend, but like everyone including me, he was there to make money. That meant keeping how much he hated Mona and Clark to himself and playing along nicely. He said it himself: he had watched Mona force me out of the loft, and it was only a matter of time before she turned on him.

Now that I was out, I had no problem breaking the rules. I still had my clients' phone numbers in my trusty Moleskine notebook. They would be happy to see me independently, as most of them had grown tired of Jason and his lack of discretion.

One day Hulbert came to see me at my new place, really upset. He told me that he, Mona and Clark had made a decision a few weeks back to create a secret stash for Jason, as Jason never paid himself a salary—he just spent whatever he wanted out of the agency's account. But Mona's extensive knowledge of the industry, plus the law enforcement risk, convinced Hulbert that Jason needed to stop using the account as a slush fund and keep large denominations in cash, so it could be kept safe from the authorities if they were ever raided. He told me that each day, they separated out half of the cash and put it in the floor safe. At the end of each week, Clark brought the stacks to a secret storage spot, away from the agency, and therefore theoretically safe. Can you see where this is going?

Mona was just getting started. One of the girls came forward and said Hulbert had raped her. Hulbert, the shy painter and consummate gentleman, had raped a girl? I freaked. I wished there were some way I could help him. For a couple of days, the office was in crisis. All of the girls were talking about it. Finally, Jason sat the girl down, and she recanted, but insisted they'd had sex. Apparently, that part was true. It seemed that she'd fallen in love with him and with Mona's support and guidance had come to understand that he'd taken advantage of her. Raped her. Hulbert wasn't fired, but like me, he was banned from the office—the penalty for having sex at the loft with an employee. Queen takes knight.

Hulbert sat me down and told me he was terrified Mona and Clark were stealing all the money from the agency through the secret stash they had created for Jason. Now that Hulbert was out, nothing was stopping them from taking all of the money. I could see it was tearing Hulbert apart. He had helped Mona and Clark create the perfect crime. It's not like Jason could call the cops.

I asked who else knew. He said no one.

I said, "You've got to tell him."

But Mona and Clark were one step ahead of the game. When Hulbert approached Jason, Jason looked at him as if he were crazy for being concerned.

"I just transferred the $25,000 they put away for me to a safe spot," Jason told him, adding, "It is strange we don't have more money...our accounts are almost empty. I know we have huge overhead, but this is ridiculous."

Hulbert had no way of knowing how much Mona and Clark had been putting away, but it was certainly more than $25,000. *Poor Jason*, I thought. Then I realized what else this meant: poor me. If the accounts were almost empty, all of my money was gone, too.

To make matters even worse, while Rome was burning, Jason just fiddled harder. He started popping up in the gossip pages bragging, Howard Stern-style, that he was the "King of all Pimps." All he seemed to care about was seeing his name there alongside Madonna and Gwyneth. It was a slow-motion train wreck. We had always been able to fly under the radar: the mob left us alone; the hotels were cool with us because we were discreet; the magazines took our ads; and even the NYPD seemed to give us a pass. We were just one of dozens of high-end escort agencies operating in the semi-open in New York City. But Jason, being Jason, had to push the limits. He literally became obsessed with Page Six. In one item, he even boasted that he wasn't worried about getting shut down because "I have the cops on my side."

I'll never forget drinking my coffee early one afternoon and opening the paper to read that. I literally did a split take.

Later, a vice cop would tell *New York* magazine, "It was like he was daring us."

CHAPTER ELEVEN
THE FALL OF NEW YORK
CONFIDENTIAL

Now that I was out of favor with King Jason, the kingdom divided. Hulbert looked out for me, but he wasn't about to put his head on the chopping block. Ron had become my friend. He was going to protect his investment, the hours he'd put into filming, but he also stayed neutral. Most of the girls turned away from me. If you weren't Jason's friend, he was your enemy, and they knew it. They were there to make fast money, not friends. You're either in, or you're out, as Ms. Klum says.

Jordan was the one girlfriend who stayed loyal to me, but she was never really into the escort thing to begin with. She loved the loft and loved me, and I loved her back. So much. But that proved to be a mixed blessing. She moved into my new apartment with me and dropped out of art school, and we lived free for six months. She'd tried the escorting thing and occasionally went on bookings with me. We didn't have to split anything with an agency, and my safe was always bursting with cash.

I was finally living on my own terms, but with no loft to return to and no one to look out for me, Jordan and I slipped deeper into a dark haze. And that's when we got addicted to heroin. We woke up one December morning, and we were sick. Heroin sick. So we did more. We both knew we were in trouble, but didn't want to face it. I was broken. I'd lost my world, my fucked up Jason, my agency, and my title as reigning Internet Sex Queen. Even though I knew the escort lifestyle was wrong and destructive and unhealthy in so many ways, it was still everything I had.

This is how my subsequent fall from grace happened:

We were on a tear. We were young, rich, beautiful and in the greatest city in the world. Jordan quit school for a semester. We were convinced she was destined to be the next Kate Moss. We had the contacts to make it happen: photographers make models, and we knew all the great ones. Meanwhile, I kept seeing all my great clients, and I enlisted Jordan to be my assistant. I paid her fifteen percent of everything I earned and in return she kept me looking beautiful, helped me pack and got me to the airport on time for my almost weekly out-of-town dates.

Our average day went like this: we'd wake up from a twelve-hour sleep wrapped up in each other in my California king-size bed, and then we'd do a small, tiny bump of heroin and meth, though we both denied ever touching the latter to anyone that asked. We were chemical snobs and crystal was the Payless of illicit drugs, but it got us up and running. I'd jump on my laptop and check my emails while I flipped my cell on speaker and let my voicemails play. Jordan would connect with Gtox, our fabulous dealer, and make plans to meet up. We'd throw on some kick-ass clothes (our favorite: identical purple camouflage Adidas track suits and Oliver Peoples shades) call a car and zip downtown to Delancy Street. I'd drop five, six hundred bucks on the following:

An eight ball $200
A gram of pure heroin $150
Crystal $100

A few Valium, Ambien, Oxycontin, $50-$100

Forever the karmic soldier, Gtox would throw in a gram of the best weed ever (he was secretly trying to wean us off the hard stuff).

He'd flirt with us a little (he kept a framed black and white pic of me on the wall of his bathroom), and we'd be on our way. We'd run a few errands, taking advantage of our car service for a few hours—things like picking up dry cleaning, taking care of Jordan's passport application and paying our cell phone bills. For some reason, in Manhattan it takes all day to do half a dozen things between traffic and getting sidetracked by sample sales or latte breaks. It's never as easy as it should be.

Now for the fun stuff: tanning, manicures, late lunch at Balthazar and some shopping before going home, where we'd do bumps of heroin and coke, take a bath together, shave our legs, and then do a mini-fashion show to decide what to wear for the night. I'd receive a million phone calls along the way from half of the nightlife world, along with a booking or two from regular clients. Next, I'd go off to the hotel while Jordan hung at the apartment with some random boys from Brooklyn, smoking all of Gtox's glorious pot.

We'd meet up at our first stop of the night, say NA on 14th Street, have a few drinks, do some more H and blow, dance, make out, and flirt more with each other than any of the guys trying to get with us. We'd maybe hit another club or three and then go home, sometimes alone, sometimes with a couple of worthy party friends to make things interesting. Often it all wrapped up with a threesome, then a nap.

Our circle of friends and associates was hardcore when it came to drugs, but no one was into needles. Being on the inner-periphery of the jet-set crowd meant we had an image to maintain and sticking a needle in our arms was way too grunge. Even smoking was reserved for the veterans as almost everyone only snorted. The heroin Jordan and I got was top shelf and while it never felt good going up my nose, it worked really well. Sometimes we'd use a piece of aluminum foil and smoke it. That's called "chasing the dragon," but I almost like the high from snorting better.

Jordan was my guardian angel. While she was partying (almost) as much as I was, she was a few years younger with a cleaner liver and little to no emotional baggage. I was carrying around an ex in jail, the scars of an abusive relationship and at least a dozen clients wanting my love and attention. Jordan decided we needed to get a little healthier. She bundled me up in my new kelly-green J. Lindeberg parka and bright pink Coach winter boots, and we took a cab to Whole Foods just a few blocks away from our Chelsea apartment. I was in awe of the place and, if either of us had known how to cook, it would have been a whole new chapter for us. The produce section alone was enough to inspire you to become the next Julia Childs. I had a fantasy of Jordan and I in a beautiful granite kitchen, dressed in cute aprons and heels, preparing lots of mouthwatering gourmet meals.

Food and pretty much all the drugs we did, save pot, don't really mix, so we just bought a few things, mostly stuff that contained sugar and didn't involve cooking. Jordan fell in love with miniature candy apples in a display case. They were tiny and so cute. I asked the girl behind the counter to wrap up two, and she leaned in and whispered, "I have to warn you, they're $26 each."

My mouth dropped open.

Whoa. I won't blink at paying $600 for a pair of shoes, but $26 for a tiny candy apple?!

We bought four.

We stopped in at Bed, Bath and Beyond and bought a few more pillows (you can never have too many) and went home for the day. The snow was swirling around, and I wanted to snuggle with Jordan, do some H and watch (nod out) to a movie.

And we did, but Jordan was on a mission, and I admired her resolve. The next day she skipped over to me and shook my shoulder, waking me out of a nap, "Natalia, we need to join a gym. I was talking to Jeremy, that photographer guy, and he told me that if we want to meet casting directors and agents and people like that, we have to go to the Chelsea Equinox. They all go there."

Made sense to me. "How do we join? What do you need?"

"Well, it's probably a few hundred dollars each to join, and you should probably give me your I.D., too."

I grabbed my wallet, pulled out a thousand dollars and my Canadian I.D. and handed it to her. She kissed me on the cheek and went to Equinox. She started going almost everyday. After a week, I started to feel like I should make the effort. I did a minimal amount of heroin, popped an Adderall and threw on some leggings and a tank top.

We got to the gym, and it was nice, really nice. She showed me the locker room, and we stored our stuff. We went up the stairs and landed on a floor that had a bunch of different cardio machines and weights and typical gym stuff, including a few beautiful people working out with their personal trainers.

Jordan suggested we get on the treadmills. I started slow, and it didn't feel so bad. For about five minutes. Then I started to get nauseous. Jordan looked over at me, her ponytail bouncing up and down as she ran.

"Natalia, you should sit down."

My face had turned a shade of green, at least that's how I felt. I sat on a bench and chilled out. After a few minutes, Jordan came over to me and said, "Ok, Natalia, that was good for today. Why don't we go steam?"

We went into the eucalyptus steam room, then the regular steam room and then showered and headed home, feeling like death warmed over.

The next few months blurred together. I made it back to the gym twice and only to use the steam room while Jordan was on the treadmill. As we got deeper and deeper into our heroin addictions, all the frenetic activity of our first month as roomies began to fade away and was replaced by lots of passing out on my couch. I'd hear my cell phone ring and sometimes manage to pick it up and look at the caller I.D. before it fell from my hand and landed on the floor. I had been the life of the loft back on Worth Street and bubbled with smiles and hugs for everyone. On heroin, I didn't even have the energy to answer my phone. Clients called relentlessly, as did my mother and a few concerned friends. I did my best to make plans, to hold on to some thread of a life, but even when I did get where I was supposed to be, I was a ghost of my former self, a walking zombie.

Then I got to the point at which I would get physically sick when I ran out of H, and the panic would set it. It didn't happen often. Unlike most of the other areas of my life, when drugs were involved, I was a planner and almost never ran out. But it's inevitable that every once in a while Gtox and all my backup dealers would be M.I.A.

Jordan would get my phone calls, my crying, "help me" phone calls, and always come to my rescue, either with what I needed, or she would at least come home, climb into bed and hold me until my precious medicine arrived.

*   *   *

In the *Behind the Music* episode about my life, this is the part where the second album tanks, the drummer dies in a horrible motorcycle accident, and the lead singer's drug addiction causes the band to miss Live Aid.

I had just made my bi-monthly visit to my doctor before I left for vacation. I had all my STD tests done and had my prescriptions for Xanax (anti-anxiety), Ambien (sleeping pill) and Adderall (ADD med) filled. He checked my blood pressure, which was low, and asked me how I was doing. I told him fine. He could tell I wasn't fine. He'd been my doctor for almost the entire time I'd lived in New York. Despite being a respected doctor on the Upper East Side, he let me pay him a small cash fee. I was like his little pro bono project.

I guess I wasn't in such good shape. He told me he was cutting off my prescriptions, which really sucked. I'd have to start buying my prescriptions from my main dealer. One Ambien from a drug dealer is $10. I tried to explain that when I used the pharmaceutical stuff I did fewer street drugs. For instance, when I took Adderall (which is basically pharmaceutical speed), I did less coke. It was true. But he wasn't buying it. He suggested I get an intravenous drip of vitamins. So I got shot up like Keith Richards with a mix of B12, Vitamin C and calcium. I don't know if it really worked or if it was just a placebo, but the shot in combination with my weekly visits to the tanning salon helped me feel better.

So I went down to Miami with a Prada bag full of over-priced meds and a condom full of smack stuffed where the TSA wouldn't look.

I was down there for the Winter Music Conference, which is basically a week-long rave, featuring hundreds of the world's best electronic DJs and tens of thousands of the world's most drugged-out club kids. I was actually feeling a little better after lying in the sun for five days. I had rented out an apartment with two friends and was pretty low key the whole time. The guy was a heroin dealer to celebrities, so I didn't have to worry about getting any bad shit, and the girl was cool to suntan with.

I was planning to stay a little longer, but a call from Neil, the CEO from Cincinnati (a.k.a. my #1 client), saying he wanted to see me in New York, meant my vacation was cut short.

I sat in the bathroom at the airport with all of my pill bottles and my baggie of heroin trying to figure what my body—what my addiction—needed right then and there. I didn't want to take Ambien or Xanax, and I didn't have any coke. I definitely needed to do some downtown so I sniffed a bump and then looked at my Adderall. If I took one, I'd be wired, and I really I needed to sleep on the plane if I were going to be rested for my most lucrative client. So I wrapped what was left into a condom, knotted it and put it inside me. Crazy, I know, but it was a really small package, and I wasn't going to get caught—I'd done it at least a dozen times before.

I felt fine as we boarded. I usually leaned up against the window and let the change in cabin pressure put me to sleep. Not this time. Because I'd bought my ticket so last minute, there were no window seats left, so I got to my middle seat and tried to make myself comfortable...but I could already feel myself nodding off. I remember flopping around a little before being woken up by a Jet Blue flight attendant. She quietly told me I was going to have to get off the plane. I was in a daze. It wasn't until I was halfway down the aisle that I realized what was going on.

I have an obscure memory of the rest of the passengers staring at me with a mixture of fear and pity. At least it felt like they were looking at me. I was too high to actually focus on anyone's face.

When she left me at the gate, I vaguely came back to life and said, "Wait, I have a medical condition. Are you not letting me fly because I was falling asleep?"

She told me she couldn't stay and listen. There was a plane full of people waiting, and she had to get back on board, but she told me to go to one of the airline's customer service counters. My luggage would be waiting for me in New York.

I explained to the customer service guy that I was narcoleptic. I showed him my prescription bottle for Adderall (it just said amphetamine on the label), told him that I had forgotten to take my medication, and now I didn't have a flight. He apologized profusely, put me on the next flight and gave me a number to call right away to file a complaint. I got three round-trip vouchers and a very nice letter of apology.

It should have been a wake-up call, but in my mind, the only lesson I'd learned was how to scam the airlines.

*   *   *

It was just before Christmas. I was still talking to a few people from the agency, including Hulbert. In the midst of my heroin haze, I got a voicemail from Katie, another escort/heroin lover. She was freaking out. Apparently, Ashley had been arrested. She ranted about how we were all going down, the kind of end-of-the-world, doomsday-style stuff that I rarely paid attention to, but this time, my ears pricked up. Jail was not an option. I was so far gone with my H addiction that I thought if I were ever busted I'd just end it all—jump off a building, or mainline a huge baggie. There was no way I'd end up sober and alone in jail.

I decided to follow up on the information and made some phone calls. Everyone confirmed that Ashley had been arrested in the typical call-girl sting—a hotel room bust where she was tricked into negotiating sex acts for amounts of money, rather than a flat rate for her time, as I had instructed her. My well-informed source within the Internet sex community sent me an email confirming her bust. Nothing happened in the industry without his knowledge, and he contacted me as soon as he found out. It read:

> Law enforcement infiltrated NY Confidential on 12/1. An undercover police officer paid $990 for a provider via credit card. They booked another girl on 12/20 for $990 on a credit card. They booked two girls on 12/31. Each time they had full service and supposedly all the sessions were taped.
>
> The 12/20 session was at the W hotel and was with Victoria. This session was booked with Victoria after looking at reviews of her by the TER handle "Poller." Is this really true? If it is, I would be concerned that she is being used by LE.

Allegedly, it all started when a client known as Big Dan found an unauthorized $28,000 charge on his credit card put there by New York Confidential. He allegedly contacted law enforcement friends, and the die was cast.

Ashley, apparently, was never charged and went back to work at New York Confidential as if nothing had happened.

As far as I know, the agency never found out Ashley had been taken in, and I didn't tell Jason or Mona. Screw them, they deserved what they had coming. I was only tangentially connected to the agency at that point. I'd drop off my money from the random bookings they were still getting me and had little to no contact with anyone. I wasn't welcome. I did tell Hulbert to watch his back, but I guess he was in too deep to get out.

The news only confirmed what I had been feeling in my gut for more than a month: the end was nigh. I tried to put even more distance between me and Jason, and New York Confidential—but it wouldn't matter in the end.

*   *   *

I booked a plane ticket home to Montreal for Christmas. I went all over the city trying to find the perfect presents for my family. I wandered around for hours, then days. I was so frustrated. I had a pocketbook full of cash, but I couldn't find anything. Finally, I slumped down on the floor of Macy's and burst into tears. The holiday hordes just walked right over me. Everything hit me at once. I didn't know what to buy my family because I didn't even know them anymore. I didn't know who I was, either. I was lost.

I finally made my way to the open market at Union Square, with its dozens of funky vendors selling Christmas-y stuff like candles, hand-knit hats and scarves. I bought everything I could carry. I thought they'd like that stuff better than shiny American store-bought things—things that represented everything they hated about my lifestyle, and why I had chosen New York over them.

I wrapped everything as best I could and crammed it all into suitcases. I kissed Jordan goodbye. She was off to Mexico to meet her family for a week. She was freaking about the "no drug" situation, but I told her she'd be okay.

Christmas Eve came. My car service took me to JFK, and I got in the check-in line. And waited. For hours. They finally announced they were canceling all flights that day because the airline's radar system was messed up and gave us a number to call. I went home, in shock that my homecoming was falling apart. I sat on my bed for hours on hold, only to be told that my flight had been rescheduled for the same time the next day. I called Ron and went over to his place. We did lines and watched the De Niro/Sharon Stone flick, *Casino*. No one should ever watch that movie on Christmas Eve.

On Christmas Day I made it out to the airport again, and, again, the flight was canceled. I called my mom crying. I told her what was going on, but could sense she wasn't buying my story—she's seen right through half of the lies I'd told her. I got defensive. I told her to call the airline herself. I could hear my family in the background, opening presents, laughing, drinking. They didn't sound as though they missed me very much. They were celebrating as a family as they had been doing for years—without me. All of the birthdays, Mother's Days, Thanksgivings, Christmases. This was just another one I would miss.

I sat on my bed and did drugs alone. As I didn't have a TV, I went online. I found nothing to distract me there—I wasn't into chat rooms or porn (yet) and, at the time, Hollywood gossip hadn't reached TMZ heights— and so I cried some more. I was completely alone.

The day after Christmas, I realized I probably could have easily fixed the whole thing. If I'd really tried,

I could have found a seat on another airline or taken the train. I thought about doing it right then, but Christmas was already over. I'd missed it.

I put my family out of my mind and for the next few months, Jordan and I lived large. We celebrated my 25th birthday for two months by going to Vegas, followed by L.A., and then we partied our heads off in New York. We did photo shoots with every photographer we knew. Peter Beard came back into my life, living in my apartment for weeks at a time. One day, we went with him to have his portrait taken by Mark Seliger. In classic Peter style, he insisted we be in the photo. We ended up in a book called *In My Stairwell,* alongside Paul McCartney, Susan Sarandon, Tom Wolfe and Lou Reed. Despite my drugged out state, it's my favorite picture of me.

* * *

A month after Christmas, I was conveniently at the Bellagio in Vegas with a client when it all went down. I was with the only client I'd had seen in about a month. I was so fucked up and drug-sick that I'd missed my first flight out there, and the client almost canceled.

The drug-free flight back was torturous. When I finally made it to my apartment, Hulbert sped over in a cab and shared as many of the calamitous details as he knew.

The loft had been raided.

The cops seized all of the computers, paperwork, credit card receipts, photos of escorts, and the $50,000 sound system. I assumed they even took the disco ball and the fog machine. But the managers were all out somehow at the time, as was Jason.

"Whatever you do, don't go back to the loft, ever," Hulbert said. "You need to keep a low profile. I need to keep a low profile. We're probably next."

Did I feel any guilt that I hadn't warned them? Not really. My source had given me the info about Ashley's bust in confidence. While in hindsight, it probably would have been in my best interest to give them a heads up, but I was too full of spite to make any effort to do anything that might help Mona, and, by extension, Jason...and me.

Still, I needed to find him. As much as I had tried to distance myself from the agency, Hulbert was right: there was no doubt a target on my head as well. I needed more info. Everything was so vague. No one knew anything solid.

I knew just where to look. I found Jason having a final blow-out hurrah with a bunch of new girls I'd never met in, where else, the Gansevoort Hotel.

Looking at him, high as hell, smiling like the Cheshire cat with four semi-naked women lounging around him doing lines, I thought about how the person I had loved so much had become a complete stranger. *Who is this person? I don't know him.* But you know what? I did. I knew exactly who he was. I always just saw what I wanted to see.

I really needed to talk, in private.

"Jason, come in the bathroom with me."

"Natal, I'm not going in the bathroom. Say what you want to say."

Why didn't he get it? This was serious. The *New York Post* had run an article that day all about him, saying there was a warrant out for his arrest. It was only a matter of time before the cops found him. A suite at the Gansevoort wasn't exactly a criminal mastermind's safe house.

If he didn't want to listen to me, there was nothing I could do. I needed to get the hell out of there. I grabbed my purse, looking inside to make sure one of those dodgy girls hadn't helped themselves to my cash or drug supply.

"Natal, you're leaving?" Jason was slurring a little. What was he on?

"Yeah, I gotta go."

"Go where?"

"Jason, I just have to go."

How do you tell someone you're leaving because you don't want to be with them when the cops show up? It seemed like Jason was doing everything he could to forget that it was only a mater of time before he went down.

Sure enough, less than forty-eight hours later, the police crashed his little party, parading him in handcuffs through the sleek hotel lobby. I thought back to the day he'd humiliated me on the roof deck in front of all those people. The cops had no idea what poetic justice their little perp-walk gave me.

Jason was charged with various counts of criminal possession of a controlled substance, money laundering, and promoting prostitution. As *New York* magazine would later recount, only days before the bust, Jason, "attired in a $5,700 full-length fox coat from Jeffrey, bought himself a Mercedes S600." But with his assets (which included my unpaid paychecks) frozen, he couldn't make the $250,000 bail.

Hulbert was arrested a couple of days later, and charged with similar counts.

No one knew what happened to Mona and Clark.

New York Confidential set off a string of busts that shut down several of the city's top agencies, including American Beauties, Julie's and New York Elites, which specialized in flying porn stars around the country to service high-rolling clients. Everyone blamed Jason for the crackdown. He had become the John Gotti of the escort industry—the flashy big mouth who brought way too much unwanted attention to their underground world.

*　　*　　*

Instead of keeping a low profile, Jason just strapped his wings on a little tighter and made a beeline for the sun. While he was locked up at Rikers Island, he used his contacts at the *Post* and the *Daily News* to keep himself in the papers. Getting his name in the papers was the only thing that seemed to keep him afloat and give him a reason to live.

Jason wanted me in on everything, too. I was all part of his hype-machine: how he had the number one agency with the number one girl in the city. He gave my cell number to every reporter in the city. They called me nonstop. I'd always checked my caller I.D. before answering the phone, but now I just let all my calls go to voicemail. The worst part was he was quoted as saying I made $1.5 million a year. It was almost like he was admitting his guilt for not paying me. Maybe in his mind he really believed he was going to pay me what I was owed someday. Either way, the cops and the IRS were going to wonder where all that money had gone.

CHAPTER TWELVE
COVERGIRL

This wasn't happening. I sat in my apartment, getting high, not knowing what to do. I lived in fear that the cops were going to show up with a warrant for me, but that didn't stop Jordan and I from going down to Delancey Street each day to see our dealer. We stocked up on a bit of everything: coke, heroin, pills, MDMA, crystal. Instead of crying, I nodded out, I got high, I got happy, I got sad. I did everything to block out how much I missed Jason. I missed how much we smiled together.

The papers kept hounding me for interviews, but I just stayed inside and hid. A week later, *New York* magazine came knocking. One of their best writers, an old-school journalist named Mark Jacobson, somehow got my number and left a message saying he wanted to write a feature on Jason and me. I liked the sound of his voice.

My sublet was coming to an end. I was going to have to move. I also had to get off heroin. After weeks of finally putting it off, I brought Jordan with me to see an addiction specialist. We left his office with a stack of prescriptions. The magic heroin drug, buprenorphine, saved my life. I detoxed at Ron's house. He knew what to do with me as he'd done this for so many friends during the 70s and 80s.

It hurt. I cried and sweated through every one of his sheets and blankets and soaked the mattress right through. I didn't feel completely normal for a year. All of the bad things that would happen to me in the next couple of months were that much worse because my body still felt poisoned. I thought I was never going to feel good again. I'd fucked everything up. The needle and the damage done[4], as another Canadian put it.

It took me a week to get myself in shape to face a reporter. When I finally felt I could handle it, I called the *New York* magazine guy back. I was relieved. I liked Mark immediately. He's like a bohemian Jimmy Breslin. He wrote the book that they based the movie *American Gangster* on. He hung with Blondie at CBGB's. He holds a torch for the seedy, the forgotten, the downtrodden. Most importantly, he doesn't judge. He's my kind of reporter.

But I also knew what would make the magazine bite. As with the reality show, what made Jason and I special wasn't that we made a lot of money or that we had a huge loft and partied with the city's elite. What made Jason and I special was what we had between us. So that's what we gave him: a love story.

Part of me was playing along for the sake of the story. But part of me was also really worried about Jason. He had tried to commit suicide twice before. This was the third time he'd lost everything. Who knew what was going through his head.

Mark agreed to drive me out to Rikers to see Jason. As we were driving out to the jail, I fell asleep on his lap, and in my semi-conscious, drug-addled state, I started rubbing his leg and then moving my hand up to his crotch. I woke up as we pulled into the security gate at the bridge that takes you out to the island. He laughed and said that even in my sleep I was the ultimate sex goddess.

During the bus ride from the main building to Jason's, we chatted about the barbed wire, and he told

---

[4] I never injected, though. Too scared of needles.

me about the restaurant he was going to take me to for lunch (some little dive in Queens that served the best Middle Eastern food in the city), and anything else irrelevant to stay out of the emotional danger zone—how I felt about Jason, about jail. I wanted to be honest with Mark, but I also didn't want to betray Jason's fantasy. It was all he had left.

Jason had constructed a fantasy in his head that we were going to get married, and I wasn't about to tell him I wasn't with the program. We finally got into the visiting room. Jason was wearing a baggy jumpsuit. He looked small and weak. He had a black eye. When he started in about our alleged upcoming nuptials, I listened. I didn't really have much to say, and it was all over pretty quickly.

*   *   *

The photo shoot for the *New York* magazine cover was at Ron's loft on Broome Street. The photo editor was on her way with the photographer and a crack team of assistants and assorted stylistas. I'd received the call from Mark, with whom I'd spent almost every day of the last six weeks. He told me Adam Moss, the magazine's grand poobah, had given the green light. He loved the story—loved, loved, loved it.

I couldn't wait to hear their concept for the shoot. It was like a dream come true. I fantasized about the clothes: Head-to-toe Chanel? Yves St. Laurent tuxedo with no shirt underneath?

They set up the lights, did my makeup and hair, and finally the editor reluctantly came to see me. I got the feeling she wasn't in love with me or my story, which didn't bother me for a second. I had prepared myself for this. I knew it wasn't going to be all sunshine and rainbows. I wasn't deluded enough to think I'd be portrayed as America's newest sweetheart. People were either going to love me or hate me.

The editor asked to see my clothes. Confused, I showed her what I had hanging in Ron's closet. I had some of my stuff there, but not nearly all my good stuff. She picked them over, making no effort to hide her lack of enthusiasm. "I don't get it. I thought you were going to bring some wardrobe options."

"I thought you guys were going to dress me," I said.

"Well, Natalia, I heard and read so much about your elaborate wardrobe, I thought you'd be more comfortable in one of your own things."

WTF? I didn't want to wear my own clothes. That's like winning a dream vacation in your own city.

Then she went off-topic, "So, how does your family feel about this?"

I smiled, "Which part? The sex for money, or telling the world about it?"

She didn't answer. She obviously didn't like my sense of humor.

But she did bring up a good point. My family was going to find out. At first, I thought maybe they wouldn't, that I could somehow keep it from them. Mark even agreed to omit my last name, but things had gone way beyond that. *New York*'s publicity department had already lined up a segment with the hugely popular, syndicated gossip show *The Insider* and with Donny Deutsch on CNBC. They told me that they were working under the presumption these would just be the first of many national TV appearances and numerous follow-up interviews.

I sat with Ron the night before and talked it all out with him. How to tell my family? We had decided that if I was going to do it, I had to tell them the whole story. I agreed, in theory, but telling my mom what I had become was a lot easier said than done.

As I agonized over what to do, my mind kept coming back to my clothes. I still didn't know what I was going to wear. Then I got inspired. If this cover was going to be amazing, I needed to make it happen myself. I dialed my friend Kenny, a hip jeweler who did custom work from his office in Manhattan's Diamond District. He was my buddy. He brought me back a tee-shirt once from Aspen that read: "I like big bumps and I cannot lie." He said he saw it in the store and thought of me. We did a lot of blow together.

"How's my little Natalia? Taking over New York?" he asked.

"Well, I could be better." I told him what was up. Five minutes later, his assistant was headed downtown with a bag full of diamonds.

Next: I called up another old party pal, Andrew. I'd dropped six grand on a shirred, white mink jacket a few months back at his Madison Avenue boutique. I told him to send me down something special.

I walked over to the editor and said, "I hope you don't mind, but we can get started in about half an hour. I have some deliveries coming."

Hmmm, speaking of which, I turned on my heel and closed the bedroom door behind me. I needed to channel a little Kate Moss and call my dealer. It was all so 80s.

Finally: Mom. For some reason, in that moment, I felt I had to tell her now, or I couldn't do the shoot. I dialed. It rang, and I prayed for her to pick up. That was new. I always preferred leaving a chirpy message letting her know I was okay without having to get into twenty questions. I hated lying to her. But this was not something I could leave on a voicemail: "Hi, mom! I've been lying to you for months. I'm not modeling or acting or even bartending. I am a call girl, high-priced, mind you, but, I have sex for money. And you can read all about it in next week's *New York* magazine. Oh yeah, and my boyfriend, Jason, he's not just my boyfriend, he's the one who got me into this...he's my boss. Love you! Talk to you soon."

She picked up.

"Hi, mom," I tried to sound bright and cheery.

"Natalie, why haven't you called me back? Didn't you get my messages?"

I had definitely gotten all ten of her messages. I couldn't even listen to them anymore. They were breaking my heart. Her voice just cried "emotionally devastated mother." You could tell she knew something was very wrong. Moms always know. I had never gone this long without returning her calls.

"Well, I have some news."

Silence. I imagined what she was thinking on the other end in that split second: AIDS, accident, running away to join a cult.

I tried to lead with the positive, "I'm going to be on the cover of a magazine, *New York* magazin*e*."

Her voice was shaking, "Natalie, what's this about?"

I hadn't practiced, but the words came out surprisingly easily.

"This is going to be upsetting."

Pause.

"I've been working as an escort. I'm not anymore, but the cover and the article are about that. You know that reality show I told you I've been filming, the one with Jason? That's what it's about."

Nothing.

Silence.

"The show is going to be sold soon, and it's going to be really great, so we're doing this article to promote the show."

I could hear whimpering.

"Mom?"

I didn't know what to say. Words cannot describe how horrible I felt.

There was silence as she cried, and I held the phone, trying to find more words, but they weren't coming.

Kenny's runner burst through the door with a tray of diamonds, the photo assistant right behind him.

The assistant barked, "Natalia, we've got to get moving here."

I didn't know what to do.

"Mom? I have to go, but I'll call you in a few hours."

I hung up. I felt relieved that I had told her, but tortured by how it all went down.

Everything was happening so fast. I should have made a mental note to call her as soon as the shoot was over. But for some reason, I felt she deserved to know before it all became real with a photo of my face being taken. I had been thinking everything over, agonizing about my family and how they would feel about all this, for weeks. I knew it would be hard for them to understand, but I thought the most important thing they needed to know was that I wasn't working as an escort anymore. I was done with it. I had sent all my clients emails telling them I was doing this story for *New York* magazine and that it was probably best for us to end our relationship, as I didn't want to get anyone in trouble.

But most of all, I didn't want anyone upset or hurt, least of all my mother.

Obviously, timing was not my forte.

I flashed the editor a smile and gave Ron a quick nod.

I jumped up on the bed that was part of the set, dropped my robe and looked right at the photographer in nothing but my undies.

"What do you think about this?"

I unzipped one of the garment bags Andrew sent down and pulled out a slinky, black fur stole. It felt like chinchilla. I wrapped it around my shoulders. It was perfect—unapologetically decadent. Kenny's runner's eyes lit up, and she started fastening necklaces and bracelets.

And that was our shot. Me, naked, with $25,000 worth of diamonds hiding behind the fur.

The next week, June 10th, 2005, my face graced every newsstand in the city and hundreds of newsstands in airports and magazine stores across North America. The cover read: "NY's #1 Escort Reveals All." The interior headline for the article, which ran over 9,000 words, summed it all up:

> The $2,000-an-Hour Woman: In the bedroom, Natalia was a superstar, an escort in demand by Wall Street traders and NFL quarterbacks alike. Her boss, Jason Itzler, who called himself the "King of All Pimps," wanted to turn his brothel into a *Playboy*-style national empire, with Natalia as its crown jewel—and his wife. A love story.

It would be *New York* magazine's top-selling issue of the year, disappearing off newsstands in less than two days. My real name was now out there, and I went from being a local gossip item to a national news story. I was tossed into the whirlpool of celebrity gossip and twenty-four-hour cable news without a life preserver.

The stress and excitement were overwhelming. I dreamt of a future full of fame and fabulousness. The first Paris Hilton sex tape had just surfaced, and I thought, *Why can't this be my springboard? Unlike Paris,* I rationalized to myself, *I can actually act.*

The publicity department at the magazine started booking me on various national shows: CNN's *Paula Zahn Now, The Big Idea with Donny Deutsch,* and *The Insider,* which promised a three-night special report. The sublet ended, Jordan moved on, and I moved into Ron Sperling's apartment. He started acting as my manager and protector, doing his best to set boundaries with producers about what they could and could not ask. I tried to keep anything that could incriminate me off-limits. In retrospect, this might have been a good subject to broach with a lawyer—as opposed to relying on the legal wisdom of an out-of-work reality TV producer.

New York magazine was supposed to throw me a party, but they were so busy booking me on TV that they didn't have time, and frankly, we didn't need a party to get any more press. However, me, being me, I wanted to celebrate, so I took things into my own hands.

A club promoter I knew secured a club called Snitch and printed up invitations with my picture and the line: "Come party with the Perfect 10. Celebrate Natalia's *New York* magazine cover story: The $2,000-an-Hour Woman and party with her—for free!"

All of my friends came. It was a blast.

For the next couple of weeks, every time I went out to a club, the paparazzi took my picture, and people pointed and whispered in their friends' ears. People whom I only knew in passing from the club scene pretended to be my best friend.

One night I was with my friend Jimmy, a close friend of the owner of the super-exclusive club Bungalow 8, Amy Sacco. We walked right in and went upstairs to a table right next to hers. The energy was incredible. There were bottles of liquor everywhere, girls dancing on the couches, super-hot guys flashing million-dollar smiles. We hadn't been sitting five minutes when Amy walked over and leaned into his ear and then gave him a pointed look. He got up and walked quickly down the stairs to the back hallway leading to the bathrooms. In a few minutes, he came back up and waved his hand for me to come to him.

Wow, was I finally going to be formally introduced to the Queen of New York Nightlife? Jimmy led me all the way back into one of the bathrooms and closed the door. I looked at him, confused.

"Jesus, Natalia, people can be such assholes."

He pulled out a bag and did a key bump.

What was up?

"Listen, sweetheart, I'm so proud of you. You gave me the best blowjobs of my life. I hope you make millions of dollars off this...you're doing all the right things, but I just got into a fight with one of my oldest friends over you, and I just want you to know that I'd do it again in a second."

He stuck the key under my nose. I sniffed.

"Amy just asked me what I'm doing hanging out with you. What am I doing hanging out with you? You're my girl. And I told her straight up, I've spent enough fucking money in this place that I don't need this shit."

My hero.

That's the way it was. People either loved me or hated me.

Part of me got off on being infamous. You instantly get a certain swagger, and you grow a thicker skin. You act like you don't give a fuck, and you can focus on having fun and doing what really feels good, rather then what looks good. That night, though, was not one of those nights. I wanted to feel welcomed and loved by the ultimate in-crowd, but they weren't feeling me. I told Jimmy I'd just gotten a text from my friend C.B. He was partying with Kid Rock at a club a few blocks away.

"Fucking Kid Rock, huh? Yeah, you definitely need to fuck him, you little star-fucker. He might even end up buying you a pair of tits by the end of the night."

He kissed me on the forehead and then threw another key of coke up my nose. I laughed and looked down at my chest. I'd take the money, but keep my tits.

I caught my own reflection in the mirror. My eyes were sparkling.

As we were leaving Bungalow 8, I saw a friend of mine, a jack-of-all-New York trades. Actor, professional gambler, party promoter, he had his own radio show and, like most people in the nightlife scene, we had a history together. I'd fallen asleep at an after-hours club a few years back, and when I'd woken up we were having sex. I've had sex in my sleep before. If it's with a boyfriend, that's one thing, but he had no right. He later apologized, and we were cool. He told me he'd met some big agents from CAA who really wanted to talk to me. I froze. This was amazing. I put his number in my phone and said I'd call him the next day.

He said, "Natalia, this is your chance...you have to call me."

As I walked away, I was starting to know what it felt like to be a sought-after commodity. The newspapers, the TV shows, and all those random people wanted to get a piece of my fifteen minutes.

"Hey, Natalia! Wave to the nice man from Page Six."

I smiled for the camera.

When I got to the club, my friend C.B. yelled in my ear, "Where have you been?"

I smiled, and he looked into my eyes. I turned my head and there was Kid Rock. A bodyguard was leaning into his ear and pointed at me. Kid Rock nodded his head at me and reached out to take my hand. He helped me up onto the banquette, and the bodyguard poured me a drink. I was imagining what the bodyguard had said to him: "That's the hooker C.B. was talking about...the one on the cover of *New York* magazine."

It was fun, and I felt way more love than at Amy Sacco's playa-hater shack, but I couldn't stay long.

I had to be responsible and get home by two so I could get my beauty sleep. I had a date with my new BFF, CNN's Paula Zahn. It was the first time I'd left a club early since, well, probably since I'd moved to New York.

Paula Zahn was awesome. We filmed in the CNN studio and then did a segment outside of the loft on Worth Street. We rode together in a limo downtown, and she tried to get me to tell her who my famous clients were "just between us." I wouldn't budge, but I can't blame her for trying.

I also loved the people at *The Insider*. The producer worked with me to shape my message as if she were my campaign manager, and I were running for president. She played up the glamorous side and focused on my future as an actress. This was exactly what I thought I needed. I'd tell my story and then be swept up by Hollywood. Once again, the fairy tale was alive and well.

*   *   *

The following Monday, I woke up to three big guys I didn't know hovering over my bed in Ron's loft on 444 Broome Street, near Chinatown. I found out later that 444 is a very unlucky number in Chinese culture. My first thought was "Oh, my God, I left a cigarette burning, and the fire department is here." I even sniffed the air for smoke. They told me to get my clothes on and get out of bed. I groggily stumbled out of bed still not sure what was happening. Then I saw the NYPD stamp on their jackets. This had to be a nightmare. Ron was in the living room looking over warrants.

My cell rang, and I looked at the detective. He gestured for me to answer. It was Barbara Walters's producer from *The View*. The perky voice on the other end said Barbara was really excited about having me on the show. I told her I'd get back to her.

The detectives went through every box, drawer, envelope, nook and cranny of Ron's apartment. I wondered if we were off to my apartment next. They would definitely have a field day with all of the straws, baggies and spoons at my house, not to mention the stainless steel dining room table I had used as a giant coke mirror for the last year. The cops asked for my I.D. and told me to put my hands behind my back. As they hauled me out of Ron's, we locked eyes. He was so upset—I could see it in his eyes. I can't even imagine what he saw in mine.

"Call someone," I said.

* * *

I was taken in for questioning.

They sat me on a bench, and then the lead vice detective, a husky man with a really strong Irish brogue, said, "All right, Natalia, we're going put you in a cell for a while, but if you need anything, Jeff here," he gestured to a young guy in his twenties, "he'll take care of ya."

The detective walked away. Jeff had me stand up and took me over to a holding cell. Before he locked me in he asked, "Do you have any weapons on you?"

I shook my head no.

"Drugs?"

Again, I shook my head no. Thank God, oh, my God, thank God, I was so happy I didn't have any drugs. Drug charges do not go away. Right then and there I started praying that all of this would go away. It dawned on me that maybe I should have skipped the meeting with the media coach and talked with a lawyer about what to do in the likely event that something like this were to occur.

I was totally clueless. Do I wait for Ron to come through and call someone like I'd asked? An hour went by, then two. My eyes were heavy. I leaned against the wall and started to drift off. I couldn't fall asleep, but I wasn't awake either. I heard footsteps and sat up straight. How could I be falling asleep right now? What was wrong with me? Wasn't I supposed to be crying or something? They opened the cell and took me to a small room with a table and three chairs. I sat down in one, and the Irish detective and another really tall one sat across from me. Jeff left the room and closed the door behind him.

What was happening? Had Ron abandoned me? This was my hour of need. I knew Ron would take care of me as he'd invested a lot in me and helped me detox off heroin. But what if he left me here? We'd been shopping our footage around and hadn't signed a deal yet. Maybe Ron thought if I went to jail our story would be that much more interesting, and he'd finally get paid.

"Natalia, I just want to start this off by saying, we know everything. There's nothing we don't know. Jason,

Hulbert, Mona, Clark, Mel Sachs, Paul Bergrin, Samantha, Cheryl, Victoria, Katie."

He just kept going, kept naming name after name.

"So, here's the thing," he continued. "You're in a lot of trouble."

My lip quivered. I wanted to scream, but I didn't do anything. I felt like someone had ripped out my tongue, throat and vocal chords.

"You can make this a whole heck of a lot easier for yourself if you're honest. If you lie to me, and like I said, I already know everything, I'll know you're lying to me."

And so it went. Question after question for what seemed like hours. When I wouldn't give anything up, they changed tactics and started asking me stupid things like, "Where is the agency?" It was so obviously an attempt to get me to loosen up so that I'd just keep gabbing when they got to real questions.

But I clammed up. I knew enough to know that pretty much anything I said could help them, and that I had the right not to say anything.

When they said they had found all the booking sheets when they raided the loft in January and started throwing out clients' names, I panicked, but as they listed the names, I quickly realized that they didn't know who any of my clients were. They couldn't have found my booking sheets as I'd taken them from the loft when I moved out. We might have been a Web-savvy business, but all our bookings were done on paper.

They seemed desperate for names of big clients. In particular, they wanted the names of their nemeses: defense lawyers. I told them that my clients were off limits, defense attorneys or otherwise. Whatever I had done in the past, I still had my conscience. I wasn't going to destroy families by naming names. They respected that—for about a second. Then they pressed on. I told them I really didn't know much about my clients. I was part of their fantasy and that didn't include their wives and children, or what law firm, hedge fund or talent agency they worked for.

It was clear they were struggling to put all the pieces together. What they were constructing in their heads was way more nefarious than what New York Confidential actually was. They were convinced there had to be a mob or drug connection. They couldn't accept that a high-end escort agency could make that kind of money without the involvement of the Italians or the Russians, or some sort of ecstasy or coke connection. The truth is, while pretty much the entire staff was high a good part of the time, we never dealt drugs. Furthermore, if the cops had been able to get close to Jason at all they would have known he wasn't interested in getting involved in the drug business again. He had become obsessed with the limelight. The drug world is too underground, too lowbrow. His big mouth even kept the mobsters at bay. When the Italians and the Russians saw he was such a loose cannon, they wanted nothing to do with him. Our business model was strictly built on the law of supply and demand of the world's oldest profession.

The cops told me they were charging me with prostitution, promoting prostitution and money laundering. They asked me if I understood. I just nodded. I didn't understand what promoting prostitution or money laundering was, but I didn't think this was the time to ask. I understood that they were charging me, period. I figured my future lawyer would spell it all out for me. They put me back in the holding cell. Jeff, the young vice detective, went and got me a sandwich and a Vitamin Water. I usually drank Focus flavor, but I asked him to get me Rescue. They didn't seem to get the joke. They let me smoke a cigarette while I gulped it down and waited. The Irish detective and the tall guy came back and said they were going to take me to central booking. They were trying to make sure we got there before the judge retired for the night so that I didn't have to stay in The Tombs, the city's notorious holding cells, overnight.

When we got outside, Jeff gave me one more cigarette. I smoked it while he told me to stay calm. I could feel the stress on my face. They told me that I would be okay, and not to talk to anyone in The Tombs and to call my family as soon as I could—they would be the only ones who could help me through all this.

We got to central booking, and there was a long line down the hallway leading to the court. The tall detective went to the officer standing at a podium checking names off a list and spoke in his ear. The officer looked to where Jeff and I were standing, and I heard him say, "Oh, yeah, yeah, they're waiting for her in the courtroom."

The tall guy looked confused and came back to us.

"They need you right away," he said, looking at me suspiciously.

They led me to the front of the line. The tall one said, "Good luck," and I was led by a court officer into the courtroom. I totally bypassed The Tombs.

It was a big courtroom. There were half a dozen other girls there sitting on a bench next to the judge. A really tall, bald man wearing a very nice suit whispered "Natalia" at me.

I had no idea who he was, but he gestured to a little booth, like a large phone booth with a little table and two stools on either side of it. I looked around. Was I allowed to go in there? The bailiff saw my uncertainty and nodded yes, I could go in. As soon as we were both in with the doors closed, he said, "Hi, I'm Josh Michael Hartshorne[5]. Ron Sperling sent me to help you out."

I breathed a sigh of relief. Ron had come through.

"Have they treated you okay?" he asked me.

I nodded.

"Okay," he continued, "we don't have much time, but I need to know as much as possible. Where is your family?"

I told him my mother's full name and gave him her number. We went through about two-dozen other questions. What was my address? How old was I? That kind of thing. Josh went to call my mom, and I went back to the bench. I saw Josh come back into the courtroom and give me the thumbs up. My name was called a few minutes later, and I met Josh at the defense table and stood tall, ready to do or say what I needed to. I entered a plea of not guilty. What happened next was magic. I was having visions of going to Rikers and experiencing terrible things I knew nothing about. Instead the judge listened to Josh say things like, "Natalie is a young actress from Canada. I just spoke with her mother. She's willing to support Natalie through this process. She has an apartment and will be present and available for all court proceedings."

The judge announced he was releasing me on ROR, which I later learned means "on my own recognizance." I was free to go. No bail. I walked out of the courtroom and onto the bustling streets of lower Manhattan.

My next date was set for the end of August, more than a month away. It didn't even register. I felt like I had literally dodged a bullet. Josh gave a statement to the small gaggle of reporters that were milling around the hallway, and the next thing I knew I was climbing into Josh's giant yellow Hummer, listening to DMX and being driven back to Ron's.

---

[5] Not his real name, obviously, and you'll see soon enough why I didn't want to identify him here!

When Ron came running down to meet us, he asked Josh to join us for a drink. He declined, but he gave me his card and told me to be at his office the next day at 2:00 p.m.

"How did you know I wasn't a morning person?" I asked, laughing and giddy from my near-death experience.

"Lucky guess."

He smiled and pulled away in his giant yellow gas guzzler. Ron hugged me and wouldn't let me go.

"I think I have a crush on my lawyer," I said.

Ron laughed and picked me up in his arms and carried me up to his loft. I had a glass of wine, did a line of blow he had waiting for me, and then passed out watching *CSI: New York*.

*   *   *

The next couple of weeks, I kept partying like nothing had happened.

One night, as I downed nearly half a bottle of Grey Goose at Pink Elephant, I turned to a friend and said, "Are you sure you want to be seen with me?"

She said, "Why?"

"Don't you know? I'm a moral terrorist!"

She looked around the club and gave me a "please, look around you" look.

Karma is a bitch. I'd become a New York celebrity, but I wasn't famous. I was infamous. There's a big difference. I didn't have legions of adoring fans wearing "Free Natalia" tee-shirts. I wasn't invited to red-carpet premieres. I was the mysterious seductress who was luring the rich and powerful away from their wives. I was a threat to society, and I needed to be put away. And so did my boss.

*   *   *

It had been almost six months since Jason had been arrested, and he still couldn't make bail. Ironically, Hulbert was able to post his bail and was released right after I was arrested, after spending nearly five months in Rikers. No one had any news on Mona and Clark. Hulbert came to see me at Ron's place, and, even though we shouldn't have been in the same room, he didn't care. He gave me the biggest hug in the world and told me to be careful. I told him I missed him and asked him if he were okay.

"Fuck no, I'm not okay," he said. "This shit is beyond messed up."

Here's the difference between Hulbert and Jason: Hulbert was genuinely happy that I was not in Rikers, that I didn't have to go through what he did. I got the feeling Jason felt otherwise. So when my lawyer told me to stop talking to him on the phone, I happily obliged.

My first court date was a non-event. I went in, and the D.A. asked the judge for a continuance. My next court date was set for the following month. The D.A. was using that time, Josh explained, to gather evidence and build a case against me. This cycle continued for the next few months. At some point, Josh explained, the charges are either dropped or there is an indictment. The indictment is the D.A.'s declaration that they feel confident enough to go to trial, and a trial date is set. Josh seemed confident. He said that since they hadn't busted me in a sting, it would be difficult to convict me on the prostitution charges, and if I didn't have anything to do with the money transfers, the money laundering charges would be tough as well. The tricky thing was, he explained, I had mouthed off so much about my involvement with the agency to the press, they'd sort of had no choice but to come after me.

Jason's greatest dream, to be all over the papers, was now becoming my nightmare. The tabloids must have written us up more than twenty times over that six-month period, including a full-page story with my picture splashed across half of it. Every time something ran, I got called into the D.A.'s office. They were pissed. I could tell with each article the pressure was ratcheting up on them to land convictions.

The D.A. and lead vice detective, a.k.a. the Irishman, would call me into a meeting with my lawyer and start ranting that I was interfering with a criminal investigation by leaking those stories to the press. I would spend the next hour swearing over and over again that I had no idea how the press was getting its information, and then they would move on and start asking me about clients again. My lawyer would step in and say, "We have told you over and over again that she will not answer questions about clients. I would hope you would respect her integrity and her decision."

They would get right in my face and try to scare me into admitting that I was still escorting and was still seeing clients. It was straight out of every cop movie or TV show you've ever seen.

Finally, one day, I exploded, "I'm broke! I have no money! If I'm seeing clients, why don't I have any money? Remember how much I allegedly used to make? I can't pay my rent, my phone bill...you know I have a drug problem, and you're doing nothing to help me! You've taken my I.D. I can't work here because I don't have a working visa, and there's no way I can get one because I've been arrested. It's like you want me to start escorting again! Well, I'm not! I quit escorting before I was arrested, before the *New York* magazine article was even written."

And that was that. I could tell they were still skeptical, but they never asked me again.

In contrast, my monthly court dates were uneventful. I would go before the judge with my attorney beside me, an Assistant District Attorney would request a continuance, and we'd all go home. The police had confiscated my I.D., laptop, phone, and passport and had no plans to return anything until the investigation was over. They made Ron's life hell for a few months. When the drug angle didn't pan out, the cops contrived their own second-shooter theory—that there was a huge pornography ring behind New York Confidential and that Ron was running it.

The lawyers had been finalizing the details of a $250,000 paycheck for Ron, Jason and me from Court TV for our footage, but all copies of the footage were confiscated the day I was arrested. After a few weeks, it was clear we weren't going to become reality TV superstars anytime soon.

I could have fought everything with a kick-ass lawyer, pled not guilty and argued that I was acting for the camera. I would have had to admit that I'd gone on some bookings and have sworn that I hadn't had sex. However, after Jason and I broke up, the staff decided to save their own skins. They knew who held the key to their future, and it wasn't Jason.

CHAPTER THIRTEEN
CAGED

Cocaine makes it really hard to cry. When Jason and I would scream and yell at each other, I wouldn't cry. When I'd talk to my girlfriends about him, I would just talk, or even rant. But when I was alone, really alone, like when we broke up, and I moved out of the loft and into my own apartment in Gramercy, I would sob. I would cry so hard it hurt everywhere. I had so much bottled up inside of me that I never got that post-cry feeling of relief of the weight being lifted. I would cry for four hours nonstop and I never got there. Either my phone would ring and I'd book an appointment with a client (I had to keep working since I had saved no money and the temp agencies weren't exactly breaking down the door to have New York's most famous hooker on their rolls), or I would just do a huge line and go out partying, which helped me forget what was happening.

When I was in the loft, I was doing drugs to keep me going, but also to heighten the highs. Now drugs had become my escape. The winter was coming, and it got darker and darker.

The five or six clients I was still seeing had become my friends, my family, my everything. We had spent so much time together that they became the only ones I trusted. I had become as dependent on them as I was on the drugs. But I drifted away from them as well and went back to being alone.

I began having cocaine seizures and overdosing. Having been successful at pretty much everything I had put my mind to, I couldn't accept the lows I was now hitting. I'd had so much fun partying and living this crazy life that the only option I thought I had was to try to recapture it. I couldn't relate to anyone. I also didn't want to burden anyone. What I needed was a good rehab facility, a great therapist and then ten days on a beach. What I got were more court dates, more drugs and more guilt.

The legal nightmare was literally driving me crazy. I was getting high all day. I couldn't process what was happening. I couldn't tell when I was asleep or awake. I couldn't go to bed because when I wasn't having night terrors, I was sleepwalking and leaving my gas stove on. Weeks went by, and I camped out at my three-story Gramercy Park apartment alone.

Ron told me a story one night about how in the 80s everyone lost their septum. I gave him a strange look.

"Is that the membrane in your nose?"

"Yeah, it separates your two nostrils. When you do too much blow, it wears down and eventually disappears."

"That's why people start smoking freebase."

"Exactly," said Ron, "That's why everyone eventually smokes freebase."

Two weeks later, I was in the first-floor bathroom of my apartment (the apartment I would soon lose because I couldn't pay the rent anymore) blowing my nose. I've never had problems with my nose the way some people who party do, but this day, my nose hurt. I was blowing; it was bleeding...I kept blowing. Finally something happened, and I almost passed out. My hands were shaking. I looked at my tissue and started crying. I picked up the phone and dialed Ron.

I was hysterical.

He was scared.

"Honey, honey, are you okay? What's wrong?"

I started crying more, "I think I just lost my septum."

He relaxed on the other end. "I was so worried."

Why was he calm? This was serious.

"What do I do?"

"Well, Natty-cakes, you stop partying."

Or I could start freebasing.

Sobriety was not an option at this point. I had enough friends who partied and who liked partying with me in my gorgeous apartment to keep me stocked and happy.

At the end of each run, when I'd been up for a few days, and everyone had left to get some sleep, I'd finally have some alone time. They'd always leave me a few grams, and I would do absolutely nothing all day except a hit of freebase every fifteen minutes.

I had a sex box. It was a gorgeous, black leather cube that looked like a stool, but when you took off the top, inside were all my sex toys: my dozens of vibrators, dildos, every shape and size, the handcuffs that were almost confiscated at airport security once, scarves and restraints. I'd put on some lingerie, play some porn and fix my makeup. I'd stand my beautiful, carved-wood, full-length mirror in front of my bed, put on some music, and feeling so gorgeous, I'd masturbate for hours. Those orgasms were so strong and felt so good, I became addicted to them almost as much as freebase. Then I'd sit on the ledge of my twelve-foot window and stare at the city. Sometimes I'd bring some hits outside on my terrace and breathe the city air and hear the city noise rushing into my ears, my senses heightened by the drugs and lack of sleep.

Getting high alone is dangerous. I tried to regulate myself and not overdose by accident. Physically, I was so run down that I could barely function. I was beginning to wonder if I could recover from this. It seemed impossible that there was any way for my life to go on. I cried for everything I'd lost, everything I'd thrown away and all the things I'd never get to know. It was like I was mourning my life before it had really begun. I stood at the edge of my roof and looked down. I cried really hard. I was standing so close to the edge, I could almost curl my toes around it. The air was cool but still, even six floors up. It took everything I had left in me to keep myself from leaning forward and making it all stop.

* * *

A few nights later, I was in Marquee. It was dark and ominous, and the bass was thumping in my chest where my heart should be. When was the last time I'd slept? My head felt empty, like my brain was rattling around in a cage. My nightlife friends always said to me, "Sleep? You can sleep when you're dead." Well, I needed a nap.

I stepped down from the booth where I was partying with a gaggle of music-video directors, models, photographers and wannabe actors. I walked the length of the bar and saw the line for the bathroom was ten-girls deep. I sighed, turned and made the trek downstairs. I paused on the landing to admire the crowd below—so many young girls, so full of energy. Where had they come from? Half looked to be native New Yorkers of the underage variety, the other half were girls like me, well, me four years earlier: fun-loving hotties who had come to the city to chase a dream. They were smiling and celebrating, their arms around each other's waists or up in the air. It was like they could see their whole lives in front of them, and it was one big shiny ball of happiness. The lights were spinning fast. I broke out of my spell and continued to the bathroom. There was no line; I guessed the cokeheads were all upstairs. I locked myself in a stall, touched my nose and took a deep breath. My loneliness washed over me like a wave. I wished more than anything that I had the will to get clean. I took out my baggie and dumped a little white mountain on my hand, sniffed and felt it burn somewhere in the middle of my skull. The pain disappeared. I peed and walked back out into the pulsating club.

Someone grabbed me before I could take two steps.

"Natalia!"

She stumbled, and we almost fell in a heap on the floor.

"Ashley!"

She kissed me on the mouth and said how much she missed me. We hadn't seen each other in...wow, six months, right around the time she'd allegedly got busted, and shortly before my whole world had come crashing down around me. That's what happens when you're high on heroin. Time passes. It's different from coke where life feels like a chaotic, fun blur. With smack, you blink, and months have gone by.

Ashley's face looked bloated. Had she had her lips done? She could barely keep her eyes open.

She was obviously really high, and drunk. I felt guilty. I was the one who turned her out, as they say, and introduced her to this whole world. I was the little devil with the coke straw on her shoulder. Now she looked terrible, and it freaked me out. She was so young.

"I have to talk to you," she said.

Uh-oh, what could she want?

As much as Ashley and I hung out and partied, I also knew she was driven. She loved the money and had her dream of being the next Mariah. When everything went down, and I left the loft, being my friend hadn't helped her achieve either, and so she disappeared from my life, just like the rest of the girls.

Now she seemed desperate to hang out. Either she was being her social-climber self, angling to be next to the tabloid sensation *du jour,* or she just wanted to get back into the action and work with me again—make some of those serious stacks we used to bring in. She was probably thinking my rates were through the roof now that I was the most famous escort in America, and all. It didn't even cross my mind that maybe she just missed me and wanted to be my friend again.

She said she had to go, but managed to punch my number into her cell.

"I'm going to call you," she slurred.

As she walked away, I thought about stopping her. I wanted to tell her everything right then and there: that I was sorry for getting her into all of this and for being the world's worst mentor; that I knew about her getting busted; and that if she had talked, I didn't blame her—I would have done the same thing.

But, I didn't.

* * *

I was at a friend's apartment on the Upper East Side. I'd taken to hanging out with the underground crowd of the city, including criminals, gamblers and drug addicts. This particular friend ran a poker room in Chelsea but lived in a fancier neck of the woods. He used the thousands he earned from the card room to fuel his thousand-dollar-a-day freebase habit and had no problem supporting mine as well. We had the best bongs to smoke it out of, plus butane-torch lighters—the whole nine yards.

We'd been partying for a few days, and my body was tired and hurting. By the end of our run, I couldn't see properly and couldn't stand up. When I finally passed out, I felt my body twitching and going into convulsions like it did every time I fell asleep. My seizures had come back—it had been about two years since I was with Paul, but they were back, and I was pretty sure this time was it. I wasn't going to get any more chances.

This particular night, I was asleep and dreaming. Apparently, I got up and started sleepwalking and did a hit. Normally this would wake me up straight away, but I stayed unconscious. I woke up screaming in the bathroom, my face covered in blood. My friend rushed in the bathroom. His face was pale, his eyes wide. He picked me up, brought me back to the bed and turned on all the lights. He felt my head, checking for blood then focused on the rest of me. He breathed in quickly when he saw my mouth.

"What?" I started crying.

I wasn't really in pain. I couldn't feel anything, but the blood was freaking me out.

"You're okay," he told me, then he hugged me.

He made me lie down in bed and quickly grabbed some towels. I saw him cleaning the bathroom—he wrapped up the bloody towels and threw them in the laundry. He sat down and did a hit, breathed out and said, "You scared the shit out of me. Why were you standing on a chair in the shower?"

I looked at him like he had three heads.

"Right, well, you're okay. Go to sleep. I'm going to stay up and make sure you're okay."

By the time I woke up the next day, my party friend, clearly traumatized by my antics, was still up and not the least bit sober. I did a few hits to get myself straight and called a car service, taking my parting gift (an eight ball of the city's finest blow) with me.

My clothing-designer friend, Morgan, came over to my apartment. Someone had called her and told her to check on me. She had a key and walked in to find me freaking out. She partied, but not hard—she couldn't handle my level of excess. She'd been through everything with me—from sitting with me back when I was still addicted to heroin to make sure that I didn't burn down my apartment by nodding out with a cigarette in my hand, to an accidental Special K overdose (someone had left a water bottle full of liquid K on my counter and, thinking it was water, I'd taken a big, I mean big, swig of it).

When she arrived, I was shaking. I couldn't find a lighter.

She tried to sit me down. I told her I would, but I needed to find a lighter first...I needed to do a hit. She knew me well enough to know how to help me. Forcing me to sit down wasn't going to work. She found a lighter, I did a hit, and we sat down on the bed.

"Natalia, you're not okay."

I didn't answer. "Natalia, you're not okay. Show me your mouth."

I started crying. I did another hit. I showed her my mouth, and she said, "Look in the mirror."

I went over to the bathroom and looked in the mirror. My front tooth was broken in half. I looked like Jim Carrey in *Dumb and Dumber*. My tooth had cut right through the skin below my lower lip. I was confused. I got up to change. I was sweating hard now, the last two hits made my body temperature shoot up. I pulled off my pants and grabbed some shorts. I did another hit and lay back on the bed.

"Oh my god! Your legs!"

I looked down: my legs were covered in black-purple bruises.

"Natalia, where have you been?"

I told her, and then I told her that I had no idea how or when I'd gotten home.

"Natalia, you're shaking, you have to go to the hospital."

I was shaking. I did have to go to the hospital. My mind was clear enough to recognize that I might die. We took a cab to Beth Israel. I didn't even do another hit before I left. We got to the emergency room, and they put me in a bed immediately. They gave me a sedative to calm my nervous system, which was going haywire, and checked my vitals. Morgan came back to my side and told me she'd been talking with the doctor. She was going to stay with me for a few hours, then she'd be back in the morning. I told her I loved her and told her I was sorry. She touched my face and said that she loved me more—I was Natalia, I was the best, the best friend, with the best spirit, the best heart, and that it was okay that I wasn't okay right now. But nothing she could have said could reassure me that I was going to get better. I couldn't breathe. I was confused. Where was I? The nurse got the doctor, and they gave me more sedatives. Finally, I drifted off to sleep.

I woke up. I wasn't in emergency...I remembered that much. I wasn't in a normal hospital room. I tried to sit up, but my arms and legs got stuck. I was in restraints and not the ones I liked to use on Scott and his girlfriend. I screamed, and a nurse came running in. She put her hands on my shoulders and gently pushed me back down.

"I'm going to get the doctor."

She returned ten seconds later with a female doctor in her thirties.

"You're awake."

I just looked at her.

"You've been sleeping for three days in that bed. And two days before that in emergency."

I didn't know what to say. I wanted to ask her how I'd gone to the bathroom, but I really didn't want to know. All I knew was I had to get out of there. Where was my cell phone? I couldn't even think of whom to call. I told the doctor I wanted to go home. She said she didn't think that was possible, at least not yet. I would have to meet with the department's doctors so they could determine if I needed to be committed.

Committed?

I was in the psych ward.

The word snapped me into reality. The defiant little girl in me came roaring back.

"When can we do that?" I asked.

"Lunch is in ten minutes, so right after lunch. Let me gather your file, and we'll come for you when we're ready."

The doctor and a colleague came in with a clipboard and asked me a series of questions. They asked me about my drug use. I told them I did use drugs, but that I was seeking treatment. I gave them the name of the doctor who'd helped me kick heroin. They told me my behavior had been erratic. I must have been erratic if I'd been restrained while I was sleeping and wasn't able to move. I told them I suffered from night terrors and was a sleepwalker. A couple more questions...they checked some boxes...jotted down some notes. Then it was over. They had no choice but to let me go. I rocked the interview, and I did it all with half a tooth. I walked out the door once again impressed with myself for beating the system.

I called my dentist, a former client, and arranged to see him at his office near Carnegie Hall on 57th Street in a few hours. Then I called Morgan and told her the good news. She was not happy. "Natalia, we worked really hard to get you in there."

"Who's we?"

"Me, Ron, Jordan. You know how many phone calls we had to make, how many favors we called in? C.B. had his dad call the director of Beth Israel himself to get you in there."

Wait a minute, I said. "You guys sent me to the psych ward! Do you think I'm crazy?"

"No, not at all, honey. But it would have meant free treatment. Don't you get it? You've got no money. You can't afford rehab right now, and you need to fix this. What are you going to do, Natalia?"

She started crying.

I had to hang up the phone. I couldn't deal with this.

I couldn't deal with anything. I didn't have anything left in me.

*   *   *

A week later, I had another court date. I'd been clean a week since getting out of the psych ward—a record for this period in my life. If anyone from my past, friends or family from Canada had seen me, they would have freaked out. I was super skinny, my skin was bad, and I had no energy. But to the people who had seen me during my heroin days, I was doing better. So I dressed to kill. I knew there'd be a few dozen photographers camped outside 100 Centre Street. I'd grown used to it, and I knew how the reporters would spin my outfit into their articles. So I picked out a gorgeous, knee-length silk skirt I'd picked up at the Bellagio in Vegas, modest, yet sexy Gucci heels and what I thought was a demure, long-sleeved black sweater.

I arrived at court on time. My previous appearances had all been before Judge Budd Goodman, who's famous, or infamous, depending on which side of the courtroom you're sitting on, for being New York's strictest judge. Officially, every defendant is supposed to be in court at 9:30 a.m., but most judges don't enforce the rule. Your lawyer tells the bailiff when you've arrived, and your case is called on a first-come basis. Judge Goodman, however, did a roll call at 9:30 sharp every morning, and if you weren't there when he called your name, he would revoke your bail and immediately issue a warrant for your arrest. A few times I got stuck in traffic, cursing in the backseat of my cab the whole way downtown to Centre Street and had to get out of the taxi and run to the courthouse, up the eight flights of stairs and down the long hallway to the courtroom to make it on time. As I clanked down the hallways, I had flashbacks to mad dashes across hotel lobbies.

Judge Goodman allegedly had a special place in his heart for the New York Confidential crew. In fact, he'd come out of retirement just to try our cases, but once it became clear that none of the cases were going to go to trial, that there would be no dramatics, no moral and criminal codes challenged, he hung up his robe for good and went back to his Westchester Country Club. Needless to say, I was relieved when I found out that I'd be going in front of a new judge.

However, I was still really nervous. I wasn't really feeling all there. It had taken a lot to convince the doctors that I was okay to go home. On the surface I was trying to maintain some semblance of calm, but this latest incident set off blaring warning alarms in my brain. If I'd landed in a psych ward, even if it was just for three days, something was very wrong. Had I done so many drugs that I'd lost my grip on reality? Or was I always imbalanced, and the drugs had acted like a catalyst to finally tip me over the edge?

I tried to find comfort in my lawyer, to feel more secure in the man with his yellow Hummer. Six-five with a shaved head, he exuded power. He was the newest partner at one of the city's top criminal defense firms, but he somehow seemed to have more juice inside the system than even Mel Sachs. But I hadn't paid him yet, and we'd been through half a dozen court dates and just as many meetings with the Assistant District Attorney handling my case. That's a lot of hours. The month or two following my arrest, he called me his new favorite client in front of his partners numerous times and returned every phone call within half an hour. Every time I felt scared or uncertain, he'd talk me down or have me come in to meet with him or meet for drinks at the Four Seasons just to decompress.

But then he disappeared—a coincidence I'm sure had nothing to do with my lack of payment! All of a sudden, he was out of town or in meetings. The last time we managed to have a conversation, he seemed to have no idea what was going on with my case. I told him I was a little worried, but he assured me that my next appearance was nothing to worry about.

"Nat, this is just a formality," he had said. "Don't get worked up about it. We've been through this before. Just be on time and wear something sensible."

I was on time, but he wasn't. I waited in the hall but he didn't show.

I finally had no choice. I walked into the courtroom without representation. The new judge wasn't as scary looking as Judge Goodman, but he didn't look super friendly either. He had what looked like a permanent scowl on his face, like someone had just run over his dog and then backed over it again. He gave me a long, hard stare and then looked down, raising his eyebrows to himself, but I saw it. He clearly was not a libertine, or a libertarian. *But this was the law, right?* I thought to myself. This was a court of law. The fact that he obviously had some personal moral issues with prostitution wouldn't matter, right? I tried to reassure myself.

The minutes ticked by, and my lawyer still hadn't shown up. My bad feeling about the day that had begun when I'd woken up was growing much darker. I began noticing all of these details I hadn't in my previous appearances. The gun on the bailiff's waist. The seal of the state of New York behind the judge's head. Then I tried to concentrate on the details of my case, but I couldn't as I didn't know them. I had been so high over the last few months that I was barely paying attention to the details of my case.

I'd put absolute trust in what I thought was another strong man who would save me. Now he was nowhere to be found. And, once again, I only had myself to blame. I still only vaguely knew what money laundering and promoting prostitution meant, let alone understand what exactly the government had to prove to convict me. The best-case scenario would have been if they had decided I was a victim, or not that important, and had dropped the case against me. No such luck. I'm guessing everyone else they arrested started pointing fingers, and I was the name on everyone's lips, right after Jason's.

Josh finally showed. Two fucking hours later. I thought we'd probably have to wait around for the afternoon session, but the bailiff announced that they were working straight through the cases in order to wrap the day early. The judge was probably taking a long weekend at his house in Sag Harbor and wanted to beat the traffic.

Being sober for a week meant my mind was pretty sharp, but I didn't really understand all the legal mumbo jumbo droning on. I was only half-listening when the words "bail" and "two hundred and fifty thousand" came out of the judge's mouth. My head snapped up like someone had shocked me with a live wire, and I looked at the judge, then my lawyer. What happened to my pit bull? My protector?

"Did I just hear correctly?" I turned to my lawyer, panicking, and whispered in his ear.

His face was white. He started shuffling papers in a sort of random, look-busy sort of way. He was completely caught off guard. The wheels of justice had just kicked into gear, and my lawyer was left on the side of the road with a bike and a flat tire.

The judge had set bail at $250,000.

"What does that mean? I don't have that money! What can we do?" I asked.

He was trying to look calm, but I could see he was sweating bullets.

He didn't answer. He was frantically jotting down notes and rifling through the indictment.

Finally, he stood up and tried to make the case that such a high bail was unnecessary. He told the court that it was absurd to think I was a flight risk. I had ties to the community and was getting my life together, I had very little money, and the authorities had taken my passport—where could I go? I'd seen it all before on *Law & Order* a million times. But this was no TV show. This was my life, and my lawyer was drowning in his own words.

The judge wasn't hearing it.

I felt myself breaking down. My ears felt like they were full of water. Even though I was taking deep breaths and hyperventilating, I felt like I was about to pass out from lack of oxygen.

My lawyer summed up his case. "Your honor, she has been ROR for the past three months and has adhered to all the court's specifications. There is no need to set bail at this point."

The judge paused for a second. But then with a flick of his wrist, his gavel made a cracking noise.

"Bail is set at $250,000."

I felt the wind sucked out of my body. I was hysterical and crying loudly. I couldn't breathe. An officer approached me, and I almost collapsed on the floor. My lawyer steadied me and tried to calm me down.

"You have to stop crying," he said. "They are going to take you into a cell. I'll be right there to see you."

I wanted to run. Everything inside of me was screaming to escape, to jump out the window, to shoot myself in the head, to do anything but be put in handcuffs and locked away in a jail cell. I had never felt so alone. I felt like my soul was being ripped from my body.

I connected the dots in my head—I had no shot at raising even the 10% needed to pay a bondsman. My mother was in Canada. I had no friends who had assets. The only people I could think of were my clients. Imagine that call?

I was headed straight to jail—do not pass go. I was being held until my trial, the date of which had not been set. I had an open-ended sentence.

They took me to a little holding area down a short flight of stairs. Within a few minutes, my lawyer appeared. He looked frazzled. The confident protector had become a frazzled paper-shuffler, scrambling to find the right words to ensure the freedom of his "favorite client." I didn't have time to get mad at him, to scream, "Why didn't you tell me this could happen? Why the fuck didn't you know this could happen?"

He didn't apologize. I think "never admit to your client you screwed up" is what they teach you the first week of law school.

My hands were cuffed behind my back, and I was ushered into an empty cell.

An officer announced there was a bus leaving for Rikers in ten minutes, and they were putting me on it. I hugged my lawyer and cried. They gave me a second before they pulled me away.

I needed so much more than my lawyer—I needed my father. Well, not *my* father, but the father I should have had. In that moment, I got smacked in the face with the one thing so missing from my life. I almost felt like a huge chunk of me was not there, were it should be, like physically not there.

I knew my lawyer felt horrible. I could see it in his face. All the emotion coming out of me must have felt like a tsunami hitting him. The people with guns each took an elbow and walked me down a hallway. We got to a door, and they opened it. A gust of wind hit me. It was cold. The last time I'd been in handcuffs had been the end of July, sunny and hot. It was cold now, and I was wearing a $500 sweater I thought would make me look demure.

I got onto the bus. There were only three other girls on it. I didn't know where to sit. Of all the things to panic about, I panicked about not knowing where to sit.

Right in the front? The back? Next to someone? Everyone seemed to know the drill. The bus was so small, I couldn't even stand up, and I'm not exactly Tyra Banks. I slid onto a seat and pressed myself next to the window. The girl directly behind sighed loudly and then sucked her teeth at some indignity I had apparently inflicted on her. Maybe I shouldn't have sat right in front of her? I had no idea. But I had a feeling this was only going to get worse.

I had visions of what awaited: being beaten up, my hair being pulled out, of breaking down. The doctors had been right after all. I was going to melt down and shatter. I hated that they'd been right. I should have committed myself. If I had taken the gift of recovery that my friends had set up for me, I would not have been sitting there. I wanted to go back in time and scream— scream for the help that I needed. Instead I'd been stubborn and belligerent and tried to pretend that I was fine, and now I was paying the price for it. They'd tried to help me, and I'd behaved like a child. What they had offered looked like torture, like a prison. Now I really was in prison.

Some of the windows in the bus were open and, because we were handcuffed (they'd transferred my hands from behind my back to the front), we couldn't push them up. We all started to freeze as the frigid air swirled about us. One of the girls asked the officer if she could push up a window, and she replied, "No." That's it, just "No," the first of a million "nos" I'd hear over the next month.

By the time we arrived at the skinny bridge that takes you out to Rikers Island, the overcast sky was turning a dark, deep gray. It was autumn in New York, usually one of my favorite times of year. I love the crispness that comes with fall in the city, but now the cold and the clouds took on a foreboding, almost gothic quality. It used to be that the city inspired me, pushed me to be the best I could be. But since Paul and the abuse, there were songs I couldn't listen to, restaurants I didn't want to go back to, clothes I didn't like wearing, all because they were too painful in some way or another. Now all of New York felt tainted by these waves of negativity and fear.

The guards at the bridge's security checkpoint waved us through, and we had officially left New York City behind.

As we drove past the mass of low-lying jail buildings surrounded by the maze of razor-wire fences, I started thinking about Jason. He was in there somewhere, suffering the same fate I was about to be subjected to. I hadn't been to visit him since my own arrest. My lawyer had forbidden it. Now I couldn't believe that I was going to be so close to him. It wasn't love or longing that I was feeling; it was anger. This was all his fault. Why had he had to open his mouth and get us in trouble? Why hadn't he paid me what he owed me? At least then, I might have saved enough to make my bail. I wasn't strong enough to accept any responsibility. That would come later. For now, Jason was the only villain.

We drove past Jason's building, then around to the other side of the island. I could see the tip of Manhattan in the distance across the river. The wind was starting to pick up, and the water looked choppy and dangerous. We stopped in front of the female facility building and were told to get off the bus. We shuffled out of the van, more defeated with each step. Inside, the intercom announcements, doors clanking open and shut, and loud, profanity-laced chatter pierced my ears. There was a desk smack in the middle of the room, an island unto itself raised on a platform, surrounded by caged cells and dozens of detained women. The cells surrounding the perimeter of the intake area didn't have vertical bars the way jail cells do in the movies. In fact, nothing I was seeing was anything like the jails they portray in Hollywood. They were big, square cells with chicken-wire-style metal caging—more like being at a dog kennel than a jail.

A really loud female officer asked if we had any weapons or drugs. We all meekly shook our heads no. She asked again louder and angrier.

"I say-ed, do you have any weapons, illegal drugs or drug paraphernalia on your person?"

"No!" we all answered.

"Thank you! You will be assigned to one of these cells, processed one by one, and then eventually go on to a building. But that probably will not happen tonight, ladies, so get comfortable."

She looked around at all the cages, then back at us.

"Okay, you three, right here."

She pointed to the closest one and swung open the door. It was empty.

"You," she looked at me, "come with me."

I felt my heart lift. My mind created an instant fantasy that maybe somehow it was all a mistake. I didn't belong here with these women, these criminals. I was going home. Okay, that was implausible. Forget that. But maybe they were just taking pity on my skinny white ass and were going to send me right through to my jail cell, and then I wouldn't have to stay in this dirty, smelly place with the rest of the herd.

I followed her around the huge island-like desk in the middle of the room, and she unlocked the door to the biggest cage, which was filled with at least a dozen women, and opened it. Fantasy over.

"Get in," she said. So I did.

The cage was packed. Some women were sitting on the benches that wrapped around the walls, some were lying on the floor. There were so many on the floor, there was barely any room to walk. As I wove my way through, my high heels clicked on the floor. Everyone who wasn't asleep looked up and stared at me. Several of those who were asleep were awakened by the clickety-clack of my conspicuous shoe wear. I was the only white girl. And I was surely the only one in Gucci heels.

I found a free corner on the bench. I thought that might be a safe spot. Maybe I could even lie down and get to sleep. I saw a few girls who were sweating and holding their stomachs, moaning.

Holy shit, I thought, *they're detoxing.*

That could have been me. I thanked God I was sober and not coming down from a night of partying, or a five-day binge, or still doing heroin and getting sick. I think I might have died. I looked at the woman closest to me, and I realized why this prime, bench real estate was free. Right at my feet was a homeless woman who looked and smelled like she hadn't bathed in months. She reeked of piss and shit. I gagged and almost threw up, but I looked around and saw there wasn't anywhere else to sit.

It went downhill from there.

Morning came in the Rose M. Singer building, or Rosie's, as everyone called it. The gears of the prison started turning—you could feel it. I didn't know what was next. One by one, women's names were called, and they were then led through to the medical wing. Everyone around me was taken away. Hours more passed. New prisoners were led in. Lunch came: peanut butter or baloney sandwiches (yes, it's true, that's what they give you) and cartons of milk. I don't eat peanut butter, didn't want baloney and can't drink milk, so I didn't eat or drink anything. Sometime in the early afternoon, I had to go to the bathroom so badly, I couldn't wait anymore. I had watched other women use the seatless metal toilet in the corner of the cage and realized that like everything else here in my new digs, I didn't have a choice—my choices were being made for me. Where I slept, what I ate, where I went, even where I went to the bathroom. Right now, that meant in a cage full of other women. I got up, walked over in my heels, pulled up my skirt and pulled down my tights. I hovered over the toilet, my thighs shaking from lack of strength, and peed as quickly as I could. I hadn't had anything to drink in more than twenty-four hours, but it still seemed like my pee lasted forever.

Finally, my name was called, and I was led down a short hallway and into a waiting area. I sat down and looked around. There were office-style cubicles everywhere. It was the medical area, and they seemed to be in a rush. I guess they were almost done for the day, but they needed to process and house me because I had been in processing for almost twenty hours now. I sat down on a hard, plastic chair in the corner of one of the cubicles, and an Indian nurse took out a clipboard and started asking me dozens of questions: Was I pregnant? Did I have any medical conditions? Was I HIV positive? Was I allergic to any food or medication? Was I on any medication? Was I under the influence of any drugs? Did I regularly use any drugs? Was I having thoughts of suicide? Did I have a history of depression or mental illness? I answered no to everything. It seemed unnecessary to share any info, like the fact that I'd been a heroin addict and was less than five-months detoxed.

I had one goal in my mind: to get out of there as soon as possible. I didn't want anything to slow me down, like being diagnosed clinically depressed and put on medication and then not allowed to be released on bail, or something like that. I didn't know if that would happen, but I wasn't interested in finding out. The depression question seemed especially comical: how could I not be depressed? I was in hell on Earth. The nurse seemed a little thrown that I was so sure of my answers and that I was being so easy. I imagined that some of the prisoners found every reason to prolong this medical process, as for some women it was probably the only way they could get medical care.

I was picked up by an officer who looked at me and barked, "Where's your I.D.?"

I looked down and pointed to the waistband of my skirt.

"It's supposed to be on your shirt."

I unclipped it and attached it to my shirt. It was a cute picture, actually. I gave them a hot angry look.

"Where are your shoes?"

"They took them," I said. On my way out, someone had noticed them and enforced the no-high-heels-in-jail rule.

"Well, you're going to have to get some shoes."

We walked down a series of long hallways, and she handed my file to a man sitting in a big, glass booth overlooking my new cell block. She never looked at or spoke to me again.

"I'm C.O. Patterson, Officer Patterson," said the male officer.

He looked at my file and said my name, "Natalie McLennan. What is that, Irish?"

"Scottish, I answered."

He looked at me amused.

"Go on inside."

He hit a buzzer, and I pushed on one of the two swinging doors.

"Other door," he said when it didn't budge.

He laughed a little and pushed the buzzer, and this time I made it inside. My new home. I wandered in. The floor was cold under my feet, with only a thin layer of nylon and spandex between my skin and the concrete.

For the first three nights, I didn't have a pillow or blanket in my cell. It was freezing, and I was shivering. I approached one of the officers. There were two: one who sat in the glass bubble and one who sat by the entrance in a chair beside a table. The one sitting told me to talk to the other guard who informed me he didn't have any extras. I would have to wait two more days for the weekly sheet/towel swap. I lay alone in my cell and froze each night, until I eventually managed to cry myself to sleep.

I spent most of my time in my cell because I didn't have anything else to do, and I felt safer there. About a week in, I decided to venture out to the main area of the building where the other inmates hung out.

*   *   *

Everyone found out that I was "that girl," or more accurately, "the hooker." The *New York Post* article with the full-page photo of me was passed around. I was instantly a pariah.

There were only two other white girls in the building whom I came across. One was named Jennifer. She was a bad ass from Queens who was at Rikers for beating up some girl over a guy. Then there was Angelica, a Sicilian chick, who was in for selling drugs. She had been in federal prison for transporting guns and drugs from Florida to New York. They would both prove to be my only friends. It's totally politically incorrect to say, but in prison you seek compassion and protection from your own kind. It's just the way things work inside.

Jennifer was a little tougher to get along with. She was really moody and seemed on the verge of getting into a brawl at any given moment. But both of them could tell I was in over my head and looked out for me. Angelica especially took the time to explain the unwritten rules that you must follow to get by in jail. She helped me get cleaning supplies for my cell when I told her it was putrid.

"Natalia!" Angelica hissed at me from the second-story balcony.

Her cell door was propped open with a bucket she was using to clean. Where did she get a bucket? Talk about resourceful. She glared at me and gestured toward her cell, meaning she wanted me to come up to see her. She grabbed my arm and pulled me inside and sat me down on her bed, cot, metal-framed-nightmare-machine, whatever you want to call it.

"Why were you talking to that nigger?"

She used the word freely. At first it really freaked me out, and I was scared I would become a target if people heard her, but over time I realized everyone in jail uses that word for everyone. That's not to say it ever came out of my mouth.

I shrugged. What did I do wrong?

"Don't fucking talk to anybody. Talk to me. The only reason these bitches are so interested in you is because they're jealous, and they want to fuck you up, you understand?"

"Jealous of what?" Of my destroyed life? They could have it.

"Of everything, Natalia. That you have a paid lawyer, that you have your picture in the newspaper, that people give a shit about you. They're jealous of your fucking hair...what does it matter? Do not talk to them."

"So, what, I just ignore it when someone speaks to me?" That didn't seem like such a good idea.

"No, you just don't put yourself there in the first place. You're a good person, Natalia. You don't belong here. And I mean that when I say it. When they say it to you, it's 'cause they want you to agree so they can say, 'what are you saying...that I *do* belong here?' and that's when they kick your ass and fuck up your pretty face."

Man, jail is complicated, I thought. Thank God for my Angelica.

* * *

My nickname, fittingly, was Tinkerbell because I'd been wearing a skirt when I was brought in, and I'd probably seemed about as tough as a fairy. Finally, on a visiting day, my friend Morgan brought me some clothes: socks and underwear, sweats, a few tee-shirts and a sweatshirt. Some of the things she brought never got through because they were blue or red, the verboten colors of the Crips and Bloods. Thank God there wasn't a gang called the Black Knights because ninety percent of my wardrobe would have been banned. I still didn't have proper shoes. I was shuffling around in a pair of orange slip-on sneakers. They were two sizes too small, and I have really small feet. I folded the back of them down and managed to get by. I washed out my tights every evening and let them dry overnight.

As I sat across from Morgan in the visiting lounge we tried to go over everything that needed to be discussed about my case. She explained that she had tried to set up a meeting with my lawyer, but he wasn't returning her calls. I had barely spoken to him as well. I guess I couldn't blame him. I hadn't paid him. He'd probably taken my case because he knew it would get him tons of free publicity. But now, with his celebrity client locked up, he wasn't looking like the go-to guy anymore. I don't know if he was embarrassed, or just pissed I didn't have any money. Either way, I had the feeling he just wanted me to go away.

Morgan said Ron was the only one who was offering anything constructive, but as I had found out, he wasn't exactly Perry Mason.

Morgan told me she'd also spoken to my mother who'd said she wanted to come visit. A chill went up my spine. I wanted to see her, but I didn't want her to see me like this. I changed the subject.

On her way out, Morgan remembered one more thing she had for me: a book, *Atlas Shrugged* by Ayn Rand. *New York* magazine's Mark Jacobson had bought it for me after he found out it was Jason's favorite novel. I'd never got around to starting it. I was a little intimidated—it's over a thousand pages long. But it turned out to make perfect Big House reading.

I read for hours every day, but sometimes I would realize that I'd been reading for pages and couldn't remember anything I had just read. My brain was having a really hard time focusing, but after a while, I buckled down and got into it. I began to see why Jason liked the book so much. It was all about a group of elitists who believed they could rise above the masses' self-defeating and outdated sense of morality. Jason was like a mix of Larry Flynt, P.T. Barnum and John Galt, the book's mysterious super-capitalist hero.

With my new duds and something to read, life on the inside got a smidgen better. But the status of the State of New York vs. Natalia hung over my head every waking second. The day of my first court date arrived, and I woke up super early, all nerves. The bus left for the courthouse at 6:30. We were served those mini boxes of

cereal with milk for breakfast—I just ate the dry cereal—
and herded into a gymnasium. There were four buses
going to the different boroughs. The Brooklyn bus was
always the fullest. The Manhattan bus was sparsely
populated. I was handcuffed to a tall, big black woman
who at first looked like she was going to bite my head off.
She turned to me and asked, "You want some of this Pop-
Tart?"

It was the nicest thing anyone had done for me
since I'd gotten to Rikers. It was stale and sweet. I'd
never tasted anything so good. I could barely keep down
the jail fare: mushy pasta with canned tomato sauce,
slabs of meat of unknown origin, powdery mashed
potatoes and overcooked, tasteless veggies.

We arrived at the Manhattan courthouse, driving
straight down into a caged-in parking lot, tucked in
between all the Centre Sreet buildings belonging to the
city. We were taken to holding cells to wait for our cases to
be called. Women came and went. A bus left, returning
most of the prisoners to Rikers before lunch. I waited. I ate
a few bites of a stale sandwich. They finally called me to
the courtroom, and I was led down the hall in handcuffs.

I scanned the room. I didn't want to let the small
phalanx of reporters who had gathered see the fear in
my eyes, but I wanted so badly to see a familiar friendly
face. And there they were: Morgan and Ron! They were
sitting by the front door looking really serious. I
mouthed a thanks, and they gave a quick wave and
encouraging smiles.

I turned to look ahead and face the judge. The
bailiff came over to tell me that my lawyer hadn't shown
up. The judge asked me if I'd communicated with my
lawyer. I said I didn't know why he wasn't there. Justice
waits for no one, apparently. The judge set my next
appearance for the Thursday after next. I felt myself

trembling inside. My greatest fears were coming true. My lawyer had abandoned me. I faced the same fate as Jason. I couldn't make bail either. We were both going to be held until our trials.

It sunk in that I needed to brace myself for the long haul. I remembered hearing Hulbert tell me he expected to get a sentence of three to five years. We'd been charged with the same things: money laundering and promoting prostitution. All I wanted to know was what was going to happen. More than anything else, the uncertainty was killing me. I was theoretically months, a year, or even longer away from a trial.

As I was being escorted back to the holding cell, I started crying. I couldn't stop. It wasn't the hysterical crying that I'd done when I'd first been put in cuffs in the courtroom and taken to Rikers. This was different; I could breathe; I could think. I was perfectly aware of my situation, and that's what was so devastating. The two C.O.s guarding the holding cells didn't lock me in right away. They sat me down in a chair. One of them looked at me tenderly and said, "Let it out. You gotta let it out. Just cry baby."

So I did. I cried my fucking heart out.

When I started to come out of it, she said to me, "Don't you worry, God will take care of you."

She gave me a few napkins. I wiped my face and used my sleeve. It felt soft against my skin. I'd take any compassion I could get at this point.

Do you think God could be my lawyer? I asked myself—because mine had disappeared.

The bus ride back to Rikers felt like it took forever. I looked out the window, watching all the free people whiz by in their shiny cars.

When I saw Angelica and Jennifer at dinner, they could sense that I didn't want to talk about it. If you come back from court, it usually means it didn't go well.

*   *   *

Two weeks into my island vacation, Morgan told me that my mom was finally coming to see me. I started crying. I was so happy, but I also knew she couldn't help me. She couldn't put her house up to make my bail because it was in another country. I had no idea what to expect from her. I hadn't spoken with her since before my arrest. She didn't know about my tooth or my psych-ward stay. All she had to go on was what she'd read in the papers.

My mom arrived at Rikers on Canadian Thanksgiving. I was taken into a stark, grey room, and told to strip naked. They stuck their hands into my body. It was awful and humiliating, but I didn't care at that point. I was going to see my mother, and that was all that mattered. I changed into a grey jumpsuit and walked into the visiting area.

She ran toward me and reached to hug me.

"No touching!" bellowed a nasty, bull-dyke guard.

We sheepishly sat down on brightly colored chairs opposite each other with a round, blue plastic table between us. Before she could get anything out, she started crying uncontrollably. I felt a stab of pain, but hardened by Rikers, no tears came. She pulled herself together and went into "let's talk" crisis mode. I thought we could focus on how to get me out of there. I talked about my case, and how I needed a new lawyer who could get up to speed on the details of the evidence against me.

She listened, but when she spoke, I grew infuriated.

She got all haughty and said, "Well, I need to know where you want your life to go."

I just stared at her. Go? I wanted to go anywhere that wasn't Rikers.

She said, "You can either go to rehab or stay here. I would rather see you here than on the streets of New York."

Was she insane?

I tried to explain to her how hard this place was, that every other person had Hep or AIDS and that any second I could easily get beaten to death. I was a little white girl from Canada in one of the most notorious inner-city jails in America. This wasn't therapy. This was hell.

I was so pissed off by her ultimatum that I stood up and started to walk out of the visiting room.

The C.O. raised her eyebrows as though to say, "You staying or going?"

I closed my eyes, turned around and sat back down. As furious as I was, I couldn't leave my mom alone in that room. I calmed down and tried to change my tone. I started explaining what was going on legally again, trying to get her up to date with the details of my case. With my lawyer AWOL, I needed all the help I could get.

She started to get really emotional again. I could see that she was so overwhelmed and in so much pain, she had hit an emotional brick wall. She felt helpless. I was her child, and I was in trouble. My heart broke. I knew what she'd been trying to do before. She'd been trying to be tough, to be the stand-in father, but the reality was she was as lost as I was. Finally, I took charge and told her about the one person who could potentially help—my former vocal coach, Michael.

She finally listened and agreed to get in touch with him.

She told me she was going to come back and see me the next day. She would bring me some more clothes and things from my apartment. I promised to call her on Morgan's phone.

I asked her about Morgan. She said she was waiting in the parking lot. That seemed weird. Why hadn't she come in to see me?

My mom explained. At the security gate, they'd taken a swab of the inside of Morgan's handbag, it had registered positive for cocaine, and she'd been turned away.

Great, I thought. Just another thing to add stress to my mother's life: the only friend of mine she felt remotely comfortable with was potentially now another problem, someone else to distrust.

"Does Morgan do drugs?" Her voice was shaking.

What do I do? Just tell the truth.

I remembered what the detectives at the 7th Precinct had told me that day en route to my arraignment: the only people you can trust are your family. They are the ones who will be there for you during this.

"Yes, Morgan does drugs."

My mom looked like she was going to pass out.

"But she barely does. She doesn't like them."

I asked what type of purse Morgan was carrying. My mom described my black leather D&G purse with silver zippers, and I saw an out.

"That's my purse. It's lucky she didn't get in trouble. It would have been all my fault because I've put coke in that purse before."

I needed my mom to trust Morgan. I needed one friend on my side that my mom would listen to.

The next day, mom was supposed to be back, but instead of my mother, in walks Morgan. I was happy to see her, but confused.

"Your mom went home."

I felt tears well up.

"We talked and decided she would go see your new lawyer this morning, then take the bus home, and I would come see you."[6]

I guess she couldn't take it anymore. I couldn't blame her.

*   *   *

My mom kept her word and got in touch with Michael. He'd given me voice lessons in my theater days and had been intrigued by all of the crazy stories from my pre-New York Confidential nightclubbing days. When he heard I was in jail, he contacted my lawyers, and we started talking on the phone every day. My lawyer told me he thought Michael might post my bail. My lawyer outlined his plan. He would convince the D.A. to lower the amount from $250,000 to a more reasonable $50,000, and then Michael would go to a bondsman and get a $5,000 bond.

It worked. Michael was able to get the bond. My bail was reduced, and the court issued my release papers.

Looking back, I suspect the original bail was probably nothing more than a test to see if I had a hidden stash somewhere. Why else would the judge issue it more than three months after my initial arrest? Why would I run if I hadn't run before? After a few weeks of hell at Rikers they conceded that I probably wasn't lying about my financial situation. I was as broke as I said I was.

No one ever bailed Jason out. That makes me really sad. I don't know if he deserved to spend the time he did in jail. I do know he should be kept away from everyone's daughters.

---

[6] Morgan and Ron hired me a new attorney, John Nicholas Iannuzzi, an old-school New York lawyer who rescued me, and whom I adore to this day.

After twenty-six days behind bars, I was set loose. I got dropped off at the gates at the end of the bridge and jumped into one of the many cabs lined up for the return trip over the River Styx. As we crossed the 59th Street Bridge, I asked the driver to put on 103.5 FM, one of the stations that always plays upbeat dance music. He adjusted the dial and, like a sign, a song came on. The chorus goes: "I'm free, to do what I want, any old time. I said I'm free, to do what I want, any old time."

"Love me, hold me. Love me, hold me. 'Cause I'm free."

I smiled for the first time in a month and stuck my head out the window as we sailed toward Manhattan, that magical island that had swallowed me up whole and then spat me out.

CHAPTER FOURTEEN
COMING HOME

In the weeks following my release from Rikers, I'd lost my apartment, was staying with random friends, and everyone was tip-toeing around me, wondering what would become of "Natalia." They were all expecting me to go back to heroin. Once a junkie, always a junkie, right? But I never did it again; I never wanted to have to relive the detox, but more importantly, I wasn't ready to give up, and I had an underlying need to prove everyone else wrong. I just went back to my old friend coke.

One day I checked an old email account. I had a message from my ex, Paul. Only it wasn't from Paul—it was from his dad and stepmom. This is what it said:

hello nat!!
just want to sadly inform you on the passing of paul on dec...
funeral will be held at-26 mulberry st.
january 2nd at 3 o'clock pm till 9
lv bill and mary

Paul was dead. I had missed the funeral. I called one of his fraternity brothers from MIT. He told me that Paul died of a heroin overdose at his apartment off Fulton Street just after Christmas. I broke. Paul is always on my mind.

I was lost in a drug binge when I got the call. It was my mom.

"Nat," she said, "I have breast cancer."

My already deflated faith in the future was crushed that much more.

"What do you mean?"

She didn't answer. I could hear her crying. Tears shot into my eyes. They spilled over and dripped loudly onto the carpet. I was sitting cross-legged, slouching forward, my head close to the floor, the phone pressed to my ear. I blinked and felt more heavy drops fall out. My throat was closed, and I couldn't get any words out for a few minutes.

I had no apartment, no income, few friends, and I was freebasing an eight ball a day (that's a lot). Now my mom was sick with cancer. Everything that could have gone wrong in my life, had—all at the same time. And it seemed the same was true for my mother.

"What did they say?" I finally asked.

My mom breathed and gave me the good news. "I have to have surgery, but a lumpectomy, not a mastectomy and then either chemo and radiation or just radiation. The oncologist told me she thinks I won't have to have chemo."

"Wow, okay, so that's okay." I said.

I was still reeling from the initial shock, but my mind was processing what she was telling me, and it really sounded like a best-case scenario, considering the alternatives.

My mom is a very proud woman. She never wants to be a burden to anyone. But I could hear the fear in her voice. For the first time I could remember, she confided in me.

"I'm just so scared." And then she broke, and for the third time in my life, I heard my mother cry—hard, deep crying. The first had been when her brother, my uncle, died when I was a little girl, and the second had been when she saw me at Rikers. I looked up at the ceiling. This was real. I knew the fear she was going through, and she was going through it not knowing if her daughter was going to die before her. We could both be dead in months.

"Mom, why is this happening? Why are all these bad things happening?" I was crying hard.

My mom didn't have an answer. And she couldn't console me. We just cried together, and the wall between us started melting away with each passing minute.

I matched the leap she had taken and told her that we would get well together. I would get myself healthy if she would.

I made her promise to me over and over again that she would be strong and come through this. I talked about how we had so many things to do together, that we needed each other.

She told me she wanted to come and see me before she started her treatment. Her first procedure, surgery to remove the tumor, was in two weeks. I told her to hold on for a minute. I put down my cell phone and walked over to my friend, Dane, with whom I was staying on the Upper East Side. Dartmouth educated, brilliant physicist dad, big-time psychiatrist mom, and yet he was really chemically imbalanced. He had become my latest party friend; someone who was letting me stay with him without any strings attached.

I told him my mom was sick and coming to New York to see me. Would it be okay if she stayed in the spare room?

He exhaled a big cloud of freebase smoke and nodded his head, "Of course, absolutely."

Our eyes met, and then we both looked out across his dirty, paraphernalia-filled apartment. We had our work cut out for us. It was a long railroad apartment and, as I walked the long hall back to the office and my cell phone, I looked back at Dane and saw him popping some pills, probably Lithium. Or Wellbutrin. Or Xanax. He got prescriptions for them all from his mom.

"Mom, it's totally cool. You can stay here," I said.

She couldn't afford a last-minute plane ticket, so she told me she was going to take the bus from Montreal. She'd be arriving at seven-thirty Saturday morning. I choked up. I felt so pathetic. All of those buckets of cash I had made, and I couldn't even afford to buy her a plane ticket. I probably had fifteen pairs of shoes that cost as much.

I gave her Dane's address and told her to take a cab. It would only cost about six dollars. I wanted to meet her when she arrived, but I didn't want to promise something I couldn't deliver and leave her waiting for me. The thought of being anywhere other than passed out on a couch at seven-thirty in the morning was too daunting at that point.

It was Monday, and I had less than a week to get myself presentable. I gave Dane the news that my mom had breast cancer. He asked me how bad it was, and I told him I didn't know for sure, but it sounded like they caught it really early. I told him I was going to have to make some changes. He surprised me by telling me that he really wasn't happy with his life either, that we could finish the drugs we had, go to sleep, wake up tomorrow and work on getting healthy. I had heard that story before. Few people really mean it. I don't know why, but I thought Dane was telling me the truth. Either way, I knew this was judgment day for me. I would do whatever it took to keep my promise to my mother.

We slept and sweated for the next day and a half. When I woke up, my body was aching, and my stomach was screaming for food, but I had no appetite. Even the thought of food made my stomach erupt. Dane kept his promise, and for the two days before my mom's arrival we cleaned the house. It was metaphorical and therapeutic all at once. He did the kitchen and bathroom (he insisted, it was his house and mostly his mess). I did all the other rooms: vacuuming, cleaning the windows and changing the linens. It actually looked really nice in the end, and I was proud of what we'd done. It was a good start.

My mom arrived, and we went to a diner on the corner for breakfast. We sat and talked for a few hours. We only had two days together, and I knew there was a lot of ground to cover. It was now April, and I hadn't seen her since Christmas. She knew I was still getting high, and I carefully told her that I was detoxed and determined to stay that way. I could see the hope in her eyes, and I tried to reassure her in every way I could that this was it.

"Nat, I'm just so scared. I've heard you say that so many times before."

I needed to help her understand that this time was different. I took her to meet Mia, a highly respected life coach. Mia had been leaving me messages since November, when I'd been released from Rikers: "Natalia, I really want to help you. Don't worry about money, just come see me." And so right before my mom arrived, I went for my first session. Mia is an angel.

I confided in my mom that Mia had told me, "You were on the cover of a magazine by the age of twenty-five. You are capable of achieving whatever you want."

I explained how I was going to work out some way to start earning money and resolve some of my problems.

What choice did I have? In about a week, my mom was going to be in surgery to remove a tumor from her breast. I was not a monster. I was still full of love for her, for our family, hell, for all of humanity. My addictions hadn't taken that away from me.

She told me they had confirmed that they had caught the cancer very early and that after her surgery she would start treatment. I knew she was so scared I was going to die, that we were both going to go too soon. I reminded her of my five-year-old self, the stubborn little girl who wouldn't ever let anyone tie her shoes for her.

"I feel like I don't even know you anymore," she said.

"Mom, the only thing I ever failed at was one French class and that's because I had to be there at eight in the morning. Failure is not an option for me. I'm still that person, and I love you, and this is more important than anything else."

It wasn't so much that I was saying the right things as I'd done that before. It was that for the first time in a very long time, she knew I meant it. She believed in me.

Dane woke up a few hours later, and we spent the afternoon in Central Park. I rode the carousel, and my mom took pictures. We had hot dogs at Gray's Papaya on the Upper West Side, and then we walked all the way back to the East Side. It was like some cheesy montage in a 70s family drama, and it felt beautiful.

When we were alone again, she made me promise to be a good houseguest, and she said that he seemed so nice. She knew he was a drug addict, too, but she tried to look past it and see him as a person. She kept hugging him and thanking him for all his help.

She left the next day, and I was different. Usually, before she was even on the bus or plane home I was already high, but I waited with her until she boarded the bus and gave her the biggest hug and told her I loved her. I needed her as much as she needed me.

I went back to Dane's apartment and watched movie after movie with him. We both knew the stakes.

This was judgment day.

My mom and I started talking on the phone everyday. She had her surgery. I stayed sober. She started treatment. I kept sober, and I saw Mia, the life coach, a few times a week.

I told the D.A. that my mom was sick, and I needed to go home to Montreal. It was the first time in seven years I had called Montreal "home." I showed them the respect of asking, but I wasn't going to take no for an answer. They said okay, provided I was back in New York for my court appearances.[7]

Wow. They were letting me go. Now I actually had to do it. It had been six months since my mom's visit to New York. I hadn't seen the rest of my family in about two years.

It was the scariest thing I would ever do. In New York I was Natalia. Who was I in Montreal?

The pressure of facing my family mounted, and I relapsed. I started getting high everyday again. For the next two months, I would slip back into my dangerous old habits.

I moved out of Dane's and in with a friend in the Bushwick section of Brooklyn. Not a nice part of Bushwick either. I had been awake for three days when I finally somehow got myself to the Port Authority Bus Terminal. I was bone-tired, but with so much fear and adrenaline pumping through me, there was no way I was going to fall asleep. No, this was one trip I was going to have to endure. I called my friend in New Jersey from some nice stranger's phone, and cried that I didn't want to go home. That was the addict in me talking.

Every other part of me—my physical self that was moments away from shutting down for good, my emotional self that needed my family and knew they

---

[7] They'd begun filing the paperwork, but it would take months to finally go through.

needed me, and my brain, that logically knew this was what I needed to do—pushed me to get on the bus.

I got on. But when the bus stopped in Albany, a couple of hours north of the city, I went into the bathroom and did a hit of freebase. I had to fight every instinct in my addict brain not to stay in that bathroom and wait for the bus to drive off.

During the last days of the relapse, the drugs had more or less stopped working. But in that nasty bathroom, the rush hit me hard. I had made so many promises to myself in the past, swearing that it was the last hit I would do, but when it's real, you know it. And I knew that those last few grams of coke were going to count. So when I bent over to light, what I swore would be the absolute last hit of my life, I didn't pray like I had in the past that I would overdose and die. Instead I let the drug take control over me, let it travel through my body wherever it wanted to go, and when I regained my sense of self, I cried. I tried to let that part of me finally die.

I got back on the bus, and we pulled out of the rest stop.

As we cruised through the lush countryside of upstate New York, my seven years of memories in the city rushed by like a movie. I was going back to Montreal the same way I'd left, on the bus. I tried not to take stock of what I had lost and would maybe never find again. But this wasn't about me, I told myself. This was about my promise to my mother. About making sure my mother didn't die.

When we finally pulled into Montreal, I was a complete mess. It seemed fitting. I needed to hit rock bottom. I slept for a week and then slowly started to reconnect with my family.

My mom had moved from my childhood home. She lived on the second floor of a building my grandmother had bought. My grandmother lived on the first floor. There were pieces of my old life: the bed I'd slept on as a teenager was in the guest room waiting for me, and family pictures were on the walls. It was a big improvement from the apartments we'd lived in when I was growing up. And it took the focus away from some of the more painful emotions and memories from my childhood.

I slowly came back to life as the drugs seeped out of my body.

For the next few days, my mom and I didn't talk too much. She let me sleep and gave me space to be inside myself. I was too ashamed to look in her eyes. Then after three nights passed with barely a few words shared, I started leaving my childhood bed and stumbling into hers. She would hold me while I cried. She didn't care how many guys I'd slept with or how much money I had made and lost—she loved me. I was her daughter, and she loved me.

In the second week, I let her find the freebase pipe I had brought. I couldn't be honest to her face, so I just left it out in the open as a sort of subconscious admission of guilt. She didn't say anything. She just got rid of it for me. When I wasn't around, I'm sure she cried, probably harder than I did, if that's possible.

She didn't miss a day of work. She went to the hospital every morning and then straight to work right after.

There were still plenty of doctors' appointments. I went to all of them with her: I sat in each waiting room and held back my tears. I was so thankful that she was okay, that this wasn't the end, and that I had another chance to be her daughter.

I looked at her, and she would smile at me and tell me how happy she was that I was with her. She thanked me over and over again and told me how proud of me she was.

I still felt like shit most of the time, physically and otherwise, but in those moments, I felt everything was going to get better.

I think everyone knew not to pressure me. Everyone who grew up with me knows how I react to feeling caged, so they didn't smother me. My mom's treatment became the focus, but we also took the time to talk about things. Hospital waiting rooms are good for that.

Six months after I came home, she finally said it to me:

"It's not fair. I look at all my friends and their daughters, and they don't have to deal with this."

It was finally out there. She'd had dreams of what I would become, and I had let her down. To her, I'd been the perfect child. Now she couldn't get over the nightmare memories. She couldn't see the beautiful times, like watching me perform at Juilliard. She was stuck with the images of an apartment full of burnt spoons and empty baggies and the grimy, green walls of the women's visiting room at Rikers.

She was right. It wasn't fair.

*   *   *

My mom got better. Her cancer went into remission. I guess we're both really lucky. I managed to land a job through a friend of mine from high school. As kids, we were best friends and hung out all the time. We took a trip to Maine together when we were fifteen, and I decided to confess my love to him. Instead of reciprocating, he decided to confess that he was gay—and we stayed just friends.

We went to college (to theater school) together and continued to stay in touch even while we lived so far apart. He would visit me in New York, up until I started escorting, and now he's become the best friend I've ever had. He sends me text messages and tells me he's there for me, and he loves me—all the things you dream of people saying when you're hurting.

His mother owns a spa in Montreal, and she offered me a job there. I began at the bottom of the spa ladder, starting out at the desk, answering phones, sweeping up at the end of the day, and doing anything else asked of me. It was an adjustment, and I had to swallow my pride a little, especially regarding my income. I made less in a week than I used to make in a few hours. It took a few months of me paying my dues, something I've never minded doing, but then they sat me down one day, and I climbed the steps to manager. Life got a little better—better hours, better responsibilities and much better pay.

The staff, who know only the basics of my rise and fall in New York, have been incredibly kind and understanding. I'm like a wounded bird they've taken under their wings. Early on, there were days I was too messed up emotionally to go into work, and they let me take the time I needed. Unconditional love from your bosses? That's Canada for you.

Still, it's been hard. I miss New York's energy. Montreal will never be New York, no matter how hard it tries. So I've finally slowed myself to the pace of Montreal and tried to find some kind of rhythm in my new life.

When I speak to my friends in New York, I'm so proud to tell them that I have my own apartment and a real job. I know it sounds pretty lame—I'm not nineteen—but in considering where I was a year ago, it's a minor miracle.

I have a therapist. When I called her to make an appointment, I told her to Google me before our first session. (How many clients can say that?) It's a slow, complicated process, but in each session I learn a little bit more about why I found that old life so alluring.

*   *   *

There's a picture I have of myself that for a while I used as my wallpaper on my laptop. I'm wearing a dress designed for me by my friend, Morgan. We called it the naked dress because as a joke I told her I wanted a dress made out of as little fabric as possible. She made it, and it was great. The few times I wore it, it always earned double-takes from everyone—whether it was because they thought it was fabulous or thought for a second I was actually walking around naked, I don't know.

I would open my laptop and see it, along with all my old party pictures, and I'd be transported back to the joy of partying in a club: I would be numbed by the memory of the music, the lights, the momentary memory high I would get reliving the cocaine flowing through my veins. It wasn't an entirely happy process, looking at this picture. I idolized my body at that time: how thin I was, how perfect I looked, how everything was beyond amazing, and I struggled with being happy in the here and now, the post-Natalia, the post-New York, new-me-life I'm living.

Then, one day, I zoomed in on the photo, like I wanted to see more, feel more. I'd worn out the image and the memory—it wasn't doing it for me anymore. And I finally saw the reality of what it captured. There, on my face, is a sore. It's on the bottom of my cheek near my chin, and it's covered by makeup, but it's there. I was so toxic, my skin was breaking out in sores. I'd been looking at the glossed-over version of the past I wanted to remember—the version that didn't have any pain or negativity.

I looked around me and realized that I am so much happier now than I was then, with or without the naked dress.

Doing drugs doesn't make much sense now, but it can still be hard sometimes. I had to cut almost all my friends out at a time when I really needed a friend, because most of the people from my past do drugs. No one ever talks about how lonely rebuilding a life from nothing can be.

I also stopped having sex for a while. When I was working, I siphoned all of my energy into my clients. In the end, there was little left for me, or what was left of me. My whole identity was wrapped around being a sexual goddess. By the time I got home and off drugs, sex had become so complicated and fraught with paranoia that I just quit. It felt great. Like I was finally reclaiming some kind of power over the urges and passions that had gotten me into this trouble and caused so many people intense pain.

I realized that I did what I did because I had lost faith in myself and my talent. I had always known that I was a good actor, and I was confident I would find success, but when things stalled, doubt crept in. I thought my acting would never reach Oscar level, hell, even daytime Emmy level, so I cashed in, sold out, whatever you want to call it, and grabbed a low-hanging form of celebrity and excitement as a consolation prize. Even my struggles with drugs felt fabulous (sometimes) because I was in celebrated company—Robert Downey Jr., Lindsay Lohan, Marilyn Monroe, and way too many others.

I still struggle sometimes with the morality of it all. The voices of the District Attorney, the cops and the countless other random people in authority, that told me how wrong what I did was, seep through, and I don't know where to put them. I hold on to the positive memories to pull myself through the uncertainty. I made a lot of mistakes; stupid, public, self-destructive mistakes, but mistakes. I know at heart I have a kind soul, and I don't try to hurt people. The person whom I harmed the most through all of this was me.

It's hard to defend screwing husbands who have made a commitment. But for some men, I really do believe that their marriages were saved by what we did together. If all it takes for a man to not leave his wife and kids is a few safe one-night stands with a stranger to satisfy his physical needs, then thank God for escorts. I grew up without a father, and I still struggle with the pain and confusion that comes with it. As for single guys, I'd rather they pay for sex than seduce some hopeful young thing at a bar who then spends the next two weeks wondering why he hasn't called.

Finally, you don't have to have a PhD in Freudian psychoanalysis to entertain the possibility, that maybe, just maybe, the trauma of my father's abandonment might have had something to do with my future behavior. It wasn't one of the numerous therapists, psychiatrists and life coaches I would end up talking to who raised that possibility; it was me. I've thought about it everyday of my life. My father was a raw wound that never healed. I always thought about what if instead of leaving us that night, he'd actually gone to help out a friend and had driven his plow off the road and into a partially frozen lake. Would I be happier? At least he'd live on in my mind as a father, and not as the man who left a young girl to grow up thinking that she needed to become the object of every man's desire just to prove that there was nothing wrong with her. It is a fear that I carried with me my whole life. The fear that it was my birth or something I did as a baby that drove him away—that in my purest form, as an infant, I caused him to do such a cold, cruel thing to my mother, my brother and me.

*   *   *

It was my first Christmas home in three years. There was the Christmas my flight was cancelled, and I sat on my bed with my heroin addiction as my only company and then the one that followed when I was out on bail, post-Rikers. Montreal was hit with the biggest snow storm in over thirty-five years. I loved it. It took me straight back to my childhood, with the snow banks that were three times my height.

I was in love with my job at the spa. My boss/best friend had asked me to help him decorate the spa for Christmas. We hung ribbons on the bamboo and wreaths on the exposed brick, which is really tricky, but I loved every second of it.

Now that I was home, I promised myself I'd get each of my family members something special, something that meant something. It wasn't about the money (which I didn't have any of anyway), it was about showing them I was part of the family again.

As I walked through Montreal, passing new store after new store, this empty feeling overcame me. It wasn't because Montreal isn't a friendly place. The people are amazing. But I had no recent memories of life here. I was a total stranger. I didn't know any of the stores, and the streets all seemed to have a different flavor than I remembered. I started worrying—was it going to be like this with my family?

When Christmas Eve arrived, I was a ball of nerves. I drank a little too much before dinner and had to work to keep myself together. My mom, my nana, my brother and his fiancée, and my aunt[8] were all sitting around the table—everyone I loved the most in this world.

Everything was perfect. The food was delicious, even though I didn't even have the turkey or stuffing (I had stopped eating meat or dairy). I didn't even miss it— the familiar smells were enough to get me high. I had caught a glance at the tree and the enormous pile of presents spilling out from under it, taking up half the living room. We had dessert and coffee and sat around the table for hours talking. I poured everyone some Inniskillin Icewine (my favorite) and watched as they freaked out over how great it is.

Finally, we all moved to the living room, and I saw the tree again. It was covered in handmade ornaments and glitter and lights. It shimmered. It was magical. Then I casually looked down at some of the presents, and I didn't see my name anywhere.

I panicked.

I had a flashback to when I was little. It was from a dream; the same reoccurring nightmare I'd had every Christmas Eve. I knew really young that our parents play Santa, and I knew what that meant for me and my brother. Whether we were good or bad had no effect on our haul. It all depended on what was left after mom covered the rent and bills.

The whole dream was super realistic. It went like this: I am sleeping in my bed, and then I wake up early while it's still dark and remember it's Christmas. I tentatively walk to the living room to get a peek at the tree. It's cold and dark, and I see the tree all lit up and

---

[8] My dad's sister. She'd become more a part of our family than his. I guess she just likes us better, so there!

decorated to the hilt, but when I look down, the place where the presents are supposed to be is empty. There are no presents at all. Not even stockings. This lonely sad wave of emotion would overtake me, and I remember thinking this is what it would feel like to be dead. I'd run into my brother's room to tell him what'd happened, and he wouldn't be there. I'd go to my mom's room, thinking to myself, *I know she'll be so sad that I'm sad, but I have to tell her, and she's not there.*

"Nat!"

My brother called my name, pulling me back to the here and now. I looked at him and tried to smile.

I don't deserve presents, I told myself. *My family does. They've been here all these years, being a family, and I haven't.*

When it came time to start handing them out, I jumped into the pile first, grabbing all of my gifts and handing them out.

One by one, they opened them and cried or just smiled and hugged me. I gave them another round of presents. Same thing.

"Whoa, Nat," my mom said, "Slow down."

And then it started. One by one they handed me gift after gift. There were presents for me. I just hadn't seen them. I'd never gotten so many beautiful presents in my life. I wanted to cry, but instead I just smiled the biggest, face-stretching smile I have ever smiled.

When it came to my mom, she handed me a big department store box. I opened it and blushed. It was a pair of pink Hello Kitty pajamas. I loved Hello Kitty when I was a little girl. I ran into her room to try them on and then ran back. Everyone cracked up as I posed for pictures, hamming it up for the camera.

I told them how I'd been scared when I hadn't seen any presents for me at first.

My brother just looked at me and smiled, "Nat, this is the best Christmas I've ever had."

My brother never says stuff like that.

We had a long hug...maybe the longest I've ever given him. I took a nice sip of wine and plopped down on the floor next to the tree. I felt so happy and content. Then I got this weird feeling, like my life was spinning back onto itself, kind of like déjà vu. I looked around the room, from my perfect spot under the glimmering tree, and realized that it wasn't déjà vu. I was home. The nightmare was over.

CHAPTER FIFTEEN
AFTERMATH

My legal case was resolved, and thankfully I didn't have to serve any more time in jail. I was relieved it was finally over.

I've funneled all of my addictions into healthy living. I work out five times a week, minimum, and I've kept up my vegetarian diet.

Jason got out of jail in 2007 after pleading guilty to money laundering and serving more than two years at Rikers. He has a MySpace page covered with photos of him drinking champagne with half-naked girls. He's wearing a tee-shirt that reads "Page Six Pimp." He claims that he's done with pimping and doing drugs. He's told everyone from Larry King to Howard Stern that he's going legit. He talked about starting a match-making service for the ridiculously wealthy called DNA Diamonds, but it fizzled before it got off the ground. He moved to Miami to work in marketing for one of his childhood friends.

I later found out what happened to Mona and Clark.

They had their baby.

Mona pled guilty to promoting prostitution, but never did any time.

Clark also ended up getting off more or less scot-free. The papers reported that he had allegedly cooperated with the D.A.'s office in our case. He pled guilty to one count of promoting prostitution and spent a total of three days in jail. Jason claimed, while Clark was COO of New York Confidential, he stole more than $500,000 from the company. In typical Jason fashion, he publicly threatened to sue Clark to get it back. The tabloids reported that after New York Confidential, Clark was connected to another agency called Velvet Traces. He also reportedly dated Ashley.

Hulbert ended up spending six and a half months at Rikers. As of last summer, his case was still pending. We're still in touch. Recently, I called him and asked if he wished we'd never come along that day on West Broadway and commissioned a painting. He didn't even hesitate.

He said no.

I waited for him to continue.

Then I jumped in, "Even with the consequences and bullshit you had to go through as a result?"

He answered, "No, it was the best party I ever went to."

Jason's lawyer, Paul Bergrin, was charged with a litany of crimes related to New York Confidential, including laundering over $800,000 of Jason's profits and then taking over, or more like taking, the business from Jason when he was locked up. Bergrin was also charged with "misconduct by an attorney." It turns out that, in an effort to get Jason's midnight curfew pushed back, he allegedly claimed Jason worked for him as a paralegal on one of his other cases: a soldier charged by the U.S. military in the Abu Ghraib scandal. I know. You can't make this stuff up, right?

Mel Sachs died of cancer in 2006. He is remembered as one of the city's most flamboyant defense attorneys with a client list that spanned from David Copperfield to Kanye West to Yankee pitcher David Wells.

The owner of TheEroticReview.com, David Elms, was jailed in California in June 2008 when he reportedly failed a series of drug tests and violated his probation, stemming from other charges unrelated to the site. He faces up to four years in prison. The escort industry reeled at the news.

I spoke to Scott one final time after it all went down. He had finally started making his own money doing a lot of high-profile charity work and fundraising for a certain Republican candidate. He ran for local office. He flew me out to visit a few times, and we always had fun together, but I could see his life was moving in a different direction. He had his sights set on a life in politics. He ended up marrying a tall blonde, the perfect wife for a politician.

"Natalia, should I be worried?" he asked. "Do people know I was your client?"

"Scott, on my end, you have nothing to be worried about. All of the booking sheets with your name on them, all the credit card imprint slips with your name and info on them, are gone."

"Okay," he sounded relieved.

"But," I continued, "you might want to do something about your credit card bills. If anyone looks for Gotham Steak, it will be there."

"Right," he answered. I could almost hear his wheels turning, trying to figure out if there was anyone his family knew who could make that little problem disappear.

Jeremy Piven contacted me about developing a feature film about my life at New York Confidential. He said he wanted to play Jason. I spoke to him on the phone a few times. He kept inviting me out to L.A., but I got the feeling he was more interested in sleeping with me than putting together a movie deal.

I guess some things never change.

*   *   *

When New York's governor Eliot Spitzer went down in a ball of flames for booking a $4,300 session with an escort named "Kristen," I confess I laughed my head off. Prior to being elected governor in 2007, he was New York's attorney general. He was known for being a "by-the-book" hard-ass, responsible for a string of high-profile prosecutions for white-collar crime, consumer fraud and environmental pollution. He was allegedly the driving force behind the crackdown on high-end escorting that led to my arrest and subsequent visit to Rikers Island.

Funny enough, turns out Mr. Morality had a long history of paying to play. Up until he was caught red-handed, he had allegedly spent over $80,000 (that they could trace) on escorts over an eight-year period—basically the entire time he was the state's top law enforcement and elected official. "Hypocritical" doesn't even begin to scrape the surface. Pathological, maybe.

I couldn't escape the news once it broke. As an ex-New York escort, I was bombarded with calls left, right and center asking me to come on TV shows to talk about my experiences with other politicians and comment on Eliot Spitzer's actions. Cameramen and reporters even showed up at my work. My fellow staff already knew about my past, but after all the media attention, most of our clients found out as well. My bosses were supportive of me, but I could tell they were worried about how the clientele would respond. Surprisingly they were open-minded, offering words of encouragement, and whispered in my ear that they wanted to hear all the details later.

Almost immediately after I watched the scandal unfold on CNN, I was interviewed live on the *Today Show* via satellite and was invited to be a guest on *Larry King Live* later the same day. That afternoon, before my second appearance, I got an email from Jason, (who touched base with me about once a month) titled, "Don't you know this girl?"

Oh, my God.

There was a photo of my little Ashley in a white bikini sitting on a yacht docked in what looked like the French Riviera, but what I knew better to be off the coast of Miami, where she was probably partying it up at the Winter Music Conference.

Kristen was Ashley. Ashley was Kristen. She had finally gotten her wish: she was famous. And then some.

As the story spiraled out of control, the not-quite contrite governor was forced to resign in a dramatic (and hugely pathetic) press conference with his humiliated wife, Silda, standing by his side. Ashley kept a low profile, hiding out as the press scoured the eastern seaboard trying to get a shot of the girl who had brought down the former Sheriff of Wall Street. Spitzer got his own *New York* magazine cover: the governor grinning like a schoolboy with an arrow pointing to his crotch and the caption: "Brain." Brilliant.

Ashley's only connection to the outside world was her MySpace page, which featured recordings of her songs and MySpace friends' links to Whitney Houston and Mary J. Blige. The songs sounded exactly how I expected them to sound: poppy, heavily produced club anthems. The lyrics, while not quite Alanis Morissette, said it all: "I know what you want. You got want I want. I know what you need. Can you handle me?"

Of course, the obvious question crossed my mind. Had she been turned into a government informant way back when and kept on the payroll? It seemed like an awfully big coincidence that she was allegedly let go after her arrest during her New York Confidential days and then happened to be at the center of the government's biggest prostitution sting operation in recent memory.

I have no idea if that's what happened. The official story is that someone in a bank noticed the governor's suspicious wire transfers and thought that they may have stumbled onto some kind of blackmail plot and reported it to the D.A.'s office, and they had no choice but to investigate. The whole thing smelled pretty fishy to me.

Of course, as the scandal consumed the news media, and the reporters couldn't locate Ashley, and it came out she was once with New York Confidential, they turned to Jason and me for comment. The last thing I was going to do was disparage my old friend. I never brought up the rumors about her involvement in our bust on the air. Even if it were true that Ashley was responsible, or provided the cops with info that helped them make their cases, I didn't hold a grudge. The way things were going, we were headed off a cliff with or without her help. She was young (nineteen), and if it happened the way my source said it happened, they probably threatened her with serious jail time. If she decided better us than her, and she gave them the information that helped bring us down, I really can't blame her.

I did the interviews with the *Today Show*, *Entertainment Tonight* and *Larry King Live* and tried to give an accurate representation of myself, and Ashley, and why we did what we did. If there's one person who could understand what she was feeling at that moment, it was me. I knew she might get hurt and probably wasn't allowed to speak for herself, so I talked about what a good person she was and how I hoped she would get through it. I discussed the good and bad parts of the business. I even told the story of a girl I knew who married one of her rich clients and ran off to Paris with him.

I took some flack for it. Conservative bloggers and some mainstream media outlets ripped me for being an apologist for immoral behavior—behavior that devastates lives and got me locked up. I'm nothing of the sort. I'm just not going to go around judging people. I'd faced enough of that in my own life.

Ashley will be fine. Like me, she survived a rough upbringing, and she'll survive this. She loves life and people glow when they're around her. I've read that she's signed to do a reality pilot with Reveille, the mega-producers behind *Big Brother* and, perhaps fittingly, *Who Wants to Be a Millionaire?* So maybe she'll become a reality star and/or finally get that recording contract she always dreamed about.

*   *   *

I had an amazing moment. I got the chance to audition for a play here in Montreal—a play written by Ayn Rand, my jailhouse savior, of all people. I totally freaked out at first. It had been two years since my last audition in New York. Would I even remember how to act, never mind audition?

But as the audition grew closer, I told myself that according to the method theory of acting I was Meryl Streep by this point, with everything that I had been through, right?

Then the doubts crept back in. Maybe I'd lived too much, done too many drugs, and lost my center somewhere along the way.

They handed me the monologue—something random about a girl confronting an older guy; nothing specific about what the conflict was. But I'm good at subtext. It screamed abuse to me, and that's how I performed it.

The director was blown away. He said no one else picked up on it. I was surprised. It seemed so obvious to me.

As I left the audition room, I was giddy. I'd really kicked ass, but more than that, I'd had fun—clean, non-chemical, non-porno fun. They gave me the lead, and not just the female lead. They actually flipped the main character, irony of all ironies, the role of the district attorney, from male to female.

Then came my publishing deal. I had to quit the play. It wasn't really a hard choice; everyone involved in the play understood. I was being given the chance to tell my own story and not let the tabloids and the haters and the prosecutors and Jason and everyone else have the last word on what I did, and who I am.

ACKNOWLEDGMENTS

I would first like to thank my family: my mother Susan, my brother Brent and sister-in-law Julie, my grandmother Lillian and late grandfather Edward and my aunt Audrey. Above everything else, it is your unconditional love and support that has guided me and kept me whole. I am blessed to have such a wonderful, caring family.

I'd like to thank my agent Jason Anthony, now of Lippincott Massie McQuilkin, who found me and never stopped believing in me and this book. Thank you for your patience, compassion and guidance.

Thank you to Michael Viner, my fabulous editor Henrietta Tiefenthaler, Sonia Fiore, Darby Connor and everyone else at Phoenix Books. And thank you to Brian Gross of BSG PR for helping get the word out.

I am grateful to have such an enthusiastic film agent in Judi Farkas of Judi Farkas Management, who loved this project from the very beginning.

Thank you to Terry Hughes and Chantelle Hartshorne for helping me create the cover image. You are both great at what you do, and great at who you are.

Love and thanks to Jordan for your friendship and encouragement—knowing you are always there is everything. Thank you to Carol St. James and the staff at Spa St. James for welcoming me so warmly.

Thank you to John Nicholas Iannuzzi and Peter Fields for your counsel and advice.

There are so many people who've helped, guided and supported me throughout my life. It is because of you that I am here now. I have truly been blessed and will never forget or take it for granted. I am thankful to have known and been loved by Paul and Sara.

And finally, thank you to all my friends, especially Fred, Marta, Nick and Catherine.